The Partnership Charter

How to Start Out Right with
Your New Business Partnership
(Or Fix the One You're In)

DAVID GAGE

BASIC
BOOKS
A Member of the Perseus Books Group
New York

Books published by Basic Books are available at special discounts for bulk purchases in the United States by corporations, institutions, and other organizations. For more information, please contact the Special Markets Department at the Perseus Books Group, 11 Cambridge Center, Cambridge MA 02142, or call (617) 252-5298, (800) 255-1514 or e-mail special.markets@perseusbooks.com.

Designed by Brent Wilcox
Set in 11-point Apollo MT

Library of Congress Cataloging-in-Publication Data
Gage, David.
    The partnership charter : how to start out right with your new business partnership (or fix the one you're in) / David Gage.
        p.   cm.
    Includes bibliographical references and index.
    ISBN-10: 0-7382-0898-1 (alk. paper)
    ISBN-13: 978-0-7382-0898-5 (alk. paper)
    1. New business enterprises—Management.   2. Partnership—Psychological aspects.   3. Interpersonal relations.   4. Industrial management.   I. Title.

HD62.5.G334   2004
658'.042—dc22
                                                                    2004003992

I was blessed with many wonderful teachers. Six of them will always stand out because of their enormous talent and because they cared deeply for my well-being. I dedicate this book to them.

John Shrake

Sister Elora Schmidt

Philip A. Morse

Michael Piechowski

Martin A. Safer

Colin Frank

CONTENTS

PART THREE

THE INTIMATE SIDE OF BEING PARTNERS

PART FOUR

THE FUTURE IS SOONER THAN YOU THINK

PREFACE

When people ask me why I started a company whose sole purpose was resolving disputes among business owners, I tell them that my life, like those of millions of others, has been influenced by business partnerships. The quality of partnerships can have a lasting effect—for better or worse—on the people involved, and I wanted to increase the odds that those effects would be for the better. The purpose of this book is similar: to introduce potential and current partners to a process, the Partnership Charter, that can help them create partnerships that will realize their dreams, not their nightmares.

I had three formative experiences with partnerships. The first occurred when I was around eight. My brother Larry was a thirteen-year-old entrepreneur with a paper route and, in my head at least, I was his junior partner. I believed I had the best partnership deal imaginable. Larry had all the responsibility. He was 100 percent responsible for ensuring that his customers got their Appleton *Post-Crescent* delivered to their doorstep seven days a week come rain, shine, or two feet of snow. As his junior partner, I was free to accompany him whenever I wanted. As I recall, that was only on Saturday mornings in the spring and fall when the weather was perfect, and I could ride my bicycle with him in those peaceful predawn hours. Other than that, my job was to help Larry count the money. Everything in those days was paid for in cash, and some customers paid in silver dollars. Larry had so many silver dollars, I thought he was the wealthiest brother anyone ever had. I was thrilled with my share of the profits—whatever it was—because it came in silver dollars. Partnership seemed like a pretty sweet deal.

Around the same time, my second brush with partnerships began when my father decided to join my mother's father and her four brothers in the family's construction company. That decision gave all of us kids front-row-center seats for the drama that is family business. I learned that grown-up partnerships were much more complex and difficult than my childhood idyll.

All family businesses are fascinating partnerships with amazingly complex dynamics. Family businesses form the bulk of the world's economy. But despite their marketplace success, they are notoriously unstable at the partner level. The dynamics that I witnessed at our frequent family gatherings, which finally resulted in years of litigation that I will describe in the book, were often a spillover from the workplace. My curiosity about those partner dynamics was largely responsible for my early interest in psychology and steered me into specializing in family therapy in the 1980s.

It was my third exposure to partnerships, however, that changed my career path and ultimately led to this book. It involved my wife, Cathy Bock, and her partners. As owners of a very successful travel agency, they had all the correct legal documents. Nevertheless, they hadn't agreed on some of the finer points of their "deal" and tried to finish negotiating them *after* becoming partners. Naturally, their lack of agreement strained their ability to work together, as did their different personalities. Before long, two of the partners sued Cathy and the fourth partner for breach of fiduciary duty. They dragged me into their dispute by having me deposed. Sitting in their lawyer's office, I answered questions about what I knew and when I knew it, with a transcriber recording every word. The absurdity of the proceedings was overwhelming. Two partners couldn't get along with the other two because they'd never completely worked out their arrangement, and yet they were trying to resolve their problem by attacking with blunt, legal instruments.

Approximately $100,000 in attorney's fees later, Cathy's partners dropped their complaint and agreed to be bought out. Reflecting on the experience, which I later came to understand was a garden-variety partner dispute, I decided to figure out a more rational, efficient way for partners to resolve their differences. That led to the founding of Business Mediation Associates in 1990.

The original goal of Business Mediation Associates (later renamed BMC Associates) was to help co-owners resolve their conflicts. Given the complexity of the issues I had seen in both my family's business and my wife's partnership, I knew this type of work necessitated a team approach to be effective. So we have always had a team of mediators with expertise in business, law, finance, and psychology. While mediating disputes, we saw how our clients had gotten into their predicaments. I knew it was crucial to figure out how to pass on that knowledge to other partners, especially because there were no books on the way to establish healthy partnerships. I knew that if Cathy and her partners had had a resource when they were forming their corporation, or if my family members had had guidelines for planning their ownership transition, a lot of agony and expense could have been avoided. Today thousands of books are available to help business owners with almost every conceivable aspect of starting and managing a business, from building employee teams and selecting the right office furniture to choosing the best legal entity. It seems no stone is left unturned, except for the one that sinks so many companies, namely, owners who can't work effectively together.

People in business—whether it's travel, construction, manufacturing, or consulting—are specialists in what they do; they're not specialists in how to be partners. The Partnership Charter is a short course in just that, how to be partners. It's practical, not theoretical. It walks people through the topics they need to discuss and negotiate to develop a comprehensive understanding of how the partnership is going to work. The charter process focuses on both the interpersonal and business issues that need to be addressed to remove the ambiguity from their "deal," which often concerns some sensitive issues such as money, decision making, ownership, fairness, and people's styles or values. So often, as was the case with my wife and her partners, those issues are dealt with but not thoroughly enough. Partners have a tendency to leave a sliver of ambiguity in their arrangement, which grows until one day it becomes a monster overshadowing the partners' every conversation. Those delicate issues and the sore spots that have caused partners pain have been built into the Partnership Charter process so they will not be overlooked.

While this book is explicit about the legal, business, financial, and interpersonal issues that partners need to address, it is not a technical "cookbook" about the specific commitments partners should make to one another. Rather, it raises the issues and provides suggestions for discussing and reaching agreements that are suitable for partners' unique circumstances. It includes exercises that we have developed in our mediations to help ensure that sensitive issues are not dealt with in a superficial manner.

More than a structured process, though, the charter is a product, a document that partners can give their attorney to draft legal documents and that they can use as a guide for years to come as they work together. It's a document that partners should review periodically and can revise as they and their circumstances change.

Developing a charter, like starting a business, is a creative process. No two sets of partners will have the same arrangement. No two Partnership Charters will look the same, although I have included a sample in the appendix to provide a sense of what one may look like. Your charter may not contain all of the topics described in these chapters, but you and your partners will want to read and discuss each topic. I have laid out the topics in an order that makes sense, but the order is not critical, because all the important issues are interconnected in complex ways. Feel free to read the chapters out of order, but try to cover every chapter at least cursorily. You may discover critical partner elements you didn't expect.

My goal in writing this book is to help people make a shift from needing to fix broken partnerships to strengthening partnerships and preventing destructive conflicts. While certain ideas will apply to some partners more than others, my hope is that you will find more than enough new information to avoid destructive conflicts and improve your partnership for years to come. In any given partnership, the fate of the partners affects many people, not just the partners themselves. Too much is at stake for prospective partners not to prepare better before starting out. Too many things can go wrong for partners not to spend the time and energy to make their existing partnership healthier. Using this book will immediately enable you to begin planning and building a stronger, more vital, and more resilient partnership.

PART ONE

PARTNER FUNDAMENTALS

CHAPTER 1

The Rewards (and Risks) of Going into Business Together

"PARTNERSHIP" IS A SEDUCTIVE buzzword in the business world today. My phone company wants to be my "partner in communication," and my doctor at Kaiser Permanente wants to be my "partner in health." Company owners hear constantly about the virtues of becoming partners with their customers, their employees, their vendors, and even their competitors. The overuse of the term *partner* has stripped it of traditional meaning, which in business has been two or more people joining together, pooling their money and talents, and taking a risk. Partners are people out to create or build something—*together*. They are putting something at risk in the hopes of creating a sustainable venture.

This book is about business partners, for the most part without regard to their legal status as partners. They may be in a partnership or a corporation. They may own property together or be co-producers of a Broadway musical. What matters is that they have a duty to one another, and the actions of one partner affect the others. In this sense, partnership is a state of mind. Partners sink or swim—together.

The enthusiasm for partnering is rooted in a down-to-earth fact: You're much more likely to succeed in a business with a partner than without one. Entrepreneurs who have succeeded by pooling their strengths far outnumber those romantic figures, the lone entrepreneurs who have triumphed over all odds. *Inc.* magazine's annual list of the hundred fastest-growing companies typically shows that partners founded about two-thirds of them. Every year, partnerships likewise dominate *Entrepreneur's* annual list of the "hottest" companies. The vast majority of high-performance companies are started by people with partners.

Academic studies confirm the importance of partnering. Researchers from the Center for the Study of Entrepreneurship at Marquette University investigated a sample of nearly two thousand companies and categorized the top performers as "hypergrowth" companies and those at the bottom as low-growth companies. Solo entrepreneurs founded only 6 percent of the "hypergrowth" companies. Partners founded a whopping 94 percent, and many of those companies had three or more founders. In stark contrast, solo entrepreneurs founded nearly half of the low-growth companies.

Founding partners are memorialized in the names of some of the world's most successful and visible businesses: William Hewlett and David Packard, for instance, or Charles Dow and Edward Jones (who actually had a third partner, Charles Bergstresser). Sometimes partnership origins are less obvious. EMC, the world's largest data storage manufacturer, was founded in 1979 by Richard Egan, the "E," and Roger Marino, the "M." ("C" was a third person who did not make it to the actual founding.) The company that employs more people than any other on the planet, Manpower Inc., was founded by Elmer Winter and Aaron Scheinfeld. Compaq Computer Corporation was the brainchild of three Texas Instruments engineers. Intel was cofounded by Gordon Moore and Robert Noyce. Home Depot was started by Bernie Marcus and Arthur Blank. Even Microsoft, which for years many people thought was founded only by Bill Gates, was cofounded by Paul Allen. The list goes on and on.

THE ATTRACTION OF OWNERSHIP

People usually form partnerships because they want to own a business. In a partnership, you don't own 100 percent, of course, but for most partners owning part of a business is much better than owning none at all.

Having partners is often what makes ownership possible. Partners provide the missing link—the money, expertise, ideas, skills, connections, facilities, patents, whatever it happens to be—that an entrepreneur needs to make a go of a business.

What is it about owning a business that is so appealing? One answer is freedom. People are not free when they work for someone else. Freedom may be limited in a partnership (partners are accountable to one another), but there's a world of difference between being an employee and being a co-owner when it comes to freedom.

For many people, too, the desire to own a business stems from a creative impulse. Ownership is a way for them to build something of their own. Others see ownership primarily as the path to a less-elevated goal: wealth. Wealth as a goal is potentially troublesome in a partnership. Partners who define their goals in terms of personal financial enrichment have a special obligation to be explicit about their motives, because focusing on one's own financial gain won't necessarily lead to decisions that benefit the business or one's partners.

ADVANTAGES OF PARTNERS

Being a partner gives people more than ownership. Many people prefer to share the responsibility for the business. Some businesses by their nature require that more than one person be available and accountable. For example, doctors band together for the practical purpose of sharing on-call duties. In addition, being able to divide tasks along lines of interest or ability can make an enterprise not only more successful but also more enjoyable.

Partnerships offer people a chance to do things that they would not be able to do on their own, or to do them more successfully. Opportunities open up when people combine forces. Having partners puts more intellectual power at the top of the business. If you pit three co-owners against a solo entrepreneur, the three co-owners are going to out-think and out-strategize the single owner in most cases, as long as they don't devolve into interpersonal conflict, or what some researchers call "affective conflict." Partnerships also allow people to exploit opportunities more quickly, and in business today, speed frequently means the difference between success and failure.

From a psychological perspective, having a partner means having someone to share the emotional burdens of ownership. A partner can provide feelings of safety and reduced risk, a sense that "we're in this together." One of the biggest complaints of solo entrepreneurs is that no one understands the tremendous demands made upon them. Even spouses who try to be as empathetic as possible cannot truly understand all the complexities of starting and running a business if they're not part of it. For some people, the fears that have kept them from starting a business become manageable with a partner.

Advantages of Having Partners

- Your partner shares the burdens and responsibilities.
- Someone else can do jobs that don't play to your strengths or interests.
- Partnership opens up opportunities that otherwise would be beyond your grasp, including greater success.
- You can move faster to take advantage of opportunities.
- You can enjoy camaraderie with an equal instead of feeling alone at the top.
- There's the potential for synergy and better decision making at the very top of the company.

For other people, having partners is simply more fun than owning alone. If the only option were solo ownership, they wouldn't do it; the cost, in stress and worry, wouldn't be worth it. Being on equal footing with someone else in the business, someone you can't dominate and who can't dominate you, makes for a more stimulating relationship than you can have with any employee.

Creating Synergy

The most exciting advantage of partnership is the potential it creates for synergy. By pooling their strengths, partners not only ensure the viability of their business, they also expand its possibilities.

A fine example of synergy is Enforcer Products, a Georgia company. On his own, a laboratory researcher named Wayne Biasetti founded Enforcer Products in 1977 to manufacture pesticides and home products that he had developed. Although he excelled in the lab, he needed someone else to handle sales and marketing—otherwise his creations would never leave the building. He brought on Jim Biggs as a partner to take charge of that side of the business. He could have simply hired a sales director, but Biasetti wanted someone as dedicated as he was.

As Enforcer Products grew, the two partners realized that there was a weak link in their business chain. They needed a third person to handle administrative and financial issues for which neither had the skills or patience. They found Ed Brush and made him an offer that included ownership. Like the three legs of a stool, the three partners gave the business a stability and solidity that it would have lacked had one of them not been there. Together they were able to grow Enforcer Products to the point where the whole was far greater than the sum of its parts. In 1997, the partners sold their company to National Service Industries.

Partners can also achieve synergy by taking advantage of less obvious differences. For example, Phil Higginbotham, an energetic and successful orthodontist in Spartanburg, South Carolina, had grown his professional practice to the point that he couldn't accept any more patients. He needed to bring on another orthodontist if he wanted to continue growing. Higginbotham wanted to find an orthodontist with whom he would be compatible but who would also complement him in some way; in other words, he wanted to create synergy in his practice.

Higginbotham asked me to do personal styles and values profiles of him and a candidate for partnership, Eric Nease, to see whether they would be a good fit. The tests revealed that they were very similar in their values but sharply different in their personal styles. On one test, their scores were virtually identical in three of the four categories, but they were almost diametrically opposed in the fourth. The test identified Higginbotham as a strong "feeling" person and Nease as a strong "thinking" person. The difference is significant in terms of how people look at the world, how they interpret what is going on around them, and ultimately, how they interact with others.

The crucial questions in such situations are always: Will our differences make us stronger or tear us apart? Will we get synergy or just trouble? I delve more deeply into this tricky question in chapter 8, but as a rule, the greater the differences, the greater the potential advantages, but also the greater the risk of conflict. Higginbotham discussed the test results directly with Nease. Together they used the results to hash out what the difference in their styles might mean on a day-to-day basis, how they could use the difference to their advantage, and what they would do if that difference got in their way.

Higginbotham elected to ask Nease to join his practice. Nease, having seen how thoughtfully, respectfully, and openly Higginbotham operated, decided he wanted to practice with him. How is the partnership working out? The difference in their styles "works out great," Higginbotham says, "because it is clearly advantageous to have both types in a practice. For example, we've had a couple of instances come up where I feel real sorry for a person, but I shouldn't." Some people have so much empathy for others that it gets them in trouble. Now, Nease provides a reality check and saves Higginbotham from being taken advantage of.

Synergy can be created in many ways among partners. The potential is there whenever partners are willing to explore their differences as well as their similarities and in so doing, leverage their differences to their mutual advantage. When this works, partners wind up with more than they could have had on their own. The problem is, it doesn't always work.

THE PERILS OF PARTNERSHIPS

With so much riding on the success of a partnership—the partners' day-to-day happiness, security (often their mortgages), reputations, comfort in retirement, not to mention peace of mind—it's easy to see why partnerships are considered perilous. In a poll taken a few years ago, *Inc.* asked businesspeople if they thought partnerships were a bad idea. Two-thirds of the respondents said they were. When asked why, the majority said they disliked co-ownership because of the partners' "inevitable conflicts" and "unmet expectations." A poll by researchers at the University of Minnesota uncovered similar misgivings inside family businesses. About half of the second-generation family members working at such companies had doubts about being there. The main source of their unease was, again, interpersonal conflicts. Failed business partnerships—and their attendant broken promises, financial ruin, and litigation nightmares—litter the business world and leave a deep impression.

Countless conversations with professional business advisors have convinced me that most of them are similarly against the idea of having partners. The reasons they offer are always the same: It's too difficult for partners to get along, partnerships are too hard to get out of, and when a partnership fails, the cost is enormous. (In private, some advisors jokingly admit that their own unhappy partner experiences have something to do with their skepticism.)

Of course, no one ever enters a partnership expecting serious conflicts. Advisors rightly point out that even when the probability of conflict is low, the risk may still be unacceptable if, as it often is, the cost of a failed partnership will be high.

THE COSTS OF FAILURE

People often jump blithely into partnerships because they are unaware of the costs of failure—and no wonder, since nobody contemplates failure when starting up. It may be difficult to assign hard numbers to these costs. Still, they can be enormous, and prospective partners should look at them carefully.

Every conflict among partners exacts an emotional toll. These conflicts can destroy lifelong relationships. They can consume partners' every working moment, and sometimes every waking moment, for extended periods of time. They exact a toll not just on the partners themselves. I've heard partners refer to the stress on their spouses as "collateral damage"; some say it was that kind of strain that forced them out of their partnership.

Conflicts need not be profound or dramatic. Low-intensity wars can be costly, too, because they often make partners underperform. Nagging dissatisfaction, perhaps a feeling that the partnership's terms are not fair, can result in a partner's dragging his or her feet. Underperformance can become chronic, so that for months or years the partners achieve *less* than they would have on their own. Not only is synergy absent, sometimes there isn't even basic cooperation.

I saw a classic case of this a few years ago. Two partners had not gotten along well since starting their Philadelphia consulting firm fifteen years earlier. For most of their time together, they had been in a low-grade conflict. They called BMC Associates to see if there was any hope of ever getting along.

In a nutshell, although the partnership was nominally 50–50, one of the women, "Janie," felt dominated by the other, "Roberta," and resented it. Feeling dominated and unappreciated caused Janie to put in less effort than she had initially. Pulling back was a passive-aggressive way of communicating her intense dissatisfaction to Roberta, but it was the only way she knew how to get it across. This behavior backfired, however, because Roberta took Janie's underperformance as confirmation that she was not equal to the job, so Roberta felt justified, even forced, to become more dominating. In a classic negative spiral, the partners suffered a great personal loss and the company suffered a significant, if difficult to measure, loss to its bottom line.

Even if partner underperformance is slight, the long-term cost to the underperforming partner, the other partners, and the business can be enormous. Even low-level conflict directly consumes inordinate amounts of partners' time and energy. It never ceases to amaze me how totally their time is eaten up by such conflict. Productive income-generating work by the partners can grind to a halt. When measured by partners' salaries and benefits, the total cost to the business of this lost time is staggering.

The Cost of Conflict Among Partners

- The personal emotional toll on the partners, their spouses, and others close to them
- The toll on the relationships among the partners
- The loss from having a partner underperform, sometimes for extended periods of time
- The time lost by partners who must spend hours and days away from management and income-generating activities
- Job dissatisfaction, high absenteeism, and lost productivity among employees who get swept up in owners' battles
- Costs associated with the departure of employees (often the best ones) who want to escape the conflict
- Mediation, arbitration, or litigation costs
- The expense of buying out a partner's interest
- Lost revenue from the loss of the partner
- Recruiting expenses and time to find a new partner or employee
- Lost productivity for owners and executives who must integrate a new partner or employee into the company
- Litigation after a breakup related to broken noncompete clauses

Few things are more frightening to employees than owners' internecine battles. Even when employees are not directly involved in partner conflicts, they get caught up in them. It is common to hear about employees taking sides. A key employee in one company complained that the divisiveness was so bad that the employees should have worn jerseys for one or the other partner! It does not matter how much information employees have about what is going on among the partners; they can engage in a lot of "worry talk" even if they know next to nothing. As on-the-job stress increases, so does absenteeism. Productivity and job satisfaction can plummet—and the preoccupied partners may never notice.

What *will* make partners take notice is when they hear that employees are looking for jobs elsewhere. Even if partners are oblivious to dropping productivity, they'll take notice when their valued employees begin jumping ship. Some authoritative estimates put the cost of replacing employees at about one year's salary, which includes downtime, opportunity costs, finding or recruiting new employees, training them, and getting them up to speed. For employees in critical jobs, the estimates are between one and two years' salary. Estimates for associates—not partners—in law firms, for example, are typically around $350,000.

When partners become aware of the bottom-line costs of conflict, they may try to negotiate a resolution among themselves. If that effort fails, it is not uncommon for desperate partners to recruit their own accountant or lawyer to be a mediator. This rarely works. As soon as negotiations bog down, one of the partners will cease seeing the advisor as neutral, if, in fact, he or she ever did. At that point, the advisor becomes history, both as mediator and possibly as trusted advisor.

Partners mired in stalled negotiations may hire attorneys. Frequently, one partner will surreptitiously turn to an attorney for help. Inevitably, other partners find out, or suspect as much, and hire their own counsel since no one wants to feel unprotected. Before anyone realizes it, they have all slipped into combat postures. No one feels safe speaking openly to anyone else. In fact, attorneys will advise their clients against speaking candidly to their partners. Whether that is self-serving or just zealous defense of one's client is immaterial. The possibility of partners' resolving their situation slips from their grasp as soon as they hire advocates and surrender responsibility for dealing with their problems themselves.

The cost of litigating partner disputes can be enormous. A recent legal contest between two partners in a financial services business was estimated by one of them to have cost between $1 and $2 million. A battle among the co-owners of the Haft family businesses cost around $40 million in legal fees before a settlement was reached. Co-owners of any small company who litigate a garden-variety partner dispute can rack up fees approaching $100,000 with little effort.

If partners opt for arbitration over litigation, or if a clause in their partnership agreement mandates it, they won't save much money. Arbitration, like litigation, is an adversarial process, even though it occurs outside the court system and is private rather than public. Usually, a retired judge presides, and all the parties have their own attorneys. The lawyers submit motions, conduct depositions and discovery, present their evidence and witnesses, do their best to refute the evidence and the witnesses of the opposing counsel, and make closing arguments. The process looks shockingly similar to courtroom litigation. Arbitration's only real advantage is that the partners are number one on the docket. It does not last as long from start to finish as litigation does, but that is primarily because the process is compressed. Many lawyers who are forced to arbitrate cases hate it because it's so intense: All of the same ritualized war games go on, but at a faster pace. It is no wonder that a *Harvard Business Review* article recently concluded that arbitration in business situations has become "the nightmare that it was meant to replace."

In arbitration, as in litigation, partners are asking someone else to listen to the evidence, weigh it according to existing case law and statutes, determine who is right and who is wrong, and render a decision. The point is still to win. To achieve that goal, one partner must prove that the other deserves to lose. Relationships seldom survive the inevitable hardball tactics.

Not surprisingly, at least one partner will have to be bought out as part of the resolution of knock-down-drag-out cases of arbitration and litigation. Relationships cannot survive such a beating. When partners must buy someone out of the business to resolve a conflict, there are frequently additional costs beyond the price of the ousted partner's interest. In rare cases, partners have buy-sell agreements in place that assign a value that no one contests. More commonly, however, someone disputes the price of the buyout, necessitating a costly valuation. Valuations often fail to settle the matter, though, because valuations are also frequently contested.

My own family discovered how painful this kind of scenario can be when our family's business experienced a protracted and costly buyout dispute. Because of different values, styles, and management philosophies, one of the five families in our third-generation company decided to leave, more or less voluntarily. They invoked the

buy-sell agreement, which had been drawn up years before and stip-
ulated the method for determining the price of the buyout. Even
though the valuation method was spelled out in black and white,
more than seven years of active litigation ensued as people fought
over the precise meaning of certain critical clauses. The cost in legal
fees alone was enormous.

My cousins who left the company did exactly what many partners
do when they leave: They set up shop close by and competed against
the family business. Price wars ensued. The family company suffered
because the business was disrupted. It's common in such breakups
that after partners separate, they continue doing whatever they have
always done but under a different name. It happens even with noncompete clauses in place. And because they often bear ill will toward
their former partners, they compete with a vengeance. This is another
cost of conflict among partners: having a new competitor who knows
your business inside out and attempts to take your customers and
your employees.

The toll on my family was devastating. People who had shared their
lives stopped speaking to one other, though there was no hiding their
anger and pain. The damage even extended to some people being con-
spicuously absent from family weddings and funerals.

The painful process my family went through plays out in communities everywhere. The stories are unique but sadly familiar. In Boston,
the public watched the partners in Legal Seafoods as they slogged
their way through their battles. New Yorkers watched this type of
partner conflict play out for much of the last third of the last century
as four brothers in the Dell'Orto family attacked and counterattacked
one another over the vestiges of their family's culinary legend, Manganaro Foods. Family relations were never the same after 1961, when
the brothers divided the business among them because of differences
in personal and management styles. The legalistic, Solomonesque division of the 110-year-old business did nothing for the siblings' relationships, however. As so often happens, legalistic resolutions begat
interminable legal encounters that kept the feud alive. For decades,
the brothers went head to head selling Italian delights next door to

one another, while dueling head to head in the courts over the use of the Manganaro and "Hero-Boy" names. Outside the courtroom, they didn't speak to one another. Only recently the brothers managed to reach a settlement—out of court.

One of the sons in the next generation, Anthony Dell'Orto, described how their fight poisoned their family relationships when he said he couldn't recall ever speaking to his uncle Salvatore's daughters, though they grew up side by side. "In pictures of my christening, some of my cousins are there and I don't even know who they are."

PARTNERS HAVE BEEN AN INVISIBLE GROUP

Considering the many advantages a successful partnership bestows and the horrendous costs a failed partnership can exact, you might assume there is a large body of research on what makes partners tick and what makes them stumble. Surprisingly, there isn't much written on the subject, even though business partners' success is tremendously important, not just to the individuals and companies involved but to the whole economy.

Business schools could teach students how to minimize the risk of partner disputes, but they do not. They are schools of business *administration*. They teach students how to run large companies. Although they have started doing a better job of teaching students how to be entrepreneurial, they teach next to nothing about how to be a partner. Even though they have taught students how companies can make "partners" out of employees, customers, and vendors, this "partner revolution" has to do, again, with administering a business, in this case through managing relationships to encourage loyalty to the company. Theoretically, if you are a Starbucks "partner" you will give more to the company than if management simply calls you an employee, but this has little to do with actual partnership.

Because most business schools' graduates who start their own businesses will have real partners some day, the schools' neglect of partnerships is hard to fathom. But business schools are not the only schools with this gap in their curriculum. Medical schools train physicians without regard for the fact that the vast majority of their graduates will have to struggle sooner or later with partners. The same is true of other professional schools.

Why has no one bothered to plug this obvious gap? I think the reason is that partners have been something of an invisible group, meaning that they operate beyond the range of the vast majority of researchers and consultants working in companies. While researchers are encouraged to investigate, analyze, and correct the bottlenecks, problems, and conflicts at all other levels, relationships between owners have been largely off limits. Likewise, consultants are rarely privy to the intimate details and internecine warfare among partners themselves.

Researchers and consultants do get to peek at the highest echelons (i.e., major stockholders, officers, and board members) of *publicly* held companies because laws mandate a certain level of transparency and public scrutiny. Not so with privately held companies. Co-owners of private, closely held companies do not have to file documents with the Securities and Exchange Commission about who owns how much of the company and how much each person makes. Few partners are willing to divulge this information for research purposes. Thus, they are free to remain a largely invisible group.

Mediation creates an interesting exception to the rule. Mediators, brought in expressly to help co-owners resolve conflicts in nonadversarial ways, have a unique window on the inner workings of partnerships. In mediation, nothing is off limits. Partners at loggerheads with one another cease being guarded and secretive. They will open their souls and pour out their stories. They actually have to be open and candid about their partnerships for mediation to work. Mediators cannot help them reach a resolution unless they dump all the messy details onto the table. The reality of mediating partner disputes is that when principals are wrangling over stock, money issues, or who is taking more than their fair share of perks, they are more than willing to reveal all, as long as they see a glimmer of hope that mediators can get them swiftly and safely out of their quagmire.

WARNINGS FROM PAST PARTNERS

In mediation after mediation, partners have told me about the hopes and aspirations they started with and the problems and impasses they encountered as they went forward. I learned directly from them what makes partnerships tick—or not. Seven caveats for would-be and existing partners emerged from these discussions:

- If you think you are not partner material (e.g., not a team player), don't even try.
- Exercise extreme caution when selecting a partner.
- If you do not really need a partner, don't go there.
- If it doesn't feel good before you start, don't do it.
- Don't think that legal documents will keep you out of trouble with one another.
- If you are a co-owner and it doesn't feel good working together, work to fix it.
- If you can see ambiguities in your relationships with your existing partners, address them while you're still getting along.

Some people will never make good partners because they simply could not be team players. Ginger Spencer, a Florida real estate agent, is crystal clear about herself in this regard: "I could never have partners because I have to do things my way. Furthermore, I never want to be accountable to anyone." Knowing and accepting your limitations is a real strength.

Business and professional schools, along with business advisors and consultants, should be offering such warnings to their students and clients—but most of them don't. At best they offer horror stories of failed partnerships. Given the perils of partnership, it is easy to see why so many schools and advisors—and so many businesspeople— think having partners is a bad idea, but a lot of things are bad ideas if you do them without sufficient caution and planning (cases in point: scuba diving, skydiving, and mountain climbing). Business partnerships are no different.

In the following section I present four critical questions that people should stop and ask themselves when contemplating taking on partners. I then address what people who already have partners can do.

‖ FOUR CRITICAL QUESTIONS BEFORE JUMPING IN

Because getting into a partnership is far, far easier then getting out, you must ask the critical questions—and answer them honestly—*before* signing on the dotted line. Addressing them takes people a long way toward making partnerships safe and successful. The first and second questions are so simple that they are often overlooked. They are, however, important to ask and answer honestly. Keep in mind that the initial answers sometimes do not hold up under closer scrutiny.

Why Do You Want to Own a Business?

I discussed some of the possible motivations for owning a business earlier in this chapter. When people are answering this question, they tend to say what sounds good, but a superficial or socially correct answer gets you nowhere. This question is really about goals and objectives. It's about purpose. It's about expectations for the business. Is your reason for wanting to own a business to build an empire? Bake the best croissants in town? Achieve security? Become famous? Travel? Become the largest Murano glass wholesaler in New York City? Own the most sought-after interior design studio in the region? Make a million? Not have a boss?

You have to know your own and your partners' reasons for wanting to own a business. Then you have to make sure everyone's motives are compatible. To do otherwise is like starting on a long journey without knowing your destination. It can be done, but it takes some mighty happy-go-lucky travelers to do it and not be at one another's throats. As a rule, the smaller the business, the more similar your reasons for owning must be. Larger organizations allow co-owners more freedom to achieve satisfaction in different ways.

Why Do You Want to Have a Partner?

For some people, having partners is a necessary evil. The thought of having partners nearly stops them in their tracks. Nonetheless, some of them slip into partnerships.

Others would start a business just to have peers to interact with on a daily basis. For these people, the business provides a special type of interpersonal contact that they crave. If they had to do it alone, they wouldn't bother.

Between these two extremes are those who want partners for the advantages that accrue from combining forces with others. Understanding exactly why you want partners is critical to preventing disappointment or a costly mistake. Many people have entered into partnerships without really addressing this question, only to discover, when their *need* for a partner has ceased, that they are stuck with a problem for which they had never bargained.

Peter, for example, had a novel idea for a computer software company that he thought could be worth a lot of money in a few years, but he wanted a partner to help him bring the idea to fruition. He had never started a business and did not believe he could do it on his own. Peter found a partner, Steve, whose experience in marketing appeared to be critical to growing the business. They both put in $50,000 and agreed not to take salaries for a year. Steve suggested a 55–45 split in Peter's favor, in recognition that the business was Peter's idea. Peter agreed.

Two years later, Peter and Steve received an unsolicited offer from a national company to buy them out for a huge sum of money. Peter was shocked at his good fortune but also had pangs of regret. Hindsight produced a very different picture in Peter's mind than the one he had had when he lacked confidence to be a solo entrepreneur two years earlier. He thought to himself that while Steve had done a perfectly respectable job for those two years, it was really his idea that had created the value. The $50,000 and a year without salary that Steve contributed paled in comparison to Peter's contributions. His view was that he'd relinquished almost half of his business, slightly over $2 million, in order to not feel alone.

Peter's revisionist view may have been partly due to greed; also, he may have been underestimating his own lack of confidence now that he had experienced success, and he may have been underestimating all that Steve had contributed. A partner may provide the confidence that one cannot muster on one's own. Starting a business can be scary, especially alone. A person starting a business may have employees to talk to, but that is not the same as having partners who share the responsibility for the entire venture. Shouldering 100 percent of the burdens, both financial and emotional, is a daunting challenge. If having a partner brings nothing more than the confidence to move forward, the partner may be worth every penny. Alternatively, if Peter had fully recognized that he needed a partner simply to quell his fear, he might have explored other means of calming his anxieties.

Are There Better Alternatives Than Taking on a Partner?

Despite the advantages of having partners, they complicate life. The more partners one has, the more complicated and risky things become, so it is wise to ask oneself if there are better alternatives available. Peter might have hired a consultant to walk him through his own strategy, for example. He might also have secured his own financing and searched for an employee with marketing experience.

It may seem ironic that a book on partners would stress the importance of *alternatives* to having partners, but the inherent risks of having partners are such that people need to carefully consider the alternatives before jumping in.

Is the Person You Are Choosing the Best Partner for You?

Many people might make very good business partners, but many of them would not be good business partners *for you*. The issue is not whether a prospective partner is the ideal person, but whether that prospective partner is someone with whom you have a reasonably good chance of success. Choosing a partner is one of the most important decisions a person will ever make. This is as true in business as it is in marriage. Many people will spend much more time with their partners than with their spouses. For better or worse, partners tie their fortunes and their futures to one another. One's choice of partners will affect one's life in profound ways. The quality of the partner relationship will have a huge effect on how one feels about going to work in the morning and how comfortably one sleeps at night. The choice of a partner is the single most important decision most people will ever make about their businesses.

The essential elements of a successful partnership are

- a good fit between the partners' personalities,
- similar values,
- the ability to be a team player,
- compatible goals and clear expectations, and
- mutual trust and respect.

When prospective partners have assessed these critical relationship elements, they have a tremendous head start. Personality studies have demonstrated that while physical appearance governs our first impressions of people, it is people's personal styles that make living or working together day after day, year after year, either a blessing or a curse.

Values, the underpinnings of all major decisions, usually function just beyond our awareness. Even though values are difficult to assess, they are critical to the long-term survival of all partnerships. Sooner or later, an issue will arise whose resolution will depend on the partners' values. It might be over whether to fire an employee, or whether to invest personal capital to upgrade equipment. Regardless of the issue, if partners' values are not aligned, something will eventually make the discrepancy apparent to everyone.

Many people believe that starting a business with a friend is a safe bet because friends tend to share similar values. Sometimes they do. A classic example is two long-lost friends who bumped into one another at their twenty-fifth college reunion (see sidebar, p. 22).

Close Friends—and Good Partners

Two Harvard classmates, Chuck Houghton and Bill Forster, bumped into each other at their twenty-fifth college reunion in 1993. They hadn't crossed paths since they graduated. At their five-day reunion, they discovered they were working only blocks apart in Manhattan.

Back in New York, over a series of lunches, they discovered how similar they were. They'd both climbed the corporate ladder (Forster as an investment banker, Houghton as a principal in a marketing and consulting firm); they were enjoying the good life; and they both harbored a private yearning to do something different, less conventional, more daring.

They noticed as their lunches continued that their conversations most often were about their shared passion for boats and the water. Forster had been sailing since he was a child and had a tremendous passion for wooden boats of all kinds. Houghton also had a particular affinity for wooden boats, especially ones handmade by a hundred-year-old company named the Electric Launch Company, or Elco.

Houghton's great-grandfather had bought one of the original Elco launches in 1893, and it was still running when Houghton was a young boy. But his passion encompassed more than his great-grandfather's boat, which is still seaworthy and is used every summer. Houghton cared deeply about the company and the people who made those boats.

Elco had a long and distinguished history. Founded in 1893, the company specialized in elegantly designed, handcrafted, long-lasting wooden boats with battery-powered electric motors. Many famous people owned Elco launches. Mrs. Henry Ford, who refused even to ride in one of her husband's early automobiles powered by what were known as "explosive motors," was the proud owner of an Elco electric launch that operated smoothly, quietly, and without "risk" of explosion.

A few decades later, when the boating public became enthralled with speed, the company switched to conventional powerboats and stopped making electric launches. Then, in 1949, a large corporation acquired Elco and essentially mothballed its operation. In 1988, Elco took to the water again when new owners took the company private. By 1993, though, Elco was about to sink for good.

Houghton had not only bought one of the struggling company's launches, he had befriended the company's owners. "When they met Chuck," Forster says, "they saw more than just a customer. Chuck was a devotee. He had a passion for the company's product." Houghton was already on the company's advisory board when he began trying to interest Forster in investing in Elco. At first, Forster says, he was "extremely reluctant" to get involved with Elco, "because I thought it would be a very challenging proposition, but not profitable."

Even after they had talked for over a year, Houghton knew that Forster still saw Elco as just another business venture. Then Houghton welcomed Forster aboard an Elco electric launch on beautiful Lake George in upstate New York. "We were out having a scotch and a cigar, riding along on this boat," Forster says, "and I looked at him and said, 'It's just not fair.' He knew that meant I had been seduced by this boat and that I was willing to sign on to this idea of trying to save the Electric Launch Company."

They both became shareholders in 1994. The next year Houghton became president and Forster, chairman. They assumed full control on January 1, 1996, and have worked together harmoniously since then. The partners are equal owners and hold the majority of the company's stock. They also have investor partners and employees with stock. Houghton handles day-to-day operations, and Forster spends only a few days a year at the plant but is always on call when his expertise is needed. Says Forster: "Chuck's running the show and I'm providing advice."

As for why Houghton so strongly wanted Forster as a partner, he says: "Having Bill as a partner brought certain high-level business skills to the table that I needed, and he gave me the confidence that we could succeed. He was also a good person and good friend—I could really trust him—and I knew it would be much more fun with him than without him."

As for Forster, his friendship with Houghton and the trust they had developed in each other were crucial to his entering the partnership. "I'm a realist, and I have a lot of experience in business," he says. "From a financial standpoint, this is a risky venture. I never would have done this if it hadn't been for Chuck. I've had many partners and I know how hard it can be, but I know that Chuck and I are similar enough and are looking at this from similar enough perspectives that it can really work. The two of us see eye to eye on a lot of basic values. Neither one of us is driven by greed, with respect to the Electric Launch Company."

The Houghton–Forster example shows that a friendship can be a distinct advantage. A deep friendship can keep a partner from jumping to negative conclusions when another partner says or does something that sounds derogatory and hurtful. It may be a wellspring of trust, a key ingredient of successful partnerships. True friendship can help one partner to be understanding when another has family problems that wind up shortchanging the business for an extended period of time. A strong bond of friendship may be a sign of shared values and can be the glue that holds partners together when the business is under stress.

Unfortunately, partnerships between friends don't always work as well as the Houghton and Forster partnership does. I interviewed an emergency medicine specialist who thought a friend would be a safe bet for a professional partner. "I chose a person who was a good friend, thinking that because of our years of friendship, we shared similar values. I couldn't have been more wrong!" He explained what happened. "Because he was a good friend, we didn't write anything down. We didn't think we needed to. Then, the first time we had to deal with a sticky issue, it all fell apart. We couldn't have seen the situation more differently." The friendship died. The practice died. And so did this doctor's interest in ever having another partner.

Countless friendships are destroyed by people who believe that their friendships give them a leg up in business partnerships. They often quickly discover that the business world is uncharted territory for their friendship. The social and business worlds intersect at times but are very different. What works in one can be totally inappropriate in the other. In some cases, being friends may actually handicap those who want to become co-owners. They must face a couple of additional hurdles that non-friends don't face. One is that friends often *imagine* that they know each other better than they really do. Second, friends often resist conscientiously learning more about one another. ("We're friends; we trust one another. We're not going to start 'probing.'") Third, as the case of the emergency medicine specialist suggests, friends are less inclined than non-friends to document their business deal. (Again, "We're friends; we trust one another.")

At the other end of the friendship spectrum from Houghton and Forster are Marvin Davis and Robert O'Leary, of another small upstate New York company, Romancing the Woods. They were not friends going into their two-person company, and they eschew the idea that it's helpful for business partners to be friends (see sidebar, below).

Good Partners—But Not Close Friends

Is having a strong friendship crucial for being good partners? Certainly not according to Marvin Davis, cofounder of a company called Romancing the Woods. Davis contends, in effect, that the more different partners are, the better.

"I think that good partners are not alike, do not think the same way, do not come from the same school, do not go to the same club. They have a dichotomy of thinking that contributes to the business," he says. "They don't have to drink together, they don't have to have dinner together, they don't have to socialize together."

All that they need in common, he says, "is a belief in the business." He and his partner, Robert O'Leary, really seem to have that. Davis is a former advertising executive from New York City; O'Leary is a highly skilled woodworker.

They met in 1991, when Davis hired O'Leary, who had a small woodworking shop, to build a gazebo on Davis's property in the Catskills. They decided to go into business together selling such structures, O'Leary recalls, the first time they sat down and relaxed over a glass of wine on Davis's new deck.

Says Davis: "I suggested to him that we [go into business together], and that I would put up any of the small moneys needed, and that he could continue in his business, but that if any business did come in [to the new company] we'd split the money. There was no plan, there was no written document—it was strictly off the cuff."

O'Leary describes the business as "tongue in cheek" in its origins. He recalls the initial conversation with Davis this way: "He said, 'I think I can sell this stuff,' and I said, 'Well, you know I can build it.'" Davis says he thought of their business as a "lark," hardly a real business at all. Although he and O'Leary went into business together in March 1992, Davis only began devoting much time to it in 1994, after his ad agency lost its biggest client and he decided to close down.

Romancing the Woods is the only company in the United States devoted to reproducing rustic nineteenth-century outdoor designs. It is so good at what it does that it has been hired to do large projects for clients as demanding as Walt Disney World, the Winterthur estate in Delaware, and such historic sites on the Hudson River as Hyde Park and the Vanderbilt mansion.

Although Davis and O'Leary like and respect each other, working together for more than ten years has not made them into good friends. They both acknowledge that their personalities and backgrounds are so extremely different that they have had many ferocious arguments over the years. "We're not buddies," O'Leary says. "We don't hang out together." Davis expounds on the same theme: "We lead different lives. We have different friends, we have different interests."

Davis had had partners before, in the advertising business, and he readily admits that he had problems with some of them. "I was too demanding of my partners," he says. "I expected them to be what I was, and they weren't, and couldn't be. This says that I'm really one of the culprits [in his conflicts with O'Leary]. I'm just not a very loose kind of guy when it comes to business. I came from an environment that was much more structured. We'd get into a lot of arguments because he did things in a fashion that I was never used to."

Davis offers this story as an example of their "complicated relationship": Davis asks O'Leary to let him know where he's going when he leaves the plant during the workday. O'Leary replies, "I don't have to let you know." Davis interprets his behavior this way: "He doesn't ever want to get that trapped. There are a lot of little things like that that aren't big things, but they're there." According to O'Leary, "He doesn't understand some things about me and my lifestyle, and I'm the same way about him."

However much he and Davis may argue, O'Leary says, "Nobody goes home mad." The glue that holds the partnership together, he says, is that "we both really love the business" because of its strong creative element. "It's more of an art form—that's the fun part of it. And that's really what keeps us together."

If they were to break up, he says, "I'd probably be back to having a small shop of some kind. I could make a living and get by, but it wouldn't be the same. I'd apply a lot of what I've learned from my years in the business with him, but it just wouldn't be the same."

I would agree with Marvin Davis that friendship is not a prerequisite for starting a partnership. But can it be advantageous? I would say most definitely, as the Houghton–Forster example shows. Friends or not, prospective partners need to explore the lay of the land when determining whether they should join forces. Chapter 9 examines how to discover whether values are truly aligned. People also need to explore why they want these specific partners, that is, what they think everyone will contribute and their expectations for one another.

People who are less than candid about what they want and expect from their partners are doing everyone a disservice. For example, Michael, who has a novel idea for a consulting business, asks Stuart to join him because he believes Stuart has a solid reputation and will be able to open doors easily. He does not tell Stuart his motivation or expectations. Stuart is under the impression that Michael wants someone he can trust to run the business professionally and proficiently.

After two years, Michael tells his partner that he's unhappy because he has felt personally responsible for bringing in 90 percent of the business. Stuart feels blindsided by this revelation because he had no clue what was expected of him. Furthermore, he is angry about the unspoken expectation because he believes that using social contacts for purely business purposes is unsavory, complicating and compromising friendships.

Prospective partners can reveal their motives in a way that benefits everyone. In the late 1990s, Tracy Bloom Schwartz was poised to buy her mother out of Creative Parties, Ltd., one of the most successful event-planning businesses in the Washington area. She wanted Sue Busbey to be her partner. Sue was their key employee and had proven herself for years as the one responsible for the administrative side of the company. Tracy and Sue were effectively running the company because Rita Bloom, the founder, had already transitioned herself out of management so that she could do what she loved most, planning events for clients. Even though it seemed perfectly natural for Tracy and Sue to buy Rita out and continue to run the company together, and they were already headed down that path, they decided that it would be smart to sit down and thoroughly explore the possibility of becoming partners, to make sure it really made sense.

In the course of two half-day sessions, Tracy and Sue explored a broad spectrum of issues, including what becoming partners would mean to each of them, how their roles would change, and their expectations of each other. The discussions gave Sue the opportunity to see that she did not wish to take on the mantle of ownership. She felt being a partner was not right for that time in her life. After saying that she really wanted to remain a key employee, Sue expressed her concern that Tracy might take her bowing out as a rejection, which could create resentment. But Tracy assured her that she understood and valued her candor and that continuing in her employee capacity was perfectly okay. Now, some years later, they continue to work very well together.

IF YOU ALREADY HAVE PARTNERS

The moment people sign their papers and commit themselves to co-ownership, the question of selecting the right partners is passé. It's done. For many people the process was too hasty and not well thought out, but once the papers are signed, there's no going back. The challenge of staying healthy and conflict-free has just begun. Three issues are now of paramount importance.

Are You Paying Attention to the Relationships Among the Partners?

Even though most co-owners take great pains to ensure the success of their business, few do much to ensure the success of their partnership. For example, I have seen many co-owners do more to nurture their relationships with key managers in the business than they do to nurture their relationships with each other. Partners must realize that their relationships are of paramount importance to the success of the business and serve as a model for relationships throughout the business. If the partners are cooperative and open with one another, others take that as a cue for what is expected of them. If partners are tolerant of each other's shortcomings and help each other out whenever possible, others will treat coworkers in a similar fashion. Conversely, if partners fight and don't talk, employees will follow that lead.

Thus, it behooves partners to attend closely to the quality of their relationship—something that is far easier to do when the business is running smoothly. The need to dedicate time and energy to the partnership as well as the business never really goes away. Because every partnership is a dynamic, ever-changing, living system, co-owners who ignore it for long periods do so at their peril. People who have been partners for years need to continue investing in their relationships as a way of ensuring their continued success. Relationships taken for granted are relationships at risk.

Have You Worked Out the Details?

Over the years, I have asked countless people who were co-owners of successful companies and professional practices if their arrangements with their co-owners were clearly laid out. They've typically replied, "Yes." I then ask them if they mean that they've worked through and resolved all the questions that they think might arise about money, ownership, roles, and how their partnership may change over time. Invariably they pause and hedge their initial "Yes."

I have been shocked by the ambiguity that some partners tolerate in their deal. For example, they have not clearly resolved such issues as:

- what they will do with profits;
- how they would handle a serious financial downturn;
- under what circumstances they will take on another co-owner;
- how they will determine if each of them is performing satisfactorily, and what they will do if someone is not; and
- what they will do if one of them loses interest in the work but is still entitled to receive a salary.

Why have so many partners ignored such potentially contentious issues? Partners who are in start-up mode describe the intense pressure they feel to secure office space, hire employees, find customers, develop products, and bring in enough revenue to stay afloat. That's all true. It is also true, however, that many people are uncomfortable discussing and negotiating the topics that partners should examine at start-up. Many people are more comfortable negotiating with clients than they are with their own partners. Negotiating with "outsiders" is much easier because the guidelines for reaching a successful outcome are clearer and the personal element is not as strong.

Some of the issues that partners must negotiate are unavoidably sensitive. For example, can partners hire spouses? What about that star son or daughter? Which employees will report to which partner? Many issues are provocative for one partner or another—and partners tend to avoid raising such issues because they are not good at dealing with conflict. If they see a troublesome question looming, they blink and pray that it goes away. Or they say, "We'll deal with that if and when it becomes an issue."

Do You Know Where the Future Will Take You?

While many partner arrangements are ambiguous about present circumstances (for example, it is often unclear who is really in charge of what areas), almost all partner arrangements are ambiguous about the future. Future uncertainties are rarely part of partners' initial discussions but are fraught with danger to the partnership. For many existing partnerships, stepping out of the day-to-day fray and thinking hypothetically about what lies ahead may be an ideal way to address issues that were given short shrift the first time around. People toying with the idea of partnership, as well as those who already have partners, can benefit enormously from a structured process that introduces the complete range of challenges that may await them. As I have described, the perils of partnership are well worth avoiding. The time to explore, discuss, and negotiate agreements and commitments is now. Waiting for a conflict to begin addressing the remaining ambiguities in a partnership is like waiting for a fire before contemplating fire extinguishers and exit routes. Chapter 2 describes a structured process that leads to a written document that is the best insurance plan prospective partners can buy to ensure their success as partners.

Starting down the Right Path:
A Partnership Charter

W HEN A COLLEAGUE AND I sat down at a conference table with BMC Associates' first clients—two partners, a father and a son, who were at each other's throats—they told us they had sown the seeds of their conflict when they met in their attorney's office to establish their partnership. Although the two of them fought regularly, their business was a resounding success if one just looked at the numbers. Two years after it opened, their New England seafood wholesale distribution company was running close to $15 million in annual revenues. The profit margin was high because the partners continued to operate from one cramped room, with just four people in the office and two workers in the warehouse. The new company's meteoric success surprised everyone, owners included, but the partnership was a failure, fraught with tension, frustration, and anger. The acrimony between the pair threatened to wipe out the financial success of the business, and if it crashed and burned, it was certain to take down some important relationships along with it.

The partners hit a low point one hot summer afternoon, when they slipped into a shouting match in front of their employees. It wasn't long before the son, Jimmy, stormed toward the door. His father, Mike, threatened, "If you leave now, don't come back. You're out!" Jimmy hollered back without breaking his stride, "That's impossible! I'm president and I own 50 percent of the company!"

At the insistence of both of their wives, they contacted us and we scheduled a mediation retreat for the following weekend. After we had established the ground rules for the mediation, and after they both had had a couple of minutes to vent, they described how they began experiencing difficulties shortly after becoming partners. It seemed to Mike that Jimmy was taking his title of president too seriously. He wanted his son to have the authority but hoped he would take more time growing into it—a common wish among fathers in family businesses.

Jimmy considered himself quite capable and thought he had taken more time than necessary to assume the mantle. He insisted that he had proceeded slowly just to placate his father, and whatever he was doing, he was doing well. He offered by way of example how he had successfully renegotiated their line of credit with the bank. Mike's perspective was that Jimmy made him look like a buffoon by meeting with the bank's commercial lending officer without him. He felt insulted, especially because Jimmy never informed him before attending the meeting. Jimmy, on the other hand, thought he stood a much better chance without his father at that particular meeting because Mike and two of Mike's cousins had driven a previous company into bankruptcy only a couple of years before.

The cross fire between the co-owners was not contained within their partnership. Their key employee, who was a close friend of Jimmy's from college, felt targeted. Mike and Jimmy both thought he was doing an excellent job, but in subtle and not-so-subtle ways, they competed for his loyalty. When we interviewed him in the beginning of the mediation, he complained about being caught in the middle. Their battle made the entire enterprise feel highly unstable to him.

To get to the heart of their conflict, we asked Mike and Jimmy why they had decided to go into business together. We learned that before starting this company with Jimmy, Mike had run a seafood-distributing outfit with two cousins. Mike's grandfather had founded it in the 1890s and since then it had been in the family. Mike himself had forty years of experience in the business and knew the industry inside out. Having seen all the things that went wrong under his father, uncles, and cousins, Jimmy believed he knew the pitfalls to avoid. Because Mike and Jimmy had always gotten along extremely well, including during the many summers Jimmy worked in the company while going to school, they both believed it would be gratifying to work together.

In an individual session with Mike, we asked what had moved them to set up the company the way they did, with Jimmy as president and Mike as vice president. Mike seemed a bit put off by the question. He said he really believed Jimmy would be good at this business.

We pushed Mike further on how they had decided on their management structure. He hesitated for a minute and then launched into the following story. When they had met with their attorney to answer questions regarding their shareholder agreement and articles of incorporation, the attorney had caught Mike off guard with two questions. He said the lawyer posed the two questions innocently enough. The first was, "Who will be president?" Mike told us there was only a deep silence in response. Although Mike had given considerable thought to taking Jimmy on as a partner, the lawyer's question took him by surprise. Mike had a long career in the business, had contacts and know-how, and was putting up the financing. Jimmy was a bright, freshly minted college graduate with plenty of energy. They had never thought about who would be in charge.

The question hung in the air. Mike glanced over at his son, who stared at their attorney and then shifted his gaze to the ceiling. With a pang of apprehension, Mike blurted out, "Make Jimmy president." Mike wound up being vice president and secretary by default.

The lawyer posed the second question: "And how will the stock be held?" Mike glanced again at his son again, and Jimmy—no fool—contemplated the ceiling once more and waited patiently for his father to decide. "Make it 50–50."

That seemed like a pretty remarkable story. Given their business history, the arrangement was peculiar. It created a structure that

Mike, even though it came from his lips, could not live with day to day.

Yet again, we pushed Mike harder on how he had made those decisions. At first he drew a blank. Then he became agitated as he recalled how his family had handled ownership issues in the past. When ownership of the business was passing to Mike's father and uncle, his grandfather picked Mike's uncle to run the business over Mike's father despite the fact, according to Mike, that his father was the one who was making the company successful. The uncle was considered by many to be alcoholic and irresponsible, but somehow none of this kept Mike's grandfather from making the uncle president and majority owner. The result was so much animosity between the brothers that they rarely spoke.

The poisoned relationship between them passed directly to the next generation. Mike recalled how he was forced to live with the legacy of his grandfather's decision because of his minority shareholder status and because he was forever under the management thumb of his inept cousins, who were also alcoholic, according to Mike. As Mike related this tale, his demeanor changed dramatically. He leaned back in his chair at the end and announced calmly, "Now I get it."

He explained to us that in the lawyer's office, without being aware of it, he had tried to right a wrong from two generations before. For the past two years, Mike had been wishing deep down that Jimmy would be grateful for what he had handed him on a silver platter: the presidency and half of the stock. "How could he be grateful" he remarked, "when I never even told him what his great-grandfather did and what I was trying to do to make amends? He was clueless, and it was my fault!"

When Jimmy came back in the conference room and heard the story from his father, he, too, understood their deal in a whole new light. Something instantly clicked in their relationship. They were no longer at loggerheads. They stopped sniping. Things opened up. It was as if a long-lost puzzle piece had been found. They finally had the conversation they should have had when they were establishing their partnership. We were then able to discuss their different personalities and values without any of the tension that had been in the air for so long. In fairly short order we helped them negotiate a four-page agreement that resolved their issues.

Driving home from the retreat, my associate and I marveled at the irony of what had happened to Mike and Jimmy. They had set themselves on a collision course at the very moment they were attempting to safeguard their voyage. They had unwittingly ensured conflict between themselves in the very act of nailing down the details of their deal. But they were not unique in this regard. When we listened to the stories of our second, third, and fourth clients, we realized that there was a pattern. Even when serious conflicts do not surface for years, the origin of partner conflicts can usually be traced to the origins of the partnerships. Often it can be traced directly to the drafting of the legal documents that are supposed to protect the partners if they run into conflict. (More on this irony in a moment.)

During its early years BMC Associates was completely focused on mediating partner battles. Eventually, however, I became curious about partnerships that had not experienced conflict. I interviewed partners who claimed to be getting along very well about their start-up process, specifically whether or not they had gotten everything out on the table and negotiated all of the basic issues. "Sure," they would say. If I followed up by asking them whether there were any lingering ambiguities in their partnerships, they would usually tell me that there were one or two items that had never really been resolved.

These dangling conversations had not yet resulted in calamity, but were they a problem? More often than not, partners who short-circuited their initial negotiations felt uncomfortable. Not all of them certainly, but many knew they were on shaky ground with one another and that circumstances had been kind to them. Even though they were doing fine day to day, they knew that if circumstances changed they could wind up facing off on opposite sides of the negotiating table. Their unresolved questions were the Achilles' heel of their partnership. As long as these important conversations remained unfinished, it was highly unlikely that the partners could realize their full potential as a team.

That realization of how critical it is for partners to negotiate and reach agreement on a full range of issues was the catalyst for developing the Partnership Charter. With the charter process, BMC Associates moved from conflict *resolution* to conflict *prevention*. We shifted from just repairing broken partnerships to helping partners achieve their shared goals.

REASONS FOR CREATING A PARTNERSHIP CHARTER

Some people have great ideas for businesses but never take the plunge because they are afraid of having partners and, for whatever reason, cannot do it alone. Countless co-owners operate successfully for years and then run into partnership glitches that destroy their businesses. Many other businesses never become as successful as they could be because the partners never figure out how to operate at their full potential. The Partnership Charter was designed to ensure that partnerships have a high probability of success and operate at their full potential.

A Partnership Charter is like a short course on how to create and manage a team of professional or business partners. In fact, it is the backbone of a course that I teach to MBA students at American University on how to manage a family-owned business. A charter is a necessary tool because few people have been taught how to be partners. It encompasses all of the topics partners need to cover as no other document or process does.

One of the main advantages of a Partnership Charter is that it provides a structure for people to address the issues that will make or break their partnership. Within that structure, the needs, priorities, personalities, and circumstances of the partners determine what is emphasized. The general charter structure covers three broad areas: business issues, relationship issues, and issues related to the future of the partnership. Each area is covered extensively in subsequent chapters.

Reasons for Creating a Partnership Charter

- To inform and enlighten people about the issues that create problems for partners
- **To p**rovide a structure in which to discuss sensitive, difficult issues
- To help people to be more open and honest with one another
- To remove the ambiguity that exists in many partner relationships
- To give partners or partners-to-be the time and space to focus on what they are trying to accomplish together
- To provide exercises for translating personal styles, values, expectations, and fairness into concrete action items
- To help people decide whether they really want to become partners
- To help prospective partners get to know each other better and build mutual trust and understanding so they can leverage their individual strengths
- To memorialize agreements about the partnership
- To create a document that serves as a guide for the partners in the future
- To have a clear statement of partners' intentions to give to attorneys who will draft legal documents
- To greatly diminish the likelihood of misunderstandings and conflicts

Creating a Partnership Charter gives people a much clearer sense of what they intend to do together. Many people become better communicators in the process. All partners who complete a charter feel more confident in themselves as a team because they know they have tested themselves. They've dealt with issues most partners avoid and have come through the process alive and together.

Does the process work this way for everyone? No. There are two other outcomes that we've seen. One is when people who are contemplating partnership work on a Partnership Charter and realize that they don't want to join forces. Their reaction to this realization is usually a mixture of sadness and relief: sadness that they will not be doing what they planned and relief because they see that it probably would not have worked.

The other outcome occurs when partners who have been working together for years decide to create a charter. They do it because they have experienced difficulty with their partnership, or they are in a transition, for example, taking on new partners. The people who are unhappy about their partnership use the charter process to determine whether they want to continue together. If they are able to work through their issues, then they go forward together. Partners who discover that they are incapable of working through the issues together usually conclude that they are highly likely to run into serious problems if they proceed without these agreements. They then shift gears and work on how they will dissolve their partnership in the most constructive way possible. The work they did on the charter usually helps smooth the process of separating.

For partners who are in transition, the charter process helps them figure out whether they want to go forward in their new configuration. Essentially, it operates like a road test. If you pass, that is, complete the charter, then you know you're good to go.

Partners who complete the charter process end up with a written document that records their understandings and serves as a guide as they go forward. A Partnership Charter captures their intentions, dreams, expectations, and agreements—their collective reality. It defines who they are as partners and what the vague word *partners* means to them. It does this so well, in fact, that many partners who are at the beginning of their partnership give the document to their attorneys, who rely on it to draw up partnership, or shareholder, agreements and buy-sell agreements.

A Partnership Charter is not written in stone; it's a living document that changes just as the individual partners and the partnership change. Partners must make a commitment to review it periodically and revise it as needed. The periodic reviews help ensure that partners continue to pay attention to any changes that are taking place before it's too late to do anything.

Does a Partnership Charter guarantee there will never be destructive conflict among the partners? No. But it forces partners to look more closely and thoroughly at who they are and how they want to work together. It keeps people from sidestepping the sensitive issues and allowing ambiguity to hide within their arrangement. A charter cannot totally preclude the possibility of destructive conflict, but it is probably the best insurance partners can buy. It is the most effective way to build confidence in the partnership.

WHAT A CHARTER SHOULD COVER

The topics that comprise a Partnership Charter came straight from partners themselves, not from a theory of partnerships. We listened to how our mediation clients got into trouble and constructed the charter based on their experiences. Our "theory" was simple: If an issue got those clients into trouble, it could get someone else into trouble, so we put it in the charter.

For example, over a decade ago, Mike and Jimmy's rudimentary "charter," if it could really be called that, was little more than a document of agreements that resolved their points of contention. It addressed primarily how, what, and when they would communicate important information to one another; their respective titles and what they meant; and their roles both inside and outside the company (i.e., with employees, the bank officers, and others). We added an ounce of prevention by giving them guidelines for dealing with any future conflicts. We did not realize at the time that they had given us the beginnings of a charter.

Subsequent clients taught us additional ways that partners could get stuck. In the beginning of our work, each new set of partners taught us something new, but over time, we found we were dealing with fewer and fewer new issues. Gradually, as issues and solutions both fell into increasingly distinct patterns, we developed a template for the Partnership Charter. We became confident that the charter process was covering all the bases.

HOW A PARTNERSHIP CHARTER IS
DIFFERENT FROM A LEGAL DOCUMENT

The documents that Mike and Jimmy's attorney drafted had given them a false sense of security. Having the corporate documents in hand

TABLE 2.1   Comparison Between Partnership Agreements and Partnership Charters

Partnership Agreement	Partnership Charter
Legally binding document; meant to create legal safeguards that compel certain conduct among the partners	Not legally binding; meant to instill and help maintain a collaborative partner spirit
Serves as a contract that creates partners' rights, duties, control, titles, and ownership shares	Serves as a guide for running the business and dealing with each other, as well as for expectations, fairness, and handling potential crises
The product—the written agreement—is the objective	The process of reaching understanding is primary; the product—the charter—is secondary
Written by lawyers with partners' input and contains many standard clauses	Written by the partners, sometimes with the help of mediators, and is highly idiosyncratic
Meant to withstand the test of time and not be altered excessively	Meant to be reviewed and revised on a regular basis; seen as a living document

SOURCE: David Gage, John Gromala, and Dawn Martin, "Addressing Partnership Issues as a Preventative Measure," in *The Family Business Conflict Resolution Handbook*, ed. B. Spector (Philadelphia: Family Business Publishing, 2003), 112–16.

lulled them into thinking they had done everything they needed to for their partnership to really work.

Legally, they had done what was necessary. Since they were forming a corporation, they were required to have articles of incorporation and a shareholders' agreement. Interestingly, to start a business as a legal partnership takes nothing whatsoever on paper. *No written contract is needed* for two people to become partners. *Acting* like partners is enough to do it. Even talking about being partners can suffice. Because no particular contract is necessary, any legal documentation at all makes people feel they have been extra cautious.

Prospective partners should realize that legal documents serve a narrow purpose. They establish the existence of the partnership or corporation as a legal entity and specify the legal rights and obligations of the partners. They include items such as the place, name, amount of capital to be invested by each partner, and distribution of profits. In a very real sense, they are there to protect partners from each other. They are about limiting liability. That is why they are legally binding.

It is wise for prospective partners to state clearly in the charter's preamble—where they describe their purpose for drafting the charter—that their charter is not meant to be a legally binding document. The charter often informs attorneys writing legal documents about partners' intentions, but it should not take the place of those legal documents.

While legal documents are important and necessary to have, they stop far short of the breadth and depth that partners need. Take something as basic as ownership percentages, for example. From a legal perspective, it is necessary to get the exact percentages in writing. As Mike and Jimmy learned, establishing percentages and entering the number into a legal document without understanding how they were derived can be confusing and lead to trouble. In chapter 4 I tell a story of five savvy businessmen who agreed on percentages in their corporate documents, then some of them claimed a year later that they also verbally agreed to review those percentages after one year. Mediators were brought in to clean up the mess—essentially to complete the ownership discussions. The original discussions satisfied the legal requirements but fell far short of what the partners needed to work well together. I describe in chapter 4 what it means to have a complete conversation about carving up the ownership pie.

Finally, whereas a partnership agreement is meant to withstand the test of time with minimal changes, a Partnership Charter is meant to be regularly reviewed and revised. A charter is more work to create and keep current, but it is also more useful because its purpose is creating and maintaining a solid, collaborative working relationship.

HOW COMPREHENSIVE SHOULD A
PARTNERSHIP CHARTER BE?

A Partnership Charter is comprehensive by design. It should include understandings on all the issues that could get partners in trouble at any stage of their partnership. Any given set of partners must thoroughly discuss their needs and reach consensus about what sections to include. Following are some guidelines:

1. If any one partner thinks something is important, it is usually reason enough to include it. Remember that in the life of a partnership, it only takes one unhappy camper to ruin the trip for everybody.

2. If you think you've already covered an issue, it behooves you to simply write it down and fold it into your charter. I have seen partners who believed they had already reached agreement on compensation, for example, but their agreement evaporated the moment they tried to capture the details on paper.

3. More is often better. Writing down agreements and sailing through a section that is not contentious is much wiser than skipping it and discovering later that it has become important. Any section that partners have really worked out, they can breeze through quickly.

4. If you have completed other types of documents that seem pertinent to working together, by all means add them. For example, the board of directors at SHN Engineering and Geological Consultants in California wanted to incorporate their mission statement into their charter. It fit perfectly.

5. Avoid skipping anything that feels like a sensitive issue. These are the most likely to cause problems.

6. Avoid the tendency to say, "We'll deal with that later if it ever becomes a problem." By that time it may be too late.

It is not essential for prospective partners to complete every section of the Partnership Charter; in fact, few do. What *is* essential is for them to thoroughly review each section together and discuss its relevance. This keeps partners honest about what they have and have not worked out.

I cannot warn enough against the tendency to short-circuit important discussions. It certainly seemed that Rosie O'Donnell and the publishing house Gruner & Jahr had conducted less-than-complete discussions when they created their 50–50 partnership deal in 2001. *The New York Times* filed this report on the breakdown of their high-profile partnership in August 2002:

> Whom exactly does a magazine named Rosie belong to? Is it the magazine's namesake, Rosie O'Donnell, the former talk show host and editorial director? Or Gruner & Jahr USA, the company that publishes the magazine? . . . The battle over that question has erupted into open warfare, with the erstwhile partners each hiring prominent lawyers to fight over who has ultimate control of the magazine's content. . . . The roots of the fight lie in the deal that turned the venerable but struggling McCall's into Rosie last year. Although the financial partnership is split 50–50 and Ms. O'Donnell's name is on the cover, Gruner & Jahr maintains editorial and operational control of the magazine. *It was a decision Ms. O'Donnell has rued from nearly the beginning of the partnership,* and that frustration has metastasized in recent months. . . . According to company officials at Gruner & Jahr, in the last month Ms. O'Donnell has threatened suit, behaved abusively toward employees and threatened to "bring the whole magazine down" (emphasis added).

Bring it down she did. More accurately, the partners' failure to resolve these questions up front brought the magazine down. Under either name, *McCall's* or *Rosie*, it is no longer published.

Rookies and veterans alike get into these kinds of predicaments because it is human nature to leave certain stones unturned. But that creates ambiguity, and ambiguity in the deal is a surefire recipe for disaster. Partners can go a long way toward avoiding conflict months and years later by conscientiously considering each topic of the charter and seeing how it applies to their situation.

WHY AGREEMENTS AMONG PARTNERS
NEED TO BE IN WRITING

When in business, it is best to act in a businesslike manner. Even though some people believe partners should operate on a handshake, keeping a written record of intentions and agreements facilitates smooth relationships among people who have their names on the door and their savings on the line.

Putting the spoken word on paper has an almost magical way of moving people from vagueness to clarity. It's quite common for people who are discussing what they want to do as a group to verbalize agreement *before* they fully understand each other's meaning. I'll never forget a quotation I first discovered in college: "I know you believe you understand what you think I said, but I am not sure you realize that what you heard is not what I meant." Partner discussions are replete with topics ripe for misunderstanding, so any technique that promotes understanding reduces the likelihood of conflict.

Writing things down also *organizes* discussions. Putting pen to paper forces a team planning their partnership to be more thorough about their collective thinking. Through writing, they see issues that they might otherwise have missed and nuances that they might have skipped over if they were merely talking. The result is a more complete discussion, which is never more important than when partners are discussing their deal with one another.

Having a written document is necessary because it creates a reliable record. Time corrodes the collective memory of partners even faster than it corrodes the memory of any one individual. That is because if only one partner's memory changes, the collective whole is lost.

For example, two partners nearly split their company after operating successfully for two years because they disagreed about who would run the company after the initial two-year period. The woman who was vice president for the first two years claimed that they had agreed to switch to her being president. The woman who was president for the first two years insisted that they had agreed to switch *only* if her own performance as president was lacking. Since they both thought she was doing a good job as president, she didn't want to switch and risk a turn of fortunes. The one who had been vice president for two years felt insulted and wanted her turn. She insisted that she could do at least as well as her partner had done. They became locked in a deadly battle over what hadn't been documented two years earlier.

Many disputes among partners are essentially battles of memories. It is easy to see that the circumstances and motivations of partners change over time in unpredictable and subtle ways, altering individual recollections. In this example, it may have been that the partners discussed switching the president's role after two years but never actually agreed to do it. We'll never know. The mediators who worked with them learned in a separate caucus session that the president partner had lost confidence in her vice-president partner. Though she denied it, that loss of confidence may have resulted in a conscious or unconscious shift in her memory. A written document would have saved them significant turmoil and expense.

A Partnership Charter is a very personal and private document that each partner will share with only one or two other people—a spouse, lawyer, accountant, or some other trusted advisor. Some people would argue that such information shouldn't be put in writing because they worry that it might be read by people for whom it wasn't intended. Other people believe business should be conducted on a handshake, and others believe that they can better keep their options open by not writing down what they are agreeing to.

The privacy concern is understandable. Because it embodies the basic "deal" among the partners, a charter is highly confidential and requires safekeeping. It is important to be careful not only with the end product but with interim drafts. Partners need to have a system for safekeeping of important and confidential business papers. The charter should be one of those papers.

People who fear that writing down their agreements will be misinterpreted as a lack of trust are hanging their trust on a very fragile hook. If trust is present, putting agreements in writing will not diminish it. If trust is so fragile that it will crumble if agreements are written down, then it was an illusion in the first place. *Some* partners can get by without documenting their agreements. The number of such partners, however, is much smaller than people imagine. Beware of anyone who says that he or she can't trust someone who desires more than a handshake.

People who resist putting agreements in writing because it forecloses their options are especially untrustworthy. In effect they are telling you up front that they reserve the right to renege on their agreements.

The dangers of *not* putting agreements among partners in writing far outweigh the risks of putting them in writing. They include

- not clearly understanding what the other partners mean,
- having incomplete discussions of issues,
- not having a clear record of what was agreed to, and
- partners conveying to other people different impressions of what they thought they agreed to.

Putting the partners' intentions, desires, and agreements in writing reduces the danger for all would-be and existing partners.

A CASE HISTORY

A Partnership Charter is both a process and a product. The following chapters use various partners' stories to describe the process of creating a charter. To give a clear picture of the product, I have included the entire Partnership Charter of one set of partners in the appendix. A caveat, however, is in order: No charter should be thought of as a model for anyone else's. It is not a compilation of best practices, and there is no definitive Partnership Charter. Even though Partnership Charters all cover roughly the same topics, any one charter is as unique as the partners themselves. What one set of partners agrees to is a result of their individual and collective histories, personalities and values, and business and financial situation. Their plans for themselves and their company represent their particular blend of dreams, aspirations, and circumstances. Their plans will never look the same as those of another group.

Star Systems is the name I've given to the company whose charter is in the appendix. The charter is real; I've changed the names of the company and the individuals, along with other identifying details, to present information that is very personal. I've retained the substance of their lives and circumstances. Most important, in the following chapters I describe how they actually dealt with common partner challenges and dilemmas. Even though their choices were not what someone else might choose, their process is informative and their end product is, for them, a sound one.

Here is how Star Systems' partners came together. For our purposes, it began when Jeff Davies, the financially strapped sole owner of Star Systems, told his CFO, Beth Nelson, that he was interested in her becoming his partner. In truth, it was less "interest" and more financial necessity—but Beth knew that. She'd been around when Star Systems was flush, before Jeff put himself, his family, his house, and the business itself on the line to get rid of his two former partners, his brother and sister.

Beth knew that Jeff was forcing himself to take on partners because he saw no other way to stay solvent. He'd been burned so badly by his experience with his siblings that he never wanted to hear the word partner again, but now he had no choice.

Jeff and his siblings had inherited equal portions of the business in the early 1990s when their parents died within ten months of each other. The company, then very profitable, sold medical laboratory instruments to research labs, biomedical corporations, and university hospitals. During all of the years that their parents had run the business and Jeff and his brother and sister worked for them, and even in later years when their involvement was limited and superficial, the three siblings got along reasonably well at work. There were occasional flare-ups, but they subsided quickly. The mother or father, after determining who was out of line, had to say only a few words to restore a modicum of decorum. This situation reminded Jeff of when he and his brother and sister would fight as kids. A fierce look or a sharp word from either parent and the kids would straighten up in short order.

Jeff's view was that the three siblings were a disaster waiting to happen. He believed that his older brother, who was president, felt threatened the minute Jeff entered the company and that both brothers resented what they perceived as their younger sister's histrionics and her dabbling in the company. She would come and go as she pleased, totally unpredictably.

In the ten months between their mother's and father's deaths, the siblings observed an unspoken détente. This proved to be the calm before the storm. All hell broke loose the week after they buried their father. The brothers unleashed their pent-up resentment about one another. The older brother told Jeff that he had never trusted him and believed Jeff was plotting to take over his position. Jeff did want his brother's job because he thought his brother was not up to the task and too insecure to be a good leader. The two brothers had divergent ideas about the company's direction and how finances should be managed. The older brother was much more content than Jeff with the course their parents had set for the company and more satisfied with their conservative financial approach.

When the fights broke out, there was a lot of shouting in private and some talking, but a dearth of listening. Accusations flew, some in front of employees. The power struggle between the brothers was now free to erupt without censure. The older brother tried to get his sister to side with him. He was successful, but only for a time; then she would side with Jeff. That never lasted long, however, because Jeff couldn't tolerate her capriciousness for long.

For over a year they bickered over who would buy out whom and at what price, until Jeff bought out both his siblings by leveraging almost all of his personal and business assets. The corporation would pay each of them more than a million dollars over ten years.

Jeff's personal financial situation now weighed him down severely even though the company was still highly profitable. The buyout had precipitated many of his difficulties, but his lifestyle exacerbated the situation. He was loath to downscale, as was his wife, and he wanted desperately to keep the business.

As much as Jeff hated the thought of having partners again, it seemed to be the only option available. His accountant assured him that this time could be different because he would have more control since he would not be one among three equals; moreover, he'd be able to choose his partner or partners.

Beth was a natural choice in most respects. She had been working for Star Systems since she had earned her CPA after college. She was the consummate insider, always keeping the company on the cutting edge, always on top of the smallest details of the company's critical relationships with suppliers. Jeff's father had made her the CFO. Everyone trusted her, and she had been the only non-family member on the board of directors. Beth had done an incredible job staying neutral during the siblings' wars and was trusted by all three of them to work with their accountant on the buyout. She had wanted to be Jeff's partner earlier, but he could not bear the thought of any new partners. She did not have much money, Jeff knew, but she was the one person he could remotely imagine having as a partner.

Jeff and his accountant sketched out a deal whereby he would sell the minimum amount of stock possible, receive enough cash to give him some short- and long-term financial relief, and, of course, not give up control of the company. They both knew that Beth understood what the company was worth, so neither thought that valuing a portion of it would be an issue.

Beth and Jeff met to talk numbers. They agreed that Star Systems was worth about $4 million, so if Beth were offered a 10 percent stake, it would cost her $400,000. That much was pretty straightforward. Then the conversation got interesting. Jeff suddenly realized that Beth was negotiating *with* him and not *for* him. They had always been on the same side of the table in negotiations with other companies, and now, suddenly, their relationship was shifting. Beth was saying that a 30 percent discount for a minority interest and lack of marketability was reasonable, putting the cost to her at $280,000. She also thought that given all that she had done for the company and Jeff, it would be reasonable to think of her putting up just $80,000 and paying the rest over five years. The bottom line was that this was all she could afford.

Jeff was forced back to the drawing board. The deal wouldn't work, at least not with only Beth as his partner, and Jeff knew of no one else inside or outside the company that he was comfortable considering in that role. Beth told him that she had a friend, Sarah, whom she thought would be a perfect fit from a professional standpoint; she just wasn't sure about how Jeff and she would take to each other. As Beth described her friend, images of his sister flashed into Jeff's mind. He immediately called a halt to the conversation.

A month later, Jeff asked Beth for more information about her friend. He agreed to meet her for lunch with Beth, using the pretext of possible employment (a real possibility, in fact, because Jeff needed someone who could take over sales and marketing).

The first meeting went well. All Jeff really remembered, though, was that Sarah seemed like the most outgoing person he'd ever met and that she was a natural salesperson. They didn't talk directly about the job or the possibility of anyone buying into the company. She was obviously interested, however, and so was he.

Jeff set up another meeting that he began by talking about the director of sales and marketing position. Sarah told him in detail about her experience, including her current job, which was basically the same position at a larger, public company. She had extensive contacts with university hospitals throughout the country that could prove valuable if she came to Star Systems. When he asked her why she would want to leave her present job, Sarah said she was looking for an opportunity to have an equity stake in a growing, profitable company. The meeting ended without any clear indication from Jeff that ownership was possible, but he didn't rule it out. He said he would get back to her within a week.

The idea of partners still made Jeff queasy, but he set up another meeting after more conversations with Beth, his accountant, and one of Sarah's references. He felt reassured by her stellar job history and her longtime friendship with Beth. His fear that Sarah was just like his sister had subsided.

The package Jeff offered Sarah gave her about the same salary she was currently making ($200,000) and an ownership stake similar to what Beth would get, that is, a 10 percent stake in the company for $280,000, with $100,000 up front and $180,00 over two years. Sarah asked how her deal differed from Beth's, and Jeff explained that Beth was going to pay slightly less up front and the balance over a longer period of time. Sarah suggested that if she could increase revenues by $500,000 in her first year, she should also have five years to pay the balance instead of two. Jeff quickly realized that Sarah was a good negotiator herself. He countered with a million-dollar revenue increase and two years, and they agreed to think it over.

Jeff suddenly realized that he had not yet discussed any of this with his attorney. They met and reviewed the proposals. The attorney, who had been intimately involved when Jeff was extricating himself from his sibling partner experience, said he was surprised that Jeff was taking on any partners. That again made Jeff nervous. The attorney told Jeff that he had recently heard me speak on partnerships and suggested that Jeff call me.

When I spoke with Jeff, he explained that his fear of taking on partners was a consequence of his bad partner experience with his siblings. When I described to him how the Partnership Charter works, he opened up to the possibility that his experience with Beth and Sarah could be different. I suggested that before they negotiated any more of their deal, they should have a retreat to explore the entire range of issues related to being partners. By the end of the three-day weekend retreat, I assured him, they would all have a much clearer understanding of whether or not this made sense and how they would operate as partners.

Their discussions and negotiations during the retreat fashioned the charter in the appendix. It is reproduced in its entirety so you can see what an entire Partnership Charter looks like. Keep in mind, however, that no charter, including this one, is meant to be a model for others to copy. One reason I chose this charter was its thoroughness, but not every charter needs to cover everything in such a detailed and complete manner. Each charter must reflect the individuality of its creators and the uniqueness of their partnership.

PART TWO

IT'S JUST BUSINESS

CHAPTER 3

Partners' Vision and Strategic Direction

It's okay to spend a lot of time arguing about which route to take to San Francisco when everyone wants to end up there, but a lot of time gets wasted in such arguments if one person wants to go to San Francisco and another secretly wants to go to San Diego.

STEVE JOBS, COFOUNDER OF APPLE COMPUTER

HAVING CONTROL OVER what a business does today and where it goes tomorrow is part of the thrill of closely held businesses. Owners get to decide where their business is headed, and if they want, they can change course in midstream. Co-owners of companies have tremendous control—*if they can agree*. If partners cannot agree, the feeling of having control will evaporate and the business may begin spinning its wheels. The following story of two partners illustrates what can happen.

PARTNERS GOING IN DIFFERENT DIRECTIONS

Two 50–50 owners of a thriving information services firm found themselves going in different directions when they couldn't agree on their company's future. One partner, Stan, believed the company's future was in providing a limited number of global customers with highly sophisticated software and services. The other partner, Lon, believed the company should provide simple but valuable Web-based information to a broad spectrum of customers. Each avenue had different risks and rewards associated with it, and each one played to a different partner's strengths. Without a clear plan from the outset, the two partners pursued their own strategies.

Each plan consumed company resources and different employees' attention, and neither plan received the resources and attention it needed. Employees were totally confused and said the company felt schizophrenic. Over a three-year period, Lon and certain key employees became increasingly frustrated, convinced that Stan and another key employee were autocratically taking the company in the wrong direction. Stan, the dominant personality of the pair, firmly refused to debate the issue.

The more adamant Stan became about his choice of direction, the more things deteriorated. Employees feared that a large potential client would perceive the confusion engulfing the company and terminate negotiations, effectively ending the hopes for either avenue of growth. Employees aligned themselves more forcefully with either Lon or Stan as their attention increasingly focused on the battle over the company's strategic direction. Lon, though by nature unassertive, insisted that Stan and he hire mediators to resolve the deadlock. Stan refused. Then he agreed to mediation, but only if the company accountant was the mediator. That ended in failure, which it was bound to do because no existing advisor is going to be perceived as neutral when the negotiating gets truly difficult. After the failed "mediation," Stan continued to stonewall, even after he learned that two key employees were interviewing with other companies. Clinging to the little control his position gave him, Stan seemed ready to fight to the finish.

Lon and his attorney then threatened to put the company in receivership, essentially asking a judge to take control of the company by appointing a person to take Stan's place. On the brink of being overthrown, Stan agreed to hire professional mediators. During several days of intense negotiations, the mediators helped the two owners decide that Stan would buy Lon out. Stan would thus be free to take the company in the direction he wanted. When the five key employees heard the news, four of them told the owners that that solution was unacceptable. They threatened to leave if Stan took over completely.

The mediators conducted extensive shuttle diplomacy in the next round of negotiations, which included meetings with the key employees. Meetings continued through an entire weekend. To resolve their impasse, both owners agreed to three major changes. First, they would build a real board of directors. The board they had was just the two of them. They would add one employee and two outside directors to make a total of five directors. Second, they would reduce their equity shares to 40 percent each and give 20 percent to present and future key employees. The third major restructuring element was that Stan would resign immediately as president, and they would bring in an acting president.

The warring over the company's soul ceased with the signing of a memorandum of understanding. The interim president and the new board took over, and together they set the company's direction. Five years later, fairly on schedule, a Fortune 100 company acquired the company for sixteen times its value at the time of the mediation. When the new owner took over, Stan was terminated and Lon was given a short-term contract.

These two partners, like many others who had never explicitly agreed on their company's strategic direction, were driving blindfolded. The lack of consensus regarding a direction or the means to resolve a disagreement about it leaves partners vulnerable and exacerbates any other problems. To avoid ending up in such a predicament, partners need to have a shared vision. Partners greatly improve their chances of success when they can agree on a vision, mission, and outline of a strategic plan.

VISION AND DIRECTION

The start-up stage of a company's life is critical—a time of great potential, excitement, and uncertainty. A start-up is an amorphous creature, not unlike a Rorschach inkblot, onto which everyone projects his or her own designs. People can talk at length about a start-up, get excited about its potential, even throw out "hard numbers," and still be talking about different companies. This section of the Partnership Charter is designed to ensure that people who are contemplating joining together are on the same mission.

Stating the mission, the vision, and strategic plans are all ways of communicating ideas, intentions, and expectations to many different constituents, for example, investors, employees, and bankers. However, what I call a partners' strategic plan is more of an internal plan, and it has only three purposes: to stimulate the partners' thinking, expose assumptions, and communicate among the principals. The plan prevents false starts and keeps partners from wasting time, effort, and resources. The strategic plan keeps individual partners from going off on their own tangents. While it is advisable to engage in a full planning process within a year of starting out, this partners' strategic plan is extremely helpful for launching the partnership. The most basic strategic planning process begins with several concise statements regarding the business's mission, vision, and values.

The mission.   The mission statement should capture what the enterprise is, what it does, for whom, and why. It captures this information in one clear, concise sentence.

The vision.   The vision should communicate the partners' image of the company's competitive edge. A vision does not have to describe a totally new type of company; companies do not have to be unique to succeed. FedEx was founded to do a common, mundane job: move packages from point A to point B, but to do it more swiftly and reliably than anyone had ever done it previously. Bernie Marcus and Arthur Blank started Home Depot to sell hardware, but they carry a wider range of merchandise and set competitive prices in order to sell *lots* of hardware. Southwest Airlines was one more airline. Besides competing on price in the cutthroat airline industry, a key aspect of its vision was what its founders call Positively Outrageous Service. Visions might revolve around tradition (e.g., Restoration Hardware), innovation, packaging, size, safety, quality, knowledgeable staff, response time, span of operations, convenience, quality, or creating fun.

A key to leadership in many businesses is the ability of the owners to convey their vision of the company to their employees and others. If the partners are even slightly out of sync with one another, the result can be as disquieting as looking at a slightly out-of-focus picture. Co-owners need to have a truly shared, singular vision and confirm that they share such a vision before jumping into business together.

Values.   Partners may also decide that they want their business to have a core set of values, or principles, that guide their company's actions. Patrick Lencioni, in a *Harvard Business Review* article entitled, "Make Your Values Mean Something," wrote that many companies lay claim to "values that too often stand for nothing but a desire to be au courant or, worse still, politically correct." (Consider that Kenneth Lay and other senior executives at Enron came up with the values statement, "Your Personal Best Makes Enron Best.") In addition to giving employees a rallying point, company values can also set a company apart in a competitive marketplace. "Core values often reflect the values of the company's founders—Hewlett-Packard's celebrated 'HP Way' is an example," Lencioni noted.

If partners declare a set of values, they must live by them and ensure that employees do too, because values create expectations. If the values are not adhered to, and expectations are not met, then cynicism and distrust will flourish and partners will be worse off than if they had never established company values. Partners must ensure that any values they choose for their company are in keeping with their own personal values. The "personal values" instrument discussed in chapter 9 helps partners clarify their own values.

The partners' strategic plan.   The basic strategic planning process entails combining the partners, and everything they bring to the table, with the major business factors that affect them. Variables from the partner side of the equation include the number of principals, their personal

Source: Based on John L. Ward and Craig E. Aronoff, "How Family Affects Strategy," *Small Business Forum* (Fall 1994): 85–88.

FIGURE 3.1   Partners' Strategic Planning Process

resources, personalities, leadership styles, interpersonal dynamics, expertise, past experiences, aspirations, goals, and personal values. All of these personal elements help shape the direction of the enterprise. The business factors include things like the industry, physical resources, borrowing capacity, and diversity of operations. The unique set of partners combines with their particular business context to produce a vision for their business, which shapes their strategic plans.

The strategic plan can be broad, but it must be detailed enough to bring the partners' vision back down to earth and ensure that they take the same road to a common destination. The plan should contain a limited number of business goals, with each goal supported by a few implementation strategies. Each should also have a timeline and its own yardstick. The goals relate to topics such as the company's markets; the breadth, scope, and degree of diversification; financial resources; and leadership requirements.

Gene Johnson and Paul Carlin founded Mail2000 in 1995 and sold it to UPS six years later for a reported $100 million. That does not happen without some careful planning before the launch. Carlin, a former postmaster general of the U.S. Postal Service, explained to me, "We spent three years fleshing out the concept for Mail2000, so by the time we received our initial major funding, we didn't have to go back and re-think parts of the system." At the core of their strategic plan "was the uniqueness of our distributed network. It's really the only effective mail distribution system using multiple production sites in the United States." Their vision was a company that could improve service and reduce the cost of mass mail distribution with a national printing network.

The other crucial aspects of their strategic planning included some clear management and finance components. To have the management team that they needed, Johnson said, "We recognized that we needed to bring in people who had other strengths, like a strong operating person and a strong financial person, and strong sales and marketing people." They agreed that Johnson would be CEO and Carlin chairman. They further agreed to put in significant money to start it up (including $1.5 million to buy their way out of the noncompetes they had agreed to when they sold their first company) and take out next to nothing. From the outset they also had an exit strategy clearly in view: They had set their sights on an IPO, a full sale, or a partial sale.

Carlin and Johnson claimed, "We never had a major disagreement over strategy." Undoubtedly, planning ahead paved the way for their being of one mind. For others, the conversations about vision and strategic plans may bring to the surface differences of opinion. It is better to learn of these differences during preplanning than when executive decisions have to be made quickly—or worse, after they've been made.

Becoming clear with one another about a strategic direction during the charter process does not mean that partners are stuck with that business design; far from it. Partners must periodically review and continually entertain the possibility of changing their strategic plan, that is, the way they make their money. Developing the partners' strategic plan simply ensures that the partners are in sync about where they are headed before they start out. Not all partners are on the same page, and many don't even realize it.

There are two major constraints on a company's growth that can be dealt with in the context of planning: management limitations and insufficient capital. These two topics should receive special attention when partners are defining their vision and direction.

THE MANAGEMENT CULTURE

From the company logo to office space, partners will have endless management decisions to hash out after they start their companies. Managing their business is the most all-consuming activity most co-owners will do together; therefore, before jumping in, they should have a crystal clear, ten-thousand-foot view of how they will manage their company together. Chapter 5 looks at managing from a day-to-day perspective; this chapter takes a high-level view so that prospective partners can tell if they are all in sync with the management style they are contemplating.

To achieve a clear, unified view of how to manage the company, partners have to discuss how they'll carry out their strategic plans. Without such discussions, one partner might lean toward a bureaucratic company utilizing a chain of command, while another might want a flatter organizational structure. Co-owners can also explore issues such as, Is this a company that delegates? Is it a hands-on type of management? Is it secretive or open? How interested are the partners in employee training and development? In promoting from within? Is customer service a management priority? Is there a commitment to hiring only the best people? At what point will managers be brought in from outside the company? How will the partners decide when the company has outgrown their own management skills? How involved do partners want employees to be in management decisions? The answers to questions like these define the management culture.

When Santhana Krishnan and Yash Shah told me about the management culture they wanted for their information technology infrastructure management company, InteQ, they said they knew it had to be extremely open. "Neither Santhana nor I had any hidden agendas or motives, so we didn't have anything that we were worried about or felt we had to hide," Shah explained. "At every meeting with employees we say, 'Please don't read between the lines. If something seems missing, it's probably because we overlooked it, or we didn't think it was important, or we screwed up.'" Everyone is encouraged to ask for whatever details he or she needs. The two partners believe that their management culture makes it easy for people to work with them. "The people who came with us six years ago are still here. We've gone through good times and bad, but not a single person who started the company with us has left."

Partners who are not in sync on these management issues create confusing cultures that frustrate employees and send the best ones running for the door. Partners like Krishnan and Shah, who are of one mind about managing their company and can establish and maintain a unified culture, can produce extraordinary results, as they have done.

MANAGING FINANCES

It can be a grave mistake to enter a business venture without some basic understanding about how to manage its finances. In chapter 6 I focus on how partners take money out of their business. Here I look at how the business's cash requirements, both capital requirements and expenses, can be anticipated, not in terms of specific amounts, but in approach.

People have strong feelings about the right way to manage spending and borrowing, and some are oblivious to the fact that others hold incompatible views. While it is true that people in business are there to use money to make money, partners have to define what that means to them. The goals in this section of the Partnership Charter are to understand one another's views and find as much common ground as possible on strategic financial issues so that day-to-day financial management goes as smoothly as possible.

In their approaches to spending, people range from profligate spenders to hoarders. Regarding debt, there are risk-takers and risk-avoiders. People at different ends of the spectrum can find themselves in the same partnership. Consider two partners, one of whom believes that they should save money for a down period. She sees limited access to capital as a distinct advantage because it forces them to carefully plan expenditures. Easy capital, she argues, leads to easy mistakes. Her partner believes that the more they spend, the more they'll make. He sees debt as a vehicle for growth—a necessary stimulant. Personal savings look like free money to him, borrowing against a second mortgage on his home looks cheap, and he's not the least bit shy about approaching friends and family for money. People with views this diverse really do wind up as partners. If they conduct the discussion I am suggesting here, they'll have a reasonable chance of succeeding together. Absent agreements going in, they are likely to be unwinding before they realize what is happening.

Developing a few basic agreements about managing finances going into partnership helped Richard Egan and Roger Marino of EMC, the electronic storage company, feel confident that they were on the same track. "One key agreement," Egan told me, "was what we called our 'doomsday war chest formula.'" The money on hand minus their debts had to equal six months' pay for everybody in the company. "That way," he explained, "if a catastrophe struck, all the employees and Roger and I would have six months to find new jobs." After they both agreed to this, it gave them a starting point for managing their finances.

One discussion regarding spending revolves around spending styles. Is this a first-class-everything company or a classic penny-pincher? The answer is more apt to depend on founders' values than on how much money is in the bank. When Stanford University student partners Jerry Yang and David Filo founded Yahoo, they agreed to spend corporate money with great care. Yahoo prided itself on being penny-pinching, even when it was reporting millions in operating profits. Its partners and executives, whose salaries have always been low by Silicon Valley standards, are known to leave meetings early to catch the last flight home to save the cost of a hotel room.

Another spending question involves the overall outlay of expenses, which will have a direct effect on whether there are any profits for the partners to share. This is also a timing question, because one partner might argue that more reinvestment now will mean greater profits later. The partners' vision and strategic plan should help define their stance on short-term gain versus long-term growth. Some partners also establish a corporate earnings threshold above which distributions or performance bonuses would be paid, and then set a target percentage of earnings that are earmarked for distribution.

A discussion about debt is critical. Questions to address include: How much capital are we ready to contribute to working capital? How much company debt are we willing to take on, presuming we have the borrowing capacity? How willing are we to secure company debt with personal assets such as our homes (a likely requirement)? What would we do if the business had a cash call but one partner couldn't carry his or her share? What if an attractive acquisition were available? What if we encountered real success and that created a demand for more money, as it typically does? Are we willing, as so many entrepreneurs are, to borrow from friends and family? Would we trade a good portion of the company for angel investor funding or venture capital? Partners should also agree on how differences in their personal finances and access to capital will be handled.

Given how many entrepreneurs start companies using credit cards, prospective partners' strategy discussions should include this topic. Approximately half of all small companies begin, and expand, using credit cards. This is far more than the 6 percent who rely on SBA loans or the 2 percent who receive venture capital. While credit card money is easy to obtain, it is costly in terms of interest and penalties.

Some situations I have seen lead me to offer a couple of caveats regarding borrowing. If partners make capital contributions or loans to the business at start-up or later that are not in proportion to their ownership interests, they should be clear why they are doing it and what, if any, are the consequences. If partners receive money from friends and family—which about 30 percent of all small firms do—they should document all the details of the arrangement, including how it affects the partners' interests, what would happen if the business failed, and whether the money received is a straight loan or is in exchange for equity. Some people with money have a penchant for leaving this ambiguous in the hopes of being protected on the downside (then it's a loan) and being rewarded on the upside (it was equity). Paul Carlin warned that partners should make sure other people's "expectations are realistic because the chances of things going south are very large." Financial backers need to know that they do not "have the right to step in and take over if it's not working." John May, an advisor to angel investors, has said that money coming from family and friends is sometimes humorously referred to as friends-family-fools' money. People on both the giving and receiving ends need to proceed with caution with loans, or investments, whichever they are.

Partners are wise to establish how open they want to be about their own finances, because their personal financial situations may directly affect the business's finances. In chapter 11 I discuss the unusual transparency one set of partners demanded of themselves to ensure that they would not be caught off guard when their company needed capital infusions.

The challenge in this section of the charter is developing a truly shared vision and direction that give the partners confidence that they are contemplating the same business and that it is set to move in one agreed-upon direction.

CHAPTER 4

Pieces of the Pie: Ownership Issues

A lion, a jackal, a leopard, and a gazelle kill an antelope and prepare to devour their kill. The lion roars, "We must divide our antelope into four parts. The first part goes to me because I am king of the beasts. Due to my strength, I deserve the second part. The third part goes to me because of my courage. Regarding the last quarter, any one of you who cares to dispute it with me can do so at his own risk.

VARIATION OF AN AESOP FABLE

IN THE SPRING OF 1998, a physician had an idea for a new medical device. He knew he needed partners, so he invited a friend, a savvy marketing man, to develop the idea with him. Within a couple of weeks they had brought two others—a lawyer and a CEO of a regional consulting company—into their discussions. The four entrepreneurs then enlisted a highly regarded researcher, who also became enthusiastic about the idea and the partnership.

With no time to lose, they brainstormed and went to work on their assignments to make sure the product was a viable concept. Everything looked positive, so they began making serious plans to find capital and staff. They enlisted the lawyer to guide them through the necessary discussions and draft the corporate documents. The process went smoothly until they came to their respective ownership interests. The first test of their budding partnership had arrived.

Each began jockeying for as large an interest as possible. The physician rightly maintained that none of them would even be thinking of this company without his idea. The marketing consultant claimed that he had played a key role in promoting the idea, had put up the most cash, and had the most contacts. The consulting company CEO felt that the idea would have been only that without his experience and ability. The lawyer believed he had already saved the company tens of thousands of dollars by drafting the organization's documents and agreements. The medical device researcher argued that the company could not go forward without his knowledge, reputation, and expertise.

Like forty-niners staking their claims, each of the five fought for his share of the equity. They finally came to an agreement on percentages, signed the papers, and began work. Within a month four of them were working full time in their new venture. The physician-investor continued his own practice but also worked his contacts for the benefit of the company.

One year later they were forced back to the drawing board. The consulting company CEO, now the CEO of the new company, and the researcher claimed that they had all agreed to review everyone's performance after a year's operation and adjust the ownership percentages accordingly. The lawyer and the marketing director disagreed vehemently, claiming that the idea of revisiting the percentages had been raised but then dismissed. The physician-investor, a friend of both the marketing director and the CEO, demurred, unable to remember the decision. The resulting deadlock took a toll on their relationships, their motivation, and their productivity. Worse, their employees were becoming aware of the disagreement.

Both the lawyer and the marketing director argued that the percentages were set in their documents. From a purely legal perspective they were correct, but a legal battle over ownership interests would destroy the company. They all finally agreed that their only option was to hire mediators to help them negotiate a resolution.

The convoluted dynamics among the partners became apparent in the one-on-one discussions with the mediators. The marketing director and the lawyer (with 32 and 12 percent ownership, respectively) were both afraid that the CEO was unhappy with their performances and wanted to punish them by diminishing their stock. The CEO (with 18 percent) *was* interested in reducing their percentages, as he didn't believe their work was as good as promised and even thought that they had done some detrimental things. However, he asserted that he didn't want to be vindictive and claimed that he really wanted some shares of company stock to be available as an incentive for key employees. In fact, he was willing to reduce his own shares proportionally. The physician-investor (with 26 percent), though amenable to surrendering some shares, was afraid to take sides. The researcher agreed that some partners had to reduce their shares to free up equity but believed that he shouldn't have to since he had originally received only a 12 percent stake.

The individual and joint discussions revealed how tightly the partners' egos were wrapped around these percentages. Most of them were highly competitive and hopeful that this venture might be the lucky break that would free them from having to work full time. Since they were united around the goal of growing and selling the company in a few years, they were acutely aware of the value of every percentage point.

With the help of the mediators, the owners eventually resolved the equity battle. By issuing additional shares they effectively reduced the equity of everyone except the researcher and thus had shares to use as incentives. Besides successfully navigating their equity crisis, they resolved some differences over the roles of the marketing director and the lawyer. They sold the company four years later to a British firm for a favorable return on their investment. Their struggle, and the fact that they nearly lost something so valuable, shows how hard it is to negotiate changes in ownership once things are under way.

THE CHALLENGE OF SETTING OWNERSHIP INTERESTS

It is extremely difficult to allocate ownership rights at the outset. That next to nothing is written on the subject is an indication that there are no guidelines or easy formulas. Laws govern the rights and responsibilities of partners, but they typically don't dictate ownership if the owners cannot agree among themselves. People are basically on their own, and for most this is uncharted territory.

The five partners in the example fell into a common trap—each person grasping for the best possible deal. Potential partners are entering into a long-term relationship that should be based on supporting each other, not besting each other, making this negotiation different from most others. Beginning a partnership with a contest over ownership interests can set a dangerous and unfortunate tone. Nonetheless, it is easy to fall into that trap because everybody wants what is in short supply. It's the classic problem of the fixed pie: No matter how many shares are issued—ten or ten million—they never equal more than 100 percent.

The charter process can be a great aid in establishing ownership percentages because it keeps partners from a mad rush to grab the highest number. Unless they first learn about one another and define other aspects of their deal, it won't matter that they got 99.9 percent of the ownership pie—the pie may be inedible. The charter process provides a structure for discussing ownership and tying it back to shared expectations and commitments. It helps partners see that ownership percentages are only one piece of the entire partnership deal by forcing them to step back, recognize that there are many issues to deal with, and take time to discuss the full range of topics.

WHAT OWNERSHIP MEANS TO INDIVIDUAL PARTNERS

Ownership means different things to different people. To one person it might mean a share of the profits; to another it might mean a right to part of the proceeds of the sale of the company; to another it might mean having a say in strategic decisions or board governance; to yet another it might mean day-to-day management authority. Each partner could have a distinct position on each aspect—profits, governance, employment, and management—that reflects his or her particular skills, interests, and needs more than his or her ownership interest per se. In other words, what a person gets out of being an owner need not be rigidly tied to that person's ownership interest. There is more flexibility than people imagine.

When negotiating partnership interests, each person should understand what ownership means to him or her and what it means to each of the future partners. Producer and director Steven Spielberg joined forces with Disney film executive Jeffrey Katzenberg and music industry wizard David Geffen to form the studio called DreamWorks SKG in 1994. Each initially invested $33 million and took a one-third interest. One year later, they let Microsoft cofounder Paul Allen buy an 18 percent stake in the company and join the board—for $500 million.

Obviously the percentages tell just a fraction of the story, and money, while it may dictate ownership stakes in many partnerships, is not the primary factor in others. Allen hinted at what he thought he could contribute beyond the money and what he might get out of the deal: "I'm not in there telling them who they should cast. I'm interested in learning from them. They may use me as a sounding board for some of the new multimedia areas." Of course, $500 million is a high price for a learning experience! The mere fact that three stars like Spielberg, Katzenberg, and Geffen joined forces and founded the company creates value that is greater than their initial capital investments. Allen certainly recognized that much of his partners' contribution was their creative and specialized intellectual capital, which he was not contributing.

Money commands a larger share of companies that are capital intensive, such as manufacturing companies. A capital contribution will also command a larger percentage when it is used to fund untested ideas, because of the risk involved. Many partners, like Richard Egan, who cofounded the data storage company EMC, have expressed relief that they took more time to develop their companies and prove their capabilities and profitability before taking on financial partners. They were in a better position to negotiate and not be dictated to because they had not traded stock for capital.

Four sections of the Partnership Charter help people appreciate the factors that determine ownership interests, understand what ownership means to each person, and divide ownership in a more rational and satisfying way:

1. strategic planning for the business,
2. roles and managing the business,
3. employment and compensation, and
4. fairness and interpersonal equity.

Some people have become partners only to discover that the company they envisioned was not the one their partners had in mind. As described in chapter 3, writing down the company's vision, its mission, and an outline of a strategic plan helps guarantee that the partners are dividing the same pie. Furthermore, the strategic planning helps each individual understand better whether his or her skills and background add value.

The value of some people's contributions will depend on the specific roles they will play in the business. If someone envisions herself overseeing all production, but her partners-to-be see her in a lesser role, they may be thinking of different ownership percentages. Some people are willing to take a smaller ownership percentage if they can have their desired role. Others would argue that the percentage of ownership should correspond to responsibility. The relationship between management roles and ownership is complex, but it is a variable that should be discussed prior to determining ownership. Roles are covered in chapter 5.

People often tie the amount of ownership they should have to the amount of money they put into the business. In some types of businesses that makes more sense than in others. It will depend to a large extent on the equivalence of the other contributions they will be making, the value of money, and also the relationship between ownership interests and how the partners will take money out of the business. While profit distributions and sale proceeds are closely tied to ownership interests, wages and other compensation are generally tied to employment. (Employment may be related to ownership, but even if it is, salaries should still be a function of the job performed, not of shares owned.) In chapter 6 I examine the various ways people hope to profit financially from being partners. Understanding them well will help prospective partners put ownership in a more realistic, full context.

The principle of fairness must govern all negotiations. Chapter 10 will help partners explore and appreciate the many ways that people contribute value to a business, from money to physical assets, from ideas to sweat equity. The fairness exercises in that chapter also help people to be more specific about what they wish to achieve from being a co-owner. When people appreciate the broader aspects of this complex picture, they are less apt to focus single-mindedly on percentages and more apt to achieve a sense of fairness.

OWNERSHIP AND CONTROL

Control—over operations, strategic decisions, and the ultimate disposition of the business—is a central issue in decisions about ownership percentages. The right to exercise control over a business is an undeniable part of ownership, but power struggles over control are commonplace. Because percentages of ownership play a significant role in control battles, partners-to-be must appreciate the complex relationship between ownership interests and control.

Fifty-Fifty Partners

Many people who go into business together choose to divide ownership 50–50, but many, like Mike and Jimmy (whom I described in chapter 2), are unclear about what it means to be equal owners. Does equal ownership mean that both partners will contribute the same resources to the venture? Will each bring in 50 percent of the revenue? Are they saying that their contributions will have equal value? Are they agreeing to work equally hard or be equally responsible for management?

An even split may indicate that at least one prospective partner is avoiding a serious discussion about the other's contributions. Some people are uncomfortable noticing differences, so they gloss over them and insist that everything is equal.

Fifty-fifty often represents a desire to be egalitarian: People will contribute and take out rewards approximately equally. This may work if the two people are on relatively equal footing with respect to their backgrounds, resources, commitment, ambition, and so on. If not, it may begin to look and feel lopsided. Sometimes 50–50 sounds more egalitarian than it actually is.

Fifty-fifty ownership is a way that some people try to equalize power in *operating* the business. Each partner seeks assurance that the other will not have an upper hand. This defensive maneuver can backfire, however, because 50–50 partners risk a deadlock in decision making if neither has clear authority to make the ultimate decision and they do not have a method for breaking impasses. If two partners elect to own equal interests, they need to take pains to decide and spell out clearly in their charter how they would deal with this risk.

At their heart, 50–50 partnerships are about creating and maintaining a spirit of equity. Ideally, equal owners try to bring out the best in each other and appreciate that, at any given moment, their contributions and rewards may not be equal. Over the long haul, both partners believe they will balance out and that they will achieve much more by being together than they could have on their own.

Two Partners in Majority–Minority Roles

In the mid-1980s, I had a discussion with a psychiatrist, who consulted regularly with business owners, about the mediation company I was going to start. He was intrigued by the concept and wanted to talk about our becoming partners. We discussed it over almost a year and finally decided to start a firm to offer the mediation services that I had first described. He offered to have the attorneys from whom he sublet office space draw up the necessary corporate documents.

Naïve person that I was, I was shocked to see that the documents gave the ownership percentages as 51–49. We had never talked about an unequal split. I said, "I didn't imagine that you would think we would be 51–49." To which he replied, "I would never be in a partnership in which I didn't have the controlling interest." It was, of course, a golden lesson for me.

In hindsight, I saw that I should not have been so surprised, but that incident certainly helped me understand how easy it is to spend time talking about the *business* without talking much about the *partnership*. I declined to follow through with the partnership. Other than a few thousand dollars each, we had primarily invested our time. The experience helped me begin to see the kind of preliminary work prospective partners have to do, as well as the importance of ownership percentages.

While some people insist on a majority stake because they have been told that anything less than 51 percent spells trouble (for them), often a majority–minority split indicates the presence of someone who is looking for control. Although the partner lacks the free rein of a sole owner, 51 percent or more gives that person significant control. In most states, majority partners' powers include the right to hold the executive position they choose, hire and fire employees, manage the finances, elect the board, and change the course of the business, all without even consulting their minority partners. They can employ a minority partner or not, pay that partner a reasonable wage or not.

The key is how ownership is set up. Absent any agreement, minority partners may be entitled "to no more than a copy of the annual minutes," according to attorney Henry Krasnow. He described their plight this way: "Although the owner of a minority interest is entitled to a voice, it is sometimes no more than a whisper. Often, the minority owner may say no, stomp their feet, and hold their breath until they turn blue, but the business will continue to be run as the majority owners choose."

Although majority ownership can confer broad powers, there are limits. The laws of many states will not allow majority partners to change the ownership structure or profit distributions, force minority owners into greater debt, or withhold financial or business information from them. Any of these acts could constitute a breach of fiduciary responsibility. The powers that majority partners enjoy are sometimes more illusory than real, because in practice the power depends on how much minority owners will tolerate before they decide to fight back. In most cases, Krasnow suggests, fighting back means "hiring a lawyer who will file a lawsuit that threatens the existence of the business."

In many partnerships, people are thrilled to be minority partners; some would not opt for majority status even if they could have it. Still, it is easy to see how problems can arise in unequal partnerships. Some partners with control conduct business with little consideration for their "lesser" partner. Minority partners can resent this, feel unfairly treated, and begin to thwart the interests of their majority partner by exercising what little power they have. For example, if an opportunity arises for an acquisition that the majority owner wants but that needs the minority partner's consent, the minority partner may withhold consent as a way of signaling that he or she wants to be treated with greater respect. When relationships become that strained, the partners, especially the majority partners, are at risk of breaching their fiduciary responsibility. For example, they may begin operating another business that somehow competes with the partnership, use partnership property for personal gain, or engage in transactions that create a conflict of interest. Even when a minority partner thwarts the legitimate business interests of the majority partner, the majority partner is not released from his or her fiduciary obligations.

To avoid these power struggles, partners must clarify, in their Partnership Charter and then in their legal documents, exactly how they want their partnership to function and what "majority–minority" means at the same time that they determine their percentages. They must spell out any protections they want minority partners to have, such as the right to serve on the board, voting trusts that might give them veto power over major corporate actions, or different classes of stock with different powers. In the case of the Star Systems partners (described in chapter 2), Jeff, with 80 percent of the stock, agreed to modify his majority rights in numerous ways. With respect to ownership, the partners' charter clearly states that Beth and Sarah, with 10 percent each, "will have the right of first refusal if and when he wants to sell any of his shares." It also states, "Jeff agrees not to sell the company to any buyer within 7 years without the consent of either Beth or Sarah."

After seven years he would have a "drag-along" right; that is, he could require that Beth and Sarah sell their shares but at the same price and on the same terms as his. Jeff also granted them a "tag-along" right, which assured them that they would get as good a deal as he would in any sale of stock, even a partial sale. All these protections were spelled out in the ownership section of their charter, which is in the appendix.

Partners have significant leeway when they set up the aspects of owning, governing, and operating their businesses, which is why partnerships can work well for all parties if partners carefully consider all their options. For example, if Jeff had been in marketing and he wanted to bring Sarah on board as CEO to run the company, they could have entered into an agreement that gave her—with her 10 percent ownership—day-to-day control as the managing partner. Such flexibility allows people more room for give and take because the focus can be on everything that the partners want to get out of co-owning, not simply an ownership number.

Three or More Partners with No One in Clear Control

The control issues change dramatically when there are three or more partners and no one has more than a 50 percent interest. Some equal partners have used the third person as a tiebreaker. In these situations, the partners choose a trusted person, and each gives him or her a nominal stake. This may soften the intensity of the two-partner dynamics, but it may also complicate the dynamics if the two major partners end up constantly vying for the third's loyalty. Such a swing-vote person should not be thought of as a mediator, though he or she is definitely in the middle. The third person's role is to side with one or another partner in any impasse. If this is how the partners work out their differences, however, they will be at risk of losing any real feeling of being partners.

BMC Associates was once asked to mediate a dispute between two 50–50 partners who had battled each other for years. At the heart of their resolution was an agreement to change the ownership structure to 40–40–20, with the 20 percent being split among three key employees.

Such arrangements have the advantage of allowing the principal partners to control the company when they can agree and avoid deadlocks when they cannot.

After prospective partners have explored the four sections of the Partnership Charter in this book that bear on ownership and have discussed the issue of control, they will be better prepared to have a meaningful discussion of individual percentages. We encourage each to come to his or her own conclusion about a fair ownership distribution. Then each prospective partner can share his or her ideas for an equitable split with the group. Though not foolproof, this process provides the opportunity of hearing everyone's ideas and alerts everyone if the partners are not in sync.

A great deal is at stake in establishing ownership interests. The way people go about determining their relative interests may affect whether they actually decide to become partners and will influence the tone, character, and quality of their partnership for years to come. In some cases, the percentages that people decide upon may actually determine the success or failure of their venture.

CHANGING OWNERSHIP INTERESTS

Most partners do not adequately plan for changes that will occur in ownership after they start their businesses. It is as if they assume that the partnership will last forever or that their interests will remain unchanged. If partners are lucky, unplanned changes in ownership interests occur quite easily. An example of this occurred some time after Dean Martin made his producer-director, Greg Garrison, a partner and co-owner in his business, Dean Martin the entertainer. Martin first gave Garrison 10 percent, then an additional 10 percent every succeeding year until they were 50–50. Then Martin offered Garrison another 10 percent, which would have made Martin a minority partner in his own career. In response to Garrison's puzzlement, Martin explained, "I'm here one day a week, and you're here seven." Garrison wisely declined the offer, saying, "Fifty-fifty's fine."

Partners should not count on smooth sailing, however. Transitions as easy as Martin and Garrison's are rare. Prospective partners should decide up front how to handle changes in ownership and what kinds of changes are acceptable, unacceptable, mandatory, and so forth. Many of the triggers for ownership changes are occasioned by acrimony, misfortune, or misconduct, making negotiations strained or nearly impossible. Time and again I have seen partners locked in a deadly embrace because they had not previously agreed upon how to handle these situations. When working on the ownership section of the Partnership Charter, people should discuss and agree upon the circumstances under which they would want to *alter* who is in the partnership and their relative percentages of ownership, and this should be documented in that section of the charter. Clear agreements about transferring ownership interests can save untold dollars, time, and pain.

Bob Hurwitz described a planned change of ownership percentages in one of the companies he cofounded, OfficeMax. He and his partner recognized that if the company grew significantly, the importance of the difference in their initial contributions would diminish, though the fact that Hurwitz had taken a greater capital risk would remain. So, although they made unequal capital contributions to get the office supply company off the ground, "It was always understood that the moment we reached a certain critical mass, we would create equality" in common (voting) stock. They remained unequal in preferred stock, "because that was based on our initial investments."

Hurwitz has also been a partner in numerous real estate partnerships. In one, Hurwitz and another general partner each had 40 percent by virtue of their capital investments in the property, while the operating partner had 20 percent. So the general partners received 40 percent of the profits and the operating partner 20 percent. As soon as the general partners recovered their initial investment, the operating partner got a larger ownership percentage (40 percent) and they got less (down to 30 percent each). Hurwitz said they settled on this plan because, "I didn't want the operating partner to look at this thing and say, 'This is terribly unfair.'"

As the five founders in the medical device company discovered, as challenging as establishing percentages can be, trying to alter them later can be even harder. Obviously, if they had an agreement to revisit their percentages after a year, it had to be in writing and to spell out precisely the standards that would be employed to modify the original distribution of shares. The idea of revisiting ownership percentages after partners have more information about how the business is working and what people are actually contributing is valid, but the usefulness of this concept lies in its implementation. Prospective partners need to think through the various ways they might want ownership to change and plan for the full range of situations that could arise.

One costly mistake that I have seen many owners make is deciding who will succeed them as co-owners. An owner, or a group of owners, should never pick a group of partners who will buy them out, at least not without the successors first working though *all* of the issues critical to being successful partners.

When Ralph Matsen was transferring the ownership of his California insurance brokerage company, he encouraged his four top executives, who appeared to be naturals for taking over, to complete a charter. Even though the four had worked together for ten years and had been running the company for a couple of years, Matsen understood the difference between co-executives and co-owners.

Matsen also recognized, having been their boss for years, that he had to step out of the picture and let them work out their own charter. It can be extremely difficult for owners, who are used to controlling everything, to accept the fact that their presence will greatly distort the process of a new group of partners. It is impossible for a new team of partners to work out their own partnership with a retiring owner hovering nearby.

The charter process allowed the executives to decide for themselves that it was a good idea to become partners, and they agreed on exactly how they would do it. Once they had finished their charter, they gave it to Matsen for his approval since he had the final say over them buying him out. Any owners who care about the success of the next generation of partners, or will depend on them for their buyout, should make sure the new owners have done their homework before finalizing the transfer of ownership.

Events That May Trigger Ownership Changes

There are many triggering events for ownership changes that partners should contemplate ahead of time. On the top of everyone's mind are death, disability, divorce, and retirement, but there are other events to consider, including

- a major shift in roles and responsibilities (e.g., because a partner cannot perform adequately),
- a partner quitting work,
- a partner wanting to cut back (waning interest in the business or wanting to semiretire),
- personal or family circumstances (e.g., a spouse's promotion necessitates moving, loss of a professional license, bankruptcy, a partner's need for cash),
- interpersonal incompatibility,
- irreconcilable differences over business issues (e.g., direction or operation), and
- unethical or illegal behavior (or drug or alcohol abuse or addiction).

This list includes the good, the bad, and the ugly. For each circumstance, prospective partners should define the triggering event so there is no ambiguity about it later. For example, how derelict must a partner's performance be to warrant his or her removal or to diminish his or her interest? What proof of unethical behavior would be necessary to warrant a change in ownership? Some triggering events are quite complicated. For example, some people tie the buyout of a partner's interest to an insurance company's determination of disability. People sometimes qualify for disability, however, and later recover, so an important question is how long partners are willing to wait to see whether a partner is permanently disabled.

Prospective partners also have to agree on how they would execute the changes instigated by triggering events. For example, retirement, unacceptable performance, and illegal behavior might trigger a complete buyout of a partner's interest, but the partners could decide that the method of determining the value of the partner's interest would differ in each circumstance.

To save time and energy in working out the answers to these questions, it helps to simplify the process by categorizing the list into groups like good, bad, and ugly, or voluntary and involuntary. In any case, the amount of planning time is negligible compared to the time the partners would have to spend if one of the events happened without planning. Partners can rest assured that something on their list *will* happen, and the only question is when.

Everyone hopes that his or her partners will be fully competent people of integrity and unflagging commitment, but the reality is that the principals will change over time for a host of reasons, and no one can predict those reasons. The only sure way to prevent the all-too-common reaction, "Why didn't we think of that *before!*" is with thorough planning and documentation. Many triggers look obvious after something happens. Consider the following example: Five lawyers start a law firm. One lawyer, with a history of sexual harassment that his new partners are unaware of, sexually harasses a secretary, who then sues the firm and wins a judgment against it. The firm and its insurance company (if it purchased protection for sexual harassment) are responsible for paying the award and fees to defend the firm. Then, adding insult to injury, to get the guilty partner out, the four partners who remain have to pay him the value of his interest in the partnership. If they had discussed the issue when forming, they might have agreed that any partner found guilty of a civil or criminal offense would be automatically expelled and receive nothing for his or her interest.

Discussions about changes in ownership are among the most important that partners will have. The following story of a partnership in southern California is an example of what happens regularly to partners who never get around to having these discussions. Philip Leslie and Raymond Cesmat cofounded Leslie's Poolmart Inc. by pulling together $1,500 each. Within twenty years they had a $50 million per year pool products company. They were going strong until Cesmat had to sell his 50 percent interest because of his divorce. Leslie was an interested buyer, but the two couldn't agree on a price, and since they had not spelled out what they wanted to happen in such a circumstance, their negotiations deadlocked.

Once circumstances changed, as they did when Cesmat had to sell, the partners fell into predictable, polarized positions. The selling partner wanted the highest possible price, while the remaining partner wanted the lowest. As negotiations stalled, Cesmat became desperate, so he filed a petition to dissolve the corporation, as California law allows. The court appointed a temporary, third director to help secure a buyer.

Leslie hated the idea of anyone else owning the company bearing his name, so when potential buyers would visit, he admitted, "I'd tell them that if they bought the company I'd go into business against them and pulverize them. I built this company and I wasn't going to see anyone else get hold of it." That, of course, lowered the offers considerably.

When the company finally sold, Leslie followed through on his threat to force Poolmart to go "belly up." He bought a 50 percent interest in rival Sandy's Pool Supply Inc. and had forty of his former employees join him. As chief executive of Sandy's, he not only expanded the company from three to twenty-one stores but put most of the outlets close enough to Poolmart's stores to compete head to head. He even started a competing mail-order business. Eventually, Leslie's vengefulness got the best of him, it seems, because his new company went belly up.

Divorce and death, two major hurdles for many partnerships, can precipitate crises in which nonpartners are entitled to an interest in the business. Divorce and death have finished off many closely held entities because partners were not willing to assume unacceptable people as partners. With planning, businesses or remaining partners may be obligated to buy shares that might otherwise be transferred to spouses or heirs, thereby obviating the crisis.

Putting a Value on Ownership Interests

Establishing the price of a partner's interest is an integral part of planning for ownership changes. BMC Associates was asked recently to mediate a dispute between two families who jointly own a manufacturing company in the Northeast. Years before their attorneys had drawn up an extensive buy-sell agreement that established mechanisms by which owners could buy and sell shares. Everyone agreed that it was a model buy-sell, with one tragic flaw: It failed to spell out an unambiguous procedure for establishing a price. That one omission resulted in hundreds of thousands of dollars wasted on lawyers, accountants, and valuation experts, not to mention the interfamily hostility and mental and emotional anguish it caused. For several years the company and its shareholders repeatedly hired reputable national valuation firms that established values ranging from $110 million to $200 million. As expected, the low valuations were from firms hired by the family members wanting to buy shares, and the high valuations were from firms hired by family members wanting to sell. Disparate valuation results in cases like this can be expected.

Prospective partners must work with their advisors to agree upon a clear method for determining the value of anyone's shares (not simply the value of the whole entity). The method must be capable of accomplishing this task regardless of whether partners are getting along. The method must be airtight, meaning that not one detail remains to be negotiated when the need arises.

There are many methods for valuing ownership interests. The simplest and least expensive is for partners to establish their own value and adjust it every year or two. If they select this method, they must be diligent in making the readjustments. A fail-safe provision should be added that provides for an independent appraisal if an agreed value has not been set within a certain time period. The courts have given partners vast discretion in determining the price of their interests in their business, including allowing them to bequeath their interest to their remaining partners. In one case, the partners agreed that the surviving partners could purchase the decedent's interest for $40,000 even though the book value was substantially higher. The court upheld the partners' agreement since "neither partner could predict who would survive to enjoy the benefits of these provisions."

Other methods for establishing the value of a business rely on various formulas such as book value, deemed liquidation value, appraised value, or capitalization of earnings. Each method has its advantages and disadvantages. Most methods, no matter how definitive they sound, have elements of subjectivity built into them and include commonly used terms that have multiple meanings.

Once the prospective partners agree on a method for establishing the value of the entire company, they need to agree how to value an individual partner's interest. This can be more complicated than one would think since it depends on discounts. Because partners are not usually able to sell their interests to anyone they choose, there is a "lack of marketability discount," and if the partner's interest is less than a controlling interest, there is also a "minority discount." Both discounts may be substantial. Partners can save themselves tribulation and expense later on if they can agree when completing their charter on the discounts they believe are fair.

Making Buyouts More Feasible

It may not take long for the value of a departing partner's interest to grow beyond what the remaining partners can afford to pay without taking drastic steps, such as liquidating assets or the entire business. There are various ways to avoid being forced to compromise the financial integrity of the business. The easiest, most basic way is for the partners to agree that payouts to a departing partner will be spread over a period of years with interest. The departing partner can be bought out immediately and given a secured note (thus he or she no longer owns any of the company). If the business is able, it can pay off the obligation sooner, but the option to pay over time can prevent insolvency.

Another approach in the event of a partner's death is to agree to maintain life insurance policies on the owners. The cost of the policies is usually small relative to the potential benefit. Insurance and tax advice is helpful to determine whether insurance is the best tool and whether the company or the partners should maintain the policies. In either case, the proceeds go to the deceased partner's heirs in a cash-stock exchange.

Disability insurance, though seldom used, can similarly cover the cost of buying out disabled partners. While policy proceeds may not constitute the entire value of the person's interest, they provide a necessary cash infusion.

Noncompete Covenants

I used to be surprised at how often people who leave a business immediately begin competing against their former partners. The more I saw this happen, the more I realized this should be expected unless steps are taken to prevent it. When someone leaves a particular business, that doesn't mean he or she wants to start a new career; the person usually will continue doing what he or she knows how to do in the same vicinity, either alone or with new partners.

The idea behind noncompete covenants is that people who leave a company should be prevented from harming their former partners. They could cause harm by setting up shop down the street, recruiting or hiring employees, or soliciting or doing business with former clients. To prevent any of these activities, partners should discuss the restrictions they wish to place on themselves. The courts generally uphold clauses that are structured to protect the ongoing business and do not deprive departing partners of any means to earn a living.

One caveat with a noncompete covenant is that the sanctions imposed on departing partners could have the unintended consequence of causing a dissatisfied partner to stay longer than he or she otherwise would. A balance is needed between protecting the business and making departures feasible.

Adding Partners

Although it may seem premature to contemplate *additional* partners before consummating the current partnership, it is the best time. The purpose is not to decide the issue once and for all; it is to develop an understanding on a potentially divisive issue. If partners-to-be cannot reach an agreement about adding partners, consider it a red flag. I encourage prospective partners to discuss and agree on the conditions under which adding partners would be desirable. The partners at Star Systems, for example, decided that at a minimum, any new partner must

- be needed by the existing shareholders;
- have knowledge and expertise that could add value to the corporation;
- be committed to the company;
- share the partners' values and a commitment to excellence; and
- be desirable to, and have good "chemistry" with, the existing partners.

I also encourage prospective partners to agree on whether there are any individuals they would *not* want to allow on board as partners. Most commonly, because of the complications involved, this might include family members and employees. If people are seriously entertaining adding family members to an existing partnership or hiring them for any potentially significant job, then it is wise to explore the implications, first by themselves, and then with whomever they are considering hiring or bringing on. Because hiring family members is so complicated, I always recommend that partners develop special guidelines for their employment and for what to do if it is not working.

Some partners decide to use a vesting process when adding partners. People might acquire stock options, but they would become partners only after they have achieved certain benchmarks and proven themselves.

I have seen a few instances in which cofounders sought to have key employees share in ownership, but adding them as partners grew complicated and contentious. The key issue is often the perceived value of the partnership. Existing partners usually place a much higher value on goodwill and all they have contributed than incoming partners do, while employees becoming partners see themselves working as hard as, or harder than, the owners. The result is a large discrepancy in the perceived value of what is being given and received.

A common miscalculation when adding any partners is thinking that adding "one more person" is not a significant alteration. This is always a significant event, and it is wise to spend the time and energy to do it properly. The most effective way is to rework the relevant parts of the Partnership Charter. This requires time and energy on everyone's part but may be the fastest way to get a new partner and the new partnership up to speed.

Documenting Ownership-Related Agreements

The Partnership Charter allows prospective partners to communicate clearly about how they wish to jointly own their business and handle ownership changes, because it frames the broad issues related to ownership in the larger context and stimulates discussion and negotiation *before* things become too technical. There is no way to avoid the technicalities, but the prospective partners should insist on first reaching agreement on what they would like before getting mired in technical details and before commencing work on legal documents. Getting overly technical and bogged down in legal or financial details can be the death knell for reaching an agreement.

Not long ago all six partners in the Washington law firm of Nussbaum and Wald were in court telling a judge a story with a common plot. Some years earlier the partners had had a series of meetings to determine their ownership interests and options if a partner were to leave. The meetings became rancorous and unproductive, and the partners failed to agree and then abandoned trying. They had five years of peaceful coexistence before things fell apart and they landed in court. The crux of the dispute: money and ownership.

A business reporter following the testimony wondered, "How could a group of lawyers, some of whom had represented other lawyers in partnership disputes, have operated for so long without a written agreement about how to divide the money?" The answer, of course, is that these decisions are among the toughest partners have to make, and even the most sophisticated partners can get bogged down or go hopelessly off track. Egos commonly clash over ownership. Forcing a resolution is unproductive, and partners are often too proud or stubborn to get help.

Prospective partners need to be sure that they are not fixating on percentages and missing the entire package. If they cannot move beyond their impasse, they should get help from business mediators who are experts in partner issues and at bringing partners to consensual agreements. While it is necessary to have input at certain points during the negotiations from accountants and attorneys on a host of issues (e.g., voting trusts, different classes of stock, and valuation methods), the technical aspects of the deal should move front and center *only* after the partners reach agreements on their intentions.

Once partners-to-be have gotten clear among themselves about all of the topics contained in their charter and have documented their agreements and understandings, then it is time to have them reviewed by an experienced business attorney and other trusted business advisors. They may have questions for the prospective partners about their agreements. After addressing those questions, the attorney can draw up the partnership agreements, corporate documents, and buy-sell agreements. Lawyers who assist partners with these documents, especially buy-sell agreements, should be very well versed in this area because the laws governing the transfer of ownership are not for the faint of heart. Lawyers who've received completed charters from their clients have routinely been impressed with the thoughtfulness and thoroughness that partners have given these complicated issues.

CHAPTER 5

Roles and Titles, Power and Status

It is not by the consolidation or concentration of powers, but by their distribution that good government is effected.

THOMAS JEFFERSON

STEPPING ON EACH OTHER'S TOES, turf battles, power struggles, and fights over titles are all symptoms that partners have not matched the needs of the business with their skills and interests. This is a common problem among partners, and I have seen cases where it has played out for years and created terrible losses of efficiency, not to mention great unhappiness. Of course it doesn't have to be that way; partners can avoid these problems by being proactive.

BUSINESS NEEDS AND PARTNERS' SKILLS

To begin sorting out their own roles, partners have to assess the personnel needs of the business. Then they have to look objectively at the skills and interests that they bring. Sometimes partners' interests and skills match up so perfectly with the needs of their business that working out the different roles is effortless. This happens in some two-person partnerships when the business needs an inside person and an outside person.

A classic long-lived example of this inside–outside division of labor started in 1896. The founders of one of the most famous bakeries in the United States, the Collin Street Bakery of Corsicana, Texas, based their partnership on that division of roles. Master baker Gus Wiedmann stuck to his fruitcakes, and his very outgoing, business-minded partner Tom McElwee made sure people in their booming oil town wanted to buy more fruitcakes than Wiedmann could produce. McElwee lured famous performers to the Corsicana Opera House, and when entertainers such as Enrico Caruso and Will Rogers left town, he made sure they had plenty of Wiedmann's Collin Street fruitcakes in their trunks. When McElwee convinced John Ringling's circus to buy Wiedmann's fruitcakes, which he would ship all over the world for them, a great mail-order business was born.

Although the founders are long gone, Collin Street Bakery ships its products to almost two hundred foreign countries and is still organized along the same inside–outside, production–marketing lines.

It's a blessing when people are so different and the needs of the business are similarly diverse. What it takes to do one job successfully is 180 degrees from what it takes to do the other. Each partner gets plenty of room to operate, and rarely does either contemplate meddling in the other's territory. A partnership can be a marriage made in heaven when each partner is independent of the other in one sense but dependent in another.

When people come together with similar competencies, they can still find themselves slipping comfortably into very different roles. The cut-from-the-same-cloth partners who took over the electric boat company in chapter 1 had such an experience when sorting out their roles. As the company's principal owners, Chuck Houghton and Bill Forster assumed roles that Houghton summarizes this way: "I'm close up and he's far away." They decided early on that it would be more productive for Forster to participate in management from a distance. Houghton runs the plant in Highland, New York, while the peripatetic Forster—who has homes in New York, California, and Connecticut—stays in touch through e-mail, responding to a detailed weekly report that Houghton writes not just for him but also for everyone who works for the company.

"Bill acts as kind of a watchdog, troubleshooter, and backstop for me," Houghton says. Forster visits the plant only twice a year or so, "but that's a plus. He can see the forest; I'm right in the trees, and I sometimes miss what's important. I get too involved in what's going on, and I tend not to think about the big picture." Forster is "a wonderful problem solver," Houghton says. "And when he senses that I'm frustrated, he drops whatever he's doing and comes up and helps. He's not stepping on my toes, and I'm not stepping on his." Forster's comments mirror Houghton's. "I see Chuck as running Elco. To me, the line of command is very clear: Chuck's running the show, and I'm providing advice." Formally, Houghton is the president and Forster is the chair of the board.

The most efficient way for partners to begin sorting out their roles is by clarifying the needs of the business when they are doing their strategic planning. Then they can move from the strategic level down to the operational level. Describing the operational roles in detail—essentially developing job descriptions—is key to working smoothly together for years to come. While this process does require significant time and energy, the amount is insignificant compared to the time and money people waste trying to untangle problems caused by poorly defined roles. Partners' roles—how they'll spend their time and energy—matter deeply to them. Ideally, the initial determination and assignment of roles is done in the context of all the other issues that people must deal with when forming a business.

One of the principal advantages of having partners is being able to share the workload. The more effective partners are at dividing their roles and responsibilities, the more efficient the business will be and the more satisfied they will be with their working relationships. Ben Cohen and Jerry Greenfield of Ben and Jerry's claimed that clearly defining their roles accounted for their success. "We did it early on," Ben explains. "I was doing sales and marketing, and Jerry was doing manufacturing. He had complete say over his area of the company, and I had pretty much complete say over mine."

In closely held businesses, a partner may sometimes try to put his or her desire for a particular position ahead of the needs of the company.

This can happen for a number of reasons, one of which is ego. Some people are loath to assume a lower-status position in management once they have been at the top.

POWER SHARING

The business press is full of stories of executives who create power-sharing arrangements because they cannot bear to be one down in the hierarchy. Philip Purcell of Dean Witter and John Mack of Morgan Stanley, two of Wall Street's most accomplished leaders, are a classic example of this. When they combined their firms in 1997 they announced the combined corporation as a merger of equals, pledging to make all major decisions jointly and to switch the title of CEO within two years. The agreement was viewed as one of the most successful financial services marriages in recent history. Before two years had elapsed, though, it became clear that Purcell, the first to take the reins as CEO, was reneging on the title swap, and—no surprise—Mack resigned as president. No one is immune from the disasters that can result from power-sharing arrangements.

Some people are uncomfortable with a lower-status position because they are on equal footing as owners. If they are equally responsible for the debt of the company and have parity when debating company policy and direction, the last thing they want is to be seen by others as assuming a lesser role. That was the situation for three partners who bought a profitable $100-million-a-year wholesale business operating with two distinct entities, one in New Jersey and the other in New York. The New York location was considerably larger, so two of the partners, David and Mark, decided that they would co-manage that operation and the third partner, Jeremy, would run the New Jersey location. Almost immediately, the co-presidents were stepping on each other's toes, countermanding one another's decisions. As antagonism dragged on, employees grew more and more confused and demoralized.

At the suggestion of their business advisor, the partners agreed that they would resolve the conflict by adding another title and level of management. They would now have a CEO at the top with two COOs running the two locations. In an attempt to be fair and impartial, they consented to draw straws to determine who would become the CEO. Mark won, but he felt ambivalent about it. On the one hand, his heart was really in running the New York operation, but on the other hand he hated the thought of either Jeremy or David becoming CEO over him. Regardless, they took their respective titles and went back to work.

One year later, their quick-draw method of conflict resolution lay in ruins. It had done next to nothing to stop the war. Giving a person whose heart was really in operations a new title was insufficient to resolve their problems. The CEO–COO problem is quite common, as Warren Bennis once noted in an article entitled "The Split Brain at the Top":

> The CEO is the leader, the COO the manager. The CEO is charged with doing the right thing, the COO with doing things right. The CEO takes the long view, the COO the short view. The CEO concentrates on the what and why, while the COO focuses on how. The CEO has the vision, the COO hands-on control. The CEO thinks in terms of innovation, development, the future, while the COO is busy with administration, maintenance, the present. The CEO sets the tone and direction, both inside and outside the company, while the COO sets the pace. Even when the CEO and the COO function happily together, they can run into big trouble. And when they're *unhappy* together, their unhappiness is reflected throughout the organization in major and minor ways.

Creating new titles without recognizing precisely what the titles—and the roles behind the titles—mean will never resolve anything. Partners must describe in detail what their titles mean on a day-to-day basis. I look more closely at titles later in this chapter, but first, let's get back to David, Mark, and Jeremy.

After trying a few other means to resolve their differences, they hired mediators. The business mediators helped them take a long and serious look at the company's needs and what each of them had to offer. The partners came to a simple but painful conclusion: Given their personalities and dissimilar values, the company wasn't big enough for all three of them. Slowly and methodically over the two ensuing years, they explored all options, including acquiring a company to make them bigger, starting a division in a third location, selling the entire company, and buying out one partner. Based on their inability to work together, as well as market and financial considerations, they ruled out the expansion options. Even though none of them wanted to leave the company, all eventually agreed that buying out one of them was the wisest step. Because Jeremy was happily ensconced in the New Jersey location, and the problem had always been between Mark and David, they decided that Mark and David would each submit a sealed bid to buy the other's interest. The lowest bidder would be bought out by the two remaining partners, thereby giving each remaining partner 50 percent of the stock.

Another way that unhealthy and ill-defined power-sharing agreements get started in closely held businesses is when companies' founders turn over the reins to the succeeding generation. Retiring founders turning over their businesses to adult children will sometimes create sibling teams with no differentiation of power or authority. They resort to this arrangement, not because it's what the company needs or because they believe in egalitarian management, but because they are loath to choose one child over another. Interestingly, the real flaw in their thinking is that *they* should make the decision *for* their adult children. It's a paradox that such an authoritarian approach to succession would have an egalitarian result. (At least, it's egalitarian until the power struggles and turf battles start, which is usually as soon as the parents are out of the picture, as was the case with the siblings at Star Systems.)

Such awkward arrangements amount to efforts to dodge the harsh truth that companies need to *differentiate* roles (and differentiate among people) to be efficient. This is as necessary at the top of a company as it is in the ranks. If a specific management role is so large that it requires two people, it is never efficient to split it down the middle with both people doing the same tasks.

Parents in these situations are making partners of their adult children by giving stock to those children who work in the business and sometimes to the other children as well. Ideally, parents should have sufficient confidence in their adult children to allow them to decide for themselves how to structure their management team. When adult children are told to work out their own partnership arrangement and are able to negotiate all of the issues involved, they usually come up with roles and responsibilities that match their individual differences to the various needs of the business. Adult children are often far better than their parents at recognizing their individual strengths and weaknesses.

"Charlie" Johnson, the CEO of Franklin Templeton Investments, was pushing seventy and knew his last, big assignment had nothing to do with growing his company. He had accomplished that already. His company's stock had appreciated nineteen-hundred-fold since he took his father's company public in 1971, making it the fourth-largest mutual fund company in the United States, with more than $300 billion in assets under management. Charlie knew his final assignment was selecting a successor.

Chuck Johnson, Charlie Johnson's oldest son, had been the heir apparent for years, but as often happens in family-run businesses, his younger brother joining the company greatly complicated matters. Charlie Johnson, undoubtedly with help from his advisors and the board, resorted to the traditional horse race strategy, very much befitting the intense, varsity athlete culture at Franklin. The contestants were his oldest son, a younger son, Greg, and the CFO, Martin Flanagan.

Although the younger son and the CFO were seen as long-shot contenders for the CEO's spot, they discovered what many people do in three-way contests: Joining forces creates a distinct advantage. The two outside contenders became good friends and effective business partners, ultimately isolating Chuck Johnson. A *Wall Street Journal* reporter wrote that the horse race strategy made life in and around the executive suites stressful, as one would well imagine. Three-way battles for power frequently splinter along two-against-one lines, and this one was no exception.

As this high-stakes struggle was playing out day after day at work, pitting brother against brother, the isolated one of the threesome was going downhill personally. Chuck Johnson slipped into alcoholism and was arrested and jailed for a felony assault against his wife, whom he severely injured when he picked her up and threw her against their kitchen stove. He lost his securities industry license and was sentenced to two months in jail and two months on probation. His close friends, who had written letters to the court on his behalf, said that he "had appeared lonely and dispirited" for months before the incident.

Was the competition with his own brother at work responsible for Chuck Johnson's personal demise? It's difficult for me to imagine it wasn't a major factor. Chuck Johnson followed in his father's footsteps. He was a classic workaholic who had made his work life center stage for decades. It's no surprise that an executive, who is isolated at work by the two people with whom he should be collaborating most closely, would feel exceedingly lonely and dispirited. (Acting out his anger in an inappropriate way is also no surprise.)

Could Charlie Johnson and the Franklin board have played the succession game more intelligently and effectively? I certainly think so. They could have instructed the three potential successors to explore among themselves how they could work together. The three men could have been granted the freedom to determine a management structure that would have worked for them and the company, subject to Charlie Johnson and the board's approval. Then Charlie Johnson could have negotiated with them over how to efficiently transfer power during his remaining time at the company. Unfortunately, he set up an adversarial contest instead, and such contests have unlimited corrosive potential.

"Last month," with one son washed out and trying to pick up the pieces of his life, "company patriarch Charlie Johnson finally settled on a succession plan, saying that Greg Johnson and Martin Flanagan would become co-CEOs at the start of 2004." George Anders of the *Wall Street Journal* reported that Chuck Johnson wasn't at his father's announcement and his brother's rise to power. "Chuck Johnson wasn't in the building. He has rented a small office across the street from Franklin, where he sorts out his papers and wonders what went wrong."

A more collaborative process for choosing a successor would have created a different reality for all three potential successors, and certainly a different life for Chuck Johnson. It's interesting to imagine what would have happened if the two brothers and the CFO—before they were deep into their horse race mentality—had decided to figure out for themselves how they would operate as partners and share power at the top of Franklin. Perhaps they couldn't have done it, but then again, perhaps they could have.

Partners who attempt co-equal management roles must do so with great care. Even when power-sharing arrangements do not result in someone's departure, they frequently spawn unintended negative consequences, such as creating a larger arena for power struggles and sowing confusion among both employees and outsiders. Such arrangements *can* work; they just rarely do. If partners want to proceed regardless of these caveats, they should outline in their charter (1) precisely what being co-equals means, (2) who will evaluate whether the arrangement is working properly and how they will make these evaluations, and (3) what will happen if deadlocks occur, and the arrangement is not working.

DIVIDING, REPORTING, AND COORDINATING

After partners divide their roles according to the needs of the business, they have to determine how they will coordinate those roles. It is critical to determine whether some partners will be reporting to others, or if not, how they will coordinate their efforts.

In the example of the three wholesale partners, the COO, David, should have been reporting to Mark, the CEO. In theory he was, but since they never discussed what the titles meant in practice, and because he had lost respect for Mark, he felt free to ignore him. That was unquestionably part of why Mark, as CEO, kept meddling in David's business. The person on the top in such a reporting relationship, in this case Mark, has a responsibility not to meddle and to make sure that the person reporting to him has the authority to execute his or her responsibilities. At the same time, however, the COO has to recognize the CEO's authority.

At the conclusion of partners' negotiations about roles, they should be able to put their respective jobs into an organizational chart that illustrates the hierarchy and reporting responsibilities. The chart should clearly state each partner's responsibilities. In a small start-up, an organizational chart may seem like overkill, but it adds clarity and helps the partners confirm that they are (literally) on the same page.

If partners are overseeing different business areas without directly reporting to each other, they must still establish a method of working together. There is efficiency in dividing and conquering, but only if the partners figure out a way to coordinate. Some partners can take divvying up their roles to such an extreme that they share next to nothing. Few people begin with this type of arrangement in mind, but I have seen many businesses in which partners who cannot get along resort to distance to try to manage their relationship. They become like silos, standing together, side-by-side, but totally separate.

That was the way that two partners in a highly profitable transportation company described themselves. They had divided their roles logically, with one in charge of the limousine division and the other in charge of charter bus operations. During an associate's and my first meeting with them they chronicled their relationship in terms of how far their desks were from one another; in the beginning of their company they had adjoining desks and jokingly referred to their "six inches of separation." As the company grew they had offices that shared a doorway. Then they moved down the hall from one another and finally into separate buildings.

The two were different in some classic ways. The partner running the limousine operation was an extrovert who loved socializing and spending money, but he cared not one iota about fleet maintenance. The charter bus partner was an introverted, fiscally conservative manager who paid obsessive attention to maintenance and every other detail about their business. Their differences created trouble throughout the company, especially among key personnel who operated across both divisions. The company grew; their respective responsibilities grew; but the amount of time they spent together dropped to nil.

Their ostensible reason for hiring mediators was because the limousine partner wanted to bring his daughter into the business and they had no agreements in place about how to transfer stock, add partners, or even hire family members. It was clear, though, that even without this challenge, they were unlikely to continue very long as partners. Their distance had become part of the company lore, and many people in the business had learned to work around it. While personal style differences accounted for some of their troubles, one of the reasons for the gulf between them was that they had grown lax about coordinating their efforts. Their lack of communication was a handicap that was partly responsible for the wedge of distrust between them.

One lesson from these "silent silos" is that while it is important to separate roles and responsibilities, unless partners continually reconnect and share information, the efficiencies and opportunities they hoped to gain may be lost. Whatever the structure of their partnership, they need to craft a way to give one another feedback and determine whether they are really doing the jobs they agreed to do and stay connected.

When partners initially put their energy into sorting out their roles based on the needs of the business, this can produce beneficial surprises and cause partners to make some organizational adjustments immediately. For example, when three engineers were working on a charter and discussing their roles in detail, they discovered that one of them was more interested in managing the firm than even he had previously realized. The other two partners encouraged him to pursue a management-training program to prepare him to really do that job effectively, in addition to doing a limited amount of regular client work.

As they discuss who will do what, most partners need to examine the importance of maintaining a distinction between their ownership roles and their management roles. If they intend their management roles to be determined by their ownership and not by matching their individual capabilities to the needs of the company, they need to make that explicit. The consequence, however, is that since their roles are based on ownership, not on performance, evaluation is a futile exercise.

Even worse, it becomes nearly impossible for a partner to object or complain if another partner is not doing his or her job.

All companies must delineate roles and responsibilities in order to assign the best people to specific jobs. In closely held companies, when the partners are deciding who will do what, it can easily turn out that certain jobs are more coveted than others and that there are more partners than desirable positions.

While partners often underestimate these distinctions before they begin working together, they become acutely aware of them later on. Most often, partners in the higher positions see that they are working harder, are under more stress, or are being underpaid for what they do. The situation begins to feel unfair. The inequity is sometimes obvious even to the partner in the lower position. One partner in such a position once told us, "I think it's totally unfair but that's the way we set it up and I'd be a fool to agree to change it now." (Still, as I explain in chapter 10, he may be more of a fool *not* to negotiate a change.)

There are pairs of partners in which neither can countenance being lower on the totem pole. It is anathema to them to be under the thumb of another partner in the management structure, so they try to force equality into their positions by simultaneously sharing a position or by alternating who holds it. The top level of management is structured in a way that effectively makes co-captains out of the co-owners. But there is a good reason ocean liners and naval vessels do not employ co-captains. Sometimes a captain must take decisive action. Debate, disagreement, or indecision could mean immediate and literal destruction. Usually, there are no life-or-death consequences for businesses, at least not literally, but if companies are mired in indecision at the top, opportunities will pass them by. (See the sidebar.)

A variation of co-presidents or co-CEOs is the tag-team approach. Because it takes time to settle into any job and do it well, frequent role switching is likely to result in as much confusion and inefficiency as simultaneous job sharing. The tag-team approach requires two partners who are not competitive with each other and who share a common vision. Otherwise, they wind up simply undoing what the other did, as if they were alternating Republican and Democratic presidents.

From Co-Captain to First Mate

Barry Sternlicht and Richard Nanula were the closest of friends from their days at Harvard Business School, where they played intramural basketball, talked stocks, and worked on a theme park project together. They were in each other's wedding parties, and the two families vacationed together. Nanula described them as "each other's biggest fans" and told a story about the time his wife gave birth to premature twins weighing less than a pound each. "Barry got on the first plane and was there in the emergency room. He stayed over. He's that kind of friend."

Years later, when Sternlicht desperately needed a partner to help him run Starwood Hotels & Resorts Worldwide, he naturally turned to Nanula, who was then CFO at Disney. Nanula packed his bags and left his prestigious job to become co-CEO at Starwood. A *Fortune* article featured their partnership and chronicled their short-lived adventure as co-CEOs:

> The core problem, these longtime pals have discovered, is that their "complementary" styles—Nanula is as calm and cautious as Sternlicht is intense and impetuous—aren't complementary after all. And—who could have guessed it?—they are clashing over power. Sternlicht got upset last summer when the *New York Times* ran a glowing profile of Nanula, identified as Starwood's boss, and photographed him perched regally at the company's posh St. Regis Hotel. According to insiders, Sternlicht griped that Nanula "looked like King Tut." Tut, tut. Sounds like plain old envy on the part of a kid who should learn to share credit. But Sternlicht is not a sharer. In January he demoted Nanula from CEO to president. "We're not equals," says Sternlicht, now chairman and CEO. "I think of myself as captain of the ship. Richard is my first mate."

It's tough being first mate after serving as co-captain. Nanula resigned shortly after his demotion, apparently from the friendship as well as the presidency. Reflecting on this period, Sternlicht, still CEO of the world's largest hotel chain and strung out by life at the top, lamented, "Why did I do this? . . . . Am I stupid, or am I a jerk? Half the time, I think I'm stupid. The other half, I think I'm a jerk."

Partners who resist differentiating their roles would be well advised to give up the search for the right power-sharing or power-switching approach. They are unlikely to find it. Instead they need to address the interpersonal issues head on rather than let them disrupt the organizational structure of the business. They must recognize when their own emotional needs are at odds with the needs of the business and make an adjustment. Such discussions should occur in the course of creating the Partnership Charter and be conducted with all of the partners present.

PERFORMANCE, FEEDBACK, AND ACCOUNTABILITY

Whatever roles people assume in their business, they have to perform them in a manner that is acceptable to their partners; otherwise there will be problems. They have to perform competently, and that means there must be accountability. Prospective partners should discuss in the charter process the level of accountability they want to maintain. If they wait until after they are fully in business, the partner who most needs to be held accountable may resist all manner of accountability.

Accountability means that there is a consequence when performance is not up to some expected level. But holding fellow owner-managers accountable is much harder than holding employees accountable, which is itself not easy. Partners may cringe at the prospect of being held truly accountable for their actions and performance, but they should consider the alternative. Without accountability, partners can perform in a substandard manner and can fail at what they're supposed to do. They can *cost* the business money rather than make money for it. They can—and do—destroy businesses. Nobody wants that to happen, but avoiding performance problems among partners requires careful planning.

To establish accountability, partners have to discuss what they are willing to be held accountable for. The best place to start is the same place executives start with employees, with job descriptions. In addition, prospective partners should use the exercises described in chapter 11 in which people list their expectations for each other. That process will add the things related to being partners that might not appear in job descriptions. The essentials of a job description include where the position fits in the organization, the person to whom the partner reports, the responsibilities of the partner, and the experience and skills necessary to accomplish the job. I encourage prospective partners to then discuss and decide which things are *essential* and constitute a bottom line, meaning that performance below that line is substandard and not tolerable. Finally, partners need to decide on the consequences of not meeting their performance expectations. They can specify managerial, financial, and even ownership consequences. As long as they reach an agreement in advance, they may impose whatever conditions they can all agree on. These need not be punitive but must be effective.

Can co-owners really reject one of their own for poor performance? There's a perception that this doesn't happen in closely held and family businesses. In many that do not survive, it does not happen. In many of the best, however, it does. The Follett Corporation is a highly successful company, owned by the Follett family, which sells textbooks and operates college bookstores throughout the country. A few years ago some costly errors led to the dismissal of five owner-managers for poor performance. Follett President Richard Litzinsinger commented on the dismissals in *Forbes*. He said when regular employees see that the owners do not tolerate substandard performance among themselves, it sends a powerful signal: "They say, 'Hey, this company treats everyone the same.'"

Reviewing performance does not have to mean "performance reports," but the reviews need to be well considered. Although partners hopefully give one another regular feedback, they should commit to a serious evaluation of one another's performance at least once a year, when they have their retreat and review their charter. Many partners desperately need feedback but never get it. Social psychologist David Dunning discovered in his research that one reason people—especially the least competent performers—overestimate their abilities is that they fail to get constructive criticism that would help them improve their performance. Dunning said, "It's surprising how often feedback is nonexistent or ambiguous."

The regular feedback partners give one another should include honest and constructive criticism. Teams that operate without honest feedback develop erroneous ideas about what works and what doesn't, as well as who is doing well and who isn't. Feedback should be thoughtful and specific. It should take place on a regular basis, at least every couple of weeks. It may occur when partners have a regular meeting to share information, but it must be in addition to operational matters and not skipped because there are more pressing matters at hand. I have heard many partners complain that they do not have time to give each other feedback because they are too busy putting out fires. Many of those fires, I point out, get started because of their inadequate feedback and communication with one another. A continuous flow of information and feedback among the partners is necessary for a high-functioning team.

Many partners will say, "We have meetings whenever we need them," but such ad hoc meetings are rarely as effective as regularly scheduled ones. They result in discussions that are not thorough, often do not include all of the partners, and don't give partners a real opportunity to support one another. Rick Maurer, who consults on building cooperation in organizations, has written about the importance of supporting colleagues in the workplace. "Within all of us beats the heart of a nine-year-old child. And that kid wants to know how he or she is doing. *Do you like what I did? Do you like me? Am I okay?* But, of course, as adults, we would never ask such questions." Partners need to commit, in their charter, to address these implicit questions regularly.

GRANTING TITLES

Assigning titles—whether by drawing straws, power struggles, or polite debate—often leads people to believe they have defined their respective roles and therefore should be able to work well together. As the three partners in the wholesale business described earlier illustrated, titles will not clear up underlying role conflicts. Titles like CEO, COO, president, CFO, and director of marketing sound specific, but everyone has different ideas about what they actually mean. These days, with titles such as CIO (Information), CLO (Learning), and CKO (Knowledge), the confusion about titles is growing.

Even though titles are of secondary importance if the partners have a clear understanding of their roles, they should still assign titles with care. There are traps here, too. For example, I found the following advice on the Web:

> ### Short on Cash? *"Up-Title"*
> The growing trend of "up-titling" means your receptionist might prefer being called "Head of Verbal Telecommunications" or your warehouse staff "Stock Replenishment Executives." Prestigious job titles recognize employees' contributions and can increase their commitment.

Playing these games with titles can create confusion among employees as well as friction among partners. Titles can carry multiple and hidden meanings, so they should not be granted lightly. To the extent that they are meant to inflate egos and do not accurately reflect some operational reality, they are a likely source of conflict. A better strategy is to keep the title tied as closely as possible to its meaning through a clear job description that links a title to a position, not a person. If there is a secret to titles, it is that they should reflect reality—something that the partners as a group must determine.

OUTSIDE MANAGERS

Co-owners may decide not to be co-managers, although hiring professional managers is usually not part of the landscape in the start-up phase. From either genuine interest or financial necessity, owners usually agree that they will run the company themselves. While working on the charter, prospective partners should discuss the circumstances under which partners would hire professional managers, because this sets the stage for a discussion that can be highly sensitive later on.

The issue frequently arises when a company is poised to enter a growth phase. Business growth can cause some roles to grow faster than the partners who are in them. In this case, it may not feel good to have to bring in an outside manager but at least the need is precipitated by growth and, presumably, by good performance. A second reason for bringing in an outside manager is to compensate for an ineffective owner-manager. That isn't a good situation for anyone, but if the partners cannot face the necessity of taking action in such circumstances, the business may sputter and die.

Many advisors counsel owners of closely held businesses to bring in professional managers as quickly as possible. The reason may be that there are many poor owner-managers, or it may be that it is difficult for owners to admit that they are in over their management heads. The decision to look for outside managers is for the owners to make, and it should be based on the depth of their desire to manage the company, their competence, and their long-term plans. Making an assessment on these issues may not be easy because it is influenced by very personal motivations, some of which may be completely unconscious. In addition, the owners must agree, which can be complicated because they may have totally different opinions of their own competence.

If partners wait until someone is performing incompetently, they may be ensuring that they will not be of one mind about it. That is why they must have a plan to handle the unfortunate situation in which a partner is unable or unwilling to perform his or her duties in a satisfactory manner. That plan, too, becomes part of their charter.

CHAPTER 6

Money: Taking It Out, and Sharing It

S TART-UPS DON'T USUALLY generate money, they consume it. It might seem premature, therefore, for people becoming partners to spend time thinking about a remote question like how to get money out of the business. Nevertheless, every set of partners is betting that sooner or later the tide will turn, profits will appear, and partners will start moving money out the door and into their pockets.

When partners make decisions about taking money out of their businesses, they face a far more complex situation than the one confronting sole owners. *Sole* owners can pay themselves whatever they want—and they do. The can take money out in a variety of ways. It does not matter terribly which way they do it, except for the tax implications. If they are overly generous with themselves, the business may be forced to assume greater debt, which the owner must guarantee. This is called commingling funds. Accountants hate when their clients do it, but sole owners are free to take out money whenever they want and not be held accountable, as long as they give the IRS its due.

For many *co-owners*, by contrast, determining pay, distributions, dividends, benefits, and perks is one of the toughest assignments they have. It may result in divisive and bitter meetings. One partner, talking about dividing profits at year-end, said, "It's traumatic every December." For other partnerships, if the disagreements over money occurred only annually, it would be a blessing. These conversations are stressful because the issues are complex and the range of possibilities is enormous; no hard-and-fast rules exist, nor is there one system that will work for everyone, and partners have different monetary needs and different ways of thinking about money. Yet they have to—or should—agree on everything they do. On top of all that, whatever they take out must be shared in some fashion, and sharing itself can be a challenge.

This section of the Partnership Charter helps partners achieve clarity about how they would like to take money out of their business. As part of the process, they may consult with their financial advisors, but when they have explored the issues and come to some understandings, they need to have those understandings reviewed by their accountant and lawyer.

HOW TO GET MONEY OUT

There are three major considerations for partners when discussing how and when to take money out: personal, business, and financial and tax related. Discussing these considerations helps the partners' decision-making process go more smoothly.

Personal Considerations

How partners take money out of their business is partly a function of the current personal circumstances of each partner and what each is seeking as a co-owner. If their *collective* circumstances allow the partners to put money in and forgo taking it out, the business may be in a stronger position when starting out or better able to expand later. Discussing each person's personal and financial circumstances and attitudes is important because these could adversely affect the entire group of partners.

The partners' personal considerations need to be aligned for them to have satisfying debates about how to take money out. A young partner, who stands to benefit more by leaving as much money as possible in the business in order to build it up, is likely to view the subject differently than one who is five years from retirement.

Partners who begin their businesses with a very informal manner of compensating themselves are at risk for having individual partners' personal considerations unduly influence the business's financial decisions. They may take money out whenever money is available, in effect treating their business checkbook like a personal piggy bank. A related problem occurs when partners let their personal circumstances affect their judgments about the size of their paychecks. Often partners will arrive at divergent opinions about how much they should be paid because someone is basing his or her numbers more on financial need than on the company's ability to pay.

A number of partners I interviewed told me about another personal consideration that they had discovered only after becoming partners. One of those who spontaneously mentioned it was Ken Olsen, a founding partner of Digital Equipment Corporation. He maintained that the spouses' feelings could confound the issue of compensation: "As partners, we felt fine about what we were making. It was a spouse of a partner who felt that it wasn't enough."

Business Considerations

How partners take money out is related to business considerations such as the organization's vision, values, and strategic plans; personnel needs; and the roles people will play. Clarity about these matters (see chapters 3 and 5) will provide a firmer basis for making decisions about money.

People sometimes become partners with the assumption that being co-owners entitles them to receive a paycheck and benefits without considering the business's needs, as if they were employees. But problems will arise if the business no longer needs partners with their skills, if they cannot satisfactorily perform the jobs they are billed for, the job outgrows them, or they get bored with what they are doing. This is especially true if they have become dependent on salary and perks that are more than they would be paid elsewhere.

If the partners' collective vision is to build an organization for the long term, one where earning an income is the partners' primary interest, they should ascertain how to begin taking at least modest salaries fairly soon.

Such a company provides a lifestyle for the partners. It is not the kind that will ever be sold for huge multiples of earnings; the assets walk out the door every night. If, on the other hand, the vision is to pump up a business quickly and then sell, partners are looking for their real reward at the end of the rainbow, not a steady job and regular income.

Paul Carlin and Gene Johnson are prime examples of founding partners with their eyes on the end of the rainbow. They had their sights set on selling part or all of Mail2000 from before they started the company in 1995. So, for the six years they ran the company, even though they had significant financial investors and probably could have drawn salaries, they only withdrew reimbursements for their expenses. Their personal financial situations, bolstered by the sale of an earlier company, made that possible. Most important, the two partners were in complete agreement about their strategic business goals. Carlin and Johnson and their investor partners got their money out when they sold the company to UPS for a reported $100 million.

Rick McCloskey and his partners in Systems Connection had no such understanding. Unfortunately for them, they are a prime example of how financially devastating it can be when partners fail to agree ahead of time on the strategic needs of the business. McCloskey explained to me that he believed he "had taken pains to make sure the new owners agreed with our three-to-five-year strategy and that they understood that going public was not the only possible way to exit." He admitted, though, "I erred in not putting those things down in writing and getting the others to explicitly agree to them." Literally within days of merging, he learned that the new partners "wanted to go public quickly and create liquidity for the stock," which was totally at odds with his and two of his partners' desire "to continue to grow the company and pursue a long-term exit plan."

Financial and Tax Considerations

The way partners take money out is related to various financial and tax considerations, including the business's financial performance, its obligations to others, and its organization. For example, salaries and bonuses are tax deductible, whereas distributions (in an LLC), or dividends (in a C corporation) are not. It would therefore seem wise to take out as much of the profits as possible in the form of compensation. There are many complications in following such a strategy, however. It creates a fuzzy line between salaries, bonuses, and perks (employment), and dividends and distributions (ownership). Inflating salaries or year-end bonuses can create all kinds of problems among partners, with the IRS, and with employees.

A company that awards higher compensation to partners than to non-partners for a comparable level of responsibility because of tax considerations is apt to create resentment and find it difficult to attract and retain top-level employees. This behavior also can leave employees wondering whether partners will be fair in other ways. If compensation is payment for work performed, it should not matter whether the person doing the work owns stock or not. Raises, promotions, bonuses, and performance evaluations should be independent of ownership status.

There are times in the lives of many partnerships when financial realities preclude any compensation at all. The coffers may be devouring cash instead of generating it. Many partners I interviewed reported going for extended periods without taking money out, a feat that necessitates a willingness on the part of all of the partners to live with less and to persevere. People used to regular paychecks may find this disconcerting and may resist the idea. A partner who thinks his or her company may need to operate for an extended period under such a stringent financial regime should thoroughly discuss that view with his or her partners to ensure everyone shares a similar mindset. (See the sidebar.)

DIFFERENT REWARDS FOR DIFFERENT PARTNERS

Carlin and Johnson at Mail2000, and the three architect partners in the BSW Group, decided to split the money from their partnership equally, but that is certainly not what many others do. When writing a Partnership Charter, some sensitive decisions must be made about the way partners take money out *relative to one another*. There are no rules

The co-owners of the international architectural firm BSW Group, Inc., based in Tulsa, illustrate how partners can meld personal, business, and financial considerations when making decisions about how to take money out of a closely held corporation. Bob Workman, Bob Sober, and Dave Broach dedicated time, energy, and resources to deciding how to get money out while building a successful firm.

According to Workman, "When we looked carefully at what was missing in the financial structure of an earlier partnership we had [with four other architects] that failed miserably, it was a totally open and honest conversation about our expectations—our personal, financial expectations and our business expectations—and then linking them together." This time the three architects made an "open-book partnership" a requirement of becoming equal partners. "We figured that if we didn't share our personal financial information with one another, we wouldn't know whether a partner's financial decisions about the business were clouded by his personal circumstances or not." So every quarter, as they budgeted for the business, they reviewed one another's personal financial situation as well. Workman described their plan for taking money out of the company this way:

> Our first rule was that owners always came last. The client, the company, the staff, the bank, and Uncle Sam always came first and in that order. For the owners to take dividends we had to have satisfied clients that paid their bills on time. Next, we had to have a company that was growing, in good condition, well equipped, well capitalized and current on its own obligations. Next, our staff needed to be well hired, well trained, well equipped, well paid, with great benefits and a share of the profits. Our obligations to our bank needed to be current and within our covenants. Finally, all business and personal taxes were to be kept current at all times. If all these things were in good order and distributions to owners were available (as well as all taxes on the distributions), then we would take dividends equally or not at all. Once we did take them, we each knew what part of our [personal] plans we were applying the net proceeds towards and it would be confirmed at our meeting the following month.

Of course, their salaries did not come last, only distributions, but they had agreed going into their partnership that salaries would be minimal—a "basic living wage plus a modest ROI." They were not trying to take all of their money out as salary and what they call "perverse salary," meaning perks. In fact, they made sure they never made more in salary than the highest paid staff member made in total compensation. Their salaries, like their distributions, were always equal.

The only foolproof way for them to determine a living-wage salary, they felt, was to apply the open-book concept. "Our lives and circumstances were similar enough that we could create a common, shared set of goals that we all felt was reasonable and would not harm the company or the other partners." If someone wanted something for himself that the other two felt was too much, his only recourse was to hope that the company would have enough left over in profits at the end of the year to provide for it; they would not allow the desire for luxuries to push salaries higher. But after agreeing to this system, Workman claimed, they rarely made bad personal financial decisions. Personal considerations were not allowed to influence profit distributions. Only business, financial, and tax considerations determined the amount of the distributions. Workman believes that their way of linking personal and business finances "forced us to make better decisions for the business and for our families."

All three partners concurred that their financial strategy has worked exceedingly well on both the personal and business levels. The company has managed to improve its profit margin by 300–400 percent in less than ten years. Those margins have made it possible for Workman to commence buying out his two partners and to lay the groundwork for a new team of partners who will eventually buy him out.

---

about how this should be done, but it can help to look at partnerships in terms of three broad categories:

1. Various partners making extremely diverse contributions
2. Partners making different but comparable contributions
3. Partners making nearly identical contributions

Extremely Diverse Contributions

Some partnerships are composed of partners whose contributions are so dissimilar that they defy comparison. Often in these cases little attempt is made to compare what partners take out financially. What they take out relative to one another must be fair, but there is no assumption that it will be similar in either amount or type.

An example is a restaurant where one partner supplies the financial backing and the other, the restaurateur, acts as maître d' and general manager. Another example is a real estate partnership in which one partner provides an apartment house while the other supplies management services. In both examples, one partner makes a one-time contribution of capital or a tangible asset, and the other provides an ongoing service. The partner making the capital or asset contribution will have a greater equity stake in the venture. In these partnerships, the contribution equation shifts gradually and predictably. As it begins, one partner makes his or her entire contribution. Over time contributions become more balanced as the managing partner works—in effect, building up equity—while the asset partner sits back. Among the ways partners could handle this shift in the balance is with a change in ownership, profit sharing, compensation, or a combination of the three.

Ownership percentages usually dictate how profits are split and how the proceeds will be divided when the property is eventually sold. In addition, the operating partner may take a management fee (salary)—but the bigger the fee, the smaller the ownership percentage and profit distributions are likely to be. Operating partners could negotiate a lower fee and a higher ownership percentage, which would result in a higher percentage of the operating profits and a greater stake in the underlying value of the property.

The important point is that when partners' contributions are this dissimilar, they must carefully negotiate how they each will take money out. Furthermore, it is very important to clarify expectations regarding all expenses that detract from profits, including management fees and capital improvements, because the two types of expenses will affect the two partners' earnings disproportionately.

Different, But Comparable, Contributions

Romancing the Woods' Davis and O'Leary (described in chapter 1) are an example of a partnership in which both partners are active, adding various ingredients to the mix and creating something decidedly greater than the sum of the parts. Davis described their mix succinctly: "Bob runs the factory; I run the marketing. He's responsible for getting the work out; I'm responsible for bringing it in. I'm responsible for the designs; his people are responsible for building them. What we share is a belief in the business." The business could not run without both partners' major contributions, and hiring someone to take either one's place would be difficult.

In this situation, each partner is working, bringing a separate set of expertise and skills and assuming specific responsibilities. Therefore, the partners are judged by different standards. Still, it is relatively easy to agree that each person's contribution, though different, is roughly comparable to the other's, and thus *each partner should be paid the same.* And they are. As long as people are competent in their area and everyone is comparably committed, it often works well for partners to pay themselves equally. "Partners are partners," is how Paul Carlin put it. "When partners can bring completely different skills, like operations, marketing and finance to the table, and then make things equal, it automatically eliminates an awful lot of problems." The advantage, according to Bob Hurwitz, is that, "It takes some of the jealousy factor out."

When partners pay themselves equally, as Carlin and Johnson did, competence and commitment become critical elements. If a partner turns out to be less than fully competent, or if the demands of the job eventually outgrow him or her, equal pay will become a problem. The same will happen if a partner's commitment wanes. People starting out invariably begin by putting in 100 percent effort, but some partners' interest or ambition may drop off. If the differences in commitment levels persist for long, equal pay may need to be reconsidered. Partners who pay themselves equally as they start out may want to agree to factor in commitment levels when they review their performance.

The thorny problem of setting different salaries for various jobs or positions is eliminated if partners pay themselves equally. Partners may conclude that equal salaries are not equitable, instead defining fair salaries according to the broader marketplace, relying on surveys of what people are normally paid for comparable jobs. However, this strategy can lead to competitive battles for specific positions. For example, if the president is paid 25 percent more than vice presidents, partners may vie for the presidential slot solely for that reason. The company may be the loser in this competition.

Another problem with this strategy is the necessity for agreeing on the market values of various positions. There is wide variation between the top and bottom salaries for any given position because accurate data are hard to come by for closely held companies and because of the idiosyncratic compensation structure in private companies. Partners should be aware of these complications and thoroughly discuss them before deciding which path to take.

Making Nearly Identical Contributions

In professional firms (such as engineers, architects, accountants, lawyers, and doctors), people become partners precisely because they have the *same* skills to contribute. They bring the same basic skill set, provide essentially the same kind of service, and are judged by the same set of standards. When these three pieces are nearly identical, small differences can stand out, especially when they affect the bottom line. One lawyer may be landing more clients than another. One engineer's jobs may consistently make money while another's produce only red ink. One architect can get clients to expand project concepts beyond what they had envisioned while another designs only what clients ask for. If the compensation system is structured so that all of the partners are taking money out equally and these differences persist, someone (the rainmaking lawyer, the profit-conscious engineer, the expansive architect) may begin feeling that the system isn't fair.

While many professional service firms still insist, "a partner's a partner" where compensation is concerned, many other firms have moved away from an equal pay system. Some firms that employed a lockstep approach that paid partners equally on the same level (senior, junior) have also changed. There has been a shift toward higher pay for individual partners who work exceptionally hard and for partners whose specialties are exceptionally lucrative. These firms take the view that the marketplace should define fair compensation.

It is difficult to overestimate the significance of the difference between equal and market-based compensation systems. In any partnership, tens or hundreds of thousands of dollars may shift into different partners' pockets depending on which system is embraced. The disparity in earning power and what a partner could command in the marketplace was responsible for the bifurcation of Anderson Worldwide in 1989 into partners who performed accounting work and those who performed the more lucrative consulting work. Before the split, the consultants were in essence paying the accountants hundreds of millions of dollars *annually* to equalize their paychecks.

Advocates of systems that reward individual accomplishment argue that they help a company retain its most productive people, help partners understand their expectations of one another, and help them confront poor performance. These advocates also maintain that such systems create an atmosphere in which people strive toward excellence and avoid complacency.

Partners are evaluated—and then paid—on criteria that contribute to the firms' success. The criteria include objective measures such as billable hours, business generated or managed, and profitability, as well as subjective measures such as loyalty, dedication to mentoring others, and being a team player. The essential components of individual reward systems are the criteria for appraising performance, a method for rewarding certain positive behaviors, and a review process. Partners must agree in advance on the criteria and on how to judge performance, especially on the subjective criteria.

Some partnerships believe that an individual reward system is the only fair system, while others believe that it creates more problems among partners than it solves. If partners want to use it, they need to work through the following types of issues. Partners often utilize objective and financial criteria that force them to focus more on the short term than the long term and on certain types of activities as opposed to others. Long-range planning efforts, being harder to measure, tend to get short shrift. Personnel development, research activities, even operations and administration may get less partner attention because they contribute only indirectly to the bottom line and weigh less, if factored in at all. Partners may be tempted to push the firm into strategic directions that enhance their own ability to generate revenue. (This was precisely the case with Lon and Stan, described in chapter 3. Lon wanted the firm to go in a particular direction and wanted the partners to be rewarded for the contracts they each brought in.)

Partners who choose to reward individual accomplishment have to consider that such a system for taking money out of businesses can impair or destroy the cooperative, collegial spirit that is essential to the maintenance of successful partnerships. It can cause partners to share less information and focus more on their own bottom line. Like basketball players concerned more with their own statistics than their team's, the partners may be tempted to inflate their own scores so as to get a bigger bonus. Law firms using this system have seen it erode partners' loyalty to their partners and the firm by causing lawyers to jealously guard their clients and share work only with their associates. As clients have become more closely tied to individual lawyers, the lawyers have been more able to switch firms and take their own client base with them. The promise of bigger pay incentives if partners switch firms and bring their clients with them results in firm-hopping, which exacerbates the loyalty problem.

While some partners feel more fairly treated by such a system, it is difficult to know whether it is better or worse for partnerships generally. It may work better for large partnerships that do not rely as heavily on collegiality and collaboration than for smaller professional firms. It should be clear that there is no one-size-fits-all approach when it comes to partners taking money out of their businesses. Nor is there a way for partners to circumvent the need to work through this sensitive and crucial issue. The best way is to sift through the personal, business, and finance and tax considerations before focusing on how much money to take out.

CHAPTER 7

Governance

I N THE GOVERNANCE SECTION of the Partnership Charter, co-owners clarify what they mean by oversight and governance and consider creating either a board of directors or an advisory board. If they decide to create a board, then they examine the boundaries between their roles as shareholders, executives, and board members, and address the questions of board independence, performance, and accountability.

In the most practical sense, the pressing question for partners to address in this section of the charter is, How could having *and using* a board be helpful? Many closely held corporations have boards of directors but fail to use them or even call the required meetings. What can boards do for the owners and the company?

HOW AN EFFECTIVE BOARD CAN HELP PARTNERS

Boards of directors were developed when the Industrial Revolution spawned corporations that were no longer managed by their owners. The new corporations were publicly or privately held behemoths that were run by nonowner executives. It became the responsibility of boards to oversee the executives in these corporations since the frequently diffuse ownership could not.

Today, boards of directors (or what are called boards of managers in LLCs) are charged with electing officers and ensuring that they run companies properly and in the best interests of the owners—never in their own interest at the expense of the owners. Board members are representatives of the owners and by law owe them duties of care and loyalty. Care demands that directors exercise the same degree of care that an ordinary, prudent person would exercise under the same or similar circumstances when conducting his or her own affairs. Loyalty prevents directors from self-dealing. In turn, laws protect directors from second-guessing from the courts by the business-judgment rule, which essentially says that directors are not liable for bad business decisions as long as they do not violate the duties of care and loyalty.

Board members have a fiduciary responsibility to *all* shareholders as a group and cannot show favoritism to any individual owner or class of owners (e.g., those working in the company versus those who do not; majority versus minority shareholders). Even though they may take actions that are not in the interest of some owners, they must preserve the legal rights of all, including minority owners.

Boards offer certain advantages to all types of companies including closely held businesses. They hold management, usually through the president or CEO, accountable for the performance of the company. They can also function as a resource to the executive team. A good board is able to speak with one voice for the partners to the managers, even though its members may disagree on specific issues. This way, the company's management shouldn't be thrown off if the partners are not all in sync. The board, in effect, manages the boundary between the owners and the executives.

Boards are uniquely positioned to focus their attention and energy on broad issues (such as company policies, markets, acquisitions, debt structure, and strategic planning). They are different in this way from most senior executive teams, which focus on operations and near-term matters. One of the best examples of this broader range of concerns is the board's responsibility to oversee the succession of leadership, including selecting the next CEO. In the past, boards did little more than rubber-stamp the CEO's choice of a successor, but that has changed in recent years as relationships between boards and CEOs have evolved. A *Harvard Business Review* article on the subject put it succinctly: "It is up to the board to ensure that the process is rigorous, careful, and—perhaps most important—defensible." Boards with independent, nonowner directors will put those members on CEO search committees and on compensation committees that make decisions about compensation of partners and senior executives. They can deliver a dose of objectivity, which is sometimes sorely needed.

Boards of directors have always been a bit of an enigma to owners of close corporations. A board oversees the senior management, but in closely held corporations, especially young corporations, the owners may *be* the management. It would seem nonsensical to have partners-as-board-members watching over themselves-as-managers, yet there are good reasons to have a separate governance body even when it comprises only owners.

When owners create a board agenda, don their board hats, and go off to a boardroom, they think differently. They get out of the trenches, look at the company from a new angle, and have a different goal in mind. Partners often report that the experience gets them out of their fire-fighting mindset and broadens their vision. Meeting as a board also paves the way for the time when all of the owners may not be managers. As discussed in chapter 4, partners have to explore whether they want people to remain co-owners if they are not working in the company. If they do, then the board may be a way for them to stay meaningfully connected and continue to have a say in the direction of the company.

WHO SHOULD BE ON THE BOARD

Owners.   Many partners assume that all owners should be board members. Some see this as an entitlement and others see it as a practical matter. Perhaps no one has more of a right to serve than those who founded or invested in the company. Also, no one may be more able and motivated to guide the company than its owners. Having all of the owners on the board obviates the concern that a shareholder's interest will not be heard at the board level.

There are potential drawbacks to deciding that it is a right of all owners to be on the board, however. If there are numerous owners with small percentages of ownership it becomes impractical to include everyone. The partners at SHN Consulting Engineers and Geologists, Inc., in Eureka, California, devised a plan that mitigates that problem. The partners with a small number of shares rotate through one position on the board that is held for them as a group.

Even when there are few owners, however, some may lack the talent for conceptual and high-level business thinking that is helpful on even a small company's board. When discussing board composition, partners may prefer not to create such a tight connection between ownership and governance, making it less traumatic for them to step aside if they lack the skills, lose interest in governance, or no longer feel up to the task. As companies change and grow, what they need from their board members changes (networking, strategic planning, succession planning, acquisition planning). The complexity of the position may grow faster than a partner's capacity to deal with it.

Finally, while it may look like a right of ownership to serve on the board when the owners also manage the company, it may look different some years later when an owner is no longer a manager. All of these combinations and permutations need to be discussed by the partners during the charter process.

Executives.   The reason to have executives on the board is that they know the inside of the company. When the board makes a decision, they will be the ones to carry it out. It is not necessary that executives be on the board to offer the advantage of all of their knowledge and wisdom, though, since boards may have executives make regular reports to them so that they stay fully informed of affairs within the company. Partners need to avoid loading a board so heavily with company executives that it adds little value.

Many companies assign the board chair role to the CEO; some board consultants believe this compromises both the usefulness and the independence of the board. CEOs manage company executives, and board chairs manage directors. Giving the CEO both responsibilities can water down the distinction between management and governance and make the CEO feel that his or her board chair duties are a nuisance and a distraction. Since the board has the job of overseeing the CEO, if the CEO is managing the board it can make this oversight function suspect. Owners should seriously consider having one of the outside board members serve as chair.

Advisors.   Owners frequently like their regular advisors to serve as board members. Accountants and lawyers may know a great deal about certain aspects of the company, and their experience and conceptual abilities may be an asset to the board; however, both the management and the board have unfettered access to their expertise and opinions without their serving on the board.

Professional ethics prevent accountants who audit a company's books from serving on its board. The canon of ethics of lawyers does not prohibit them from advising a company and also serving on its board. Sometimes, however, lawyers have a conflict providing legal advice because they have been directly involved in the decisions as board members. Before asking legal advisors to become board members, co-owners should discuss the possibilities of conflicts.

Outsiders.   Independent members—nonowners and nonmanagers who have no allegiances to any person or faction—bring credibility to boards. Outsiders are people who have responsibility and accountability with no apparent way of profiting from board decisions other than sometimes owning relatively small amounts of stock. Truly independent board members are not employees or friends of the CEO or peers who might have a built-in reluctance to hold them accountable. They are people with strong values and integrity and the capacity to think independently and vote their conscience even under pressure. They are often presidents or high-level executives at other companies who can provide advice born of experience, or business consultants who currently are not serving the management and would have no conflict of interest. The presence of a couple of outside board members adds credibility to the board's oversight function, which is stretched when a board is composed solely of owners.

Outsiders can often contribute expertise that may be lacking within the group of partners and within management, for example, in acquisitions, going public, restructuring, or international sales. Bringing fresh perspectives and new ideas is an additional reason for building a board with truly independent outside people. It helps avoid what is called in military jargon "incestuous amplification." *Jane's Defense Weekly* defines this as "a condition . . . where one only listens to those who are already in lockstep agreement, reinforcing set beliefs and creating a situation ripe for miscalculation"—not a safe condition for either armies or companies.

Corporate boards of publicly traded companies came under close scrutiny recently as a result of perceived abuses and lack of effective oversight. Investigations pointed a finger at boards laden with lackeys. Ronald Anderson of American University's Kogod School of Business found that independent boards (i.e., those with a majority of independent members) may be critical to the success of companies controlled by families. He discovered that companies with strong directors who take a long-term view do better than those companies whose boards lack outside directors and run the companies at the expense of minority shareholders. The key difference is the independence of the firm's board. Few closely held businesses are going to have a truly independent board, but it is helpful to know how strong, independent board members can help make companies more successful.

In the 1990s it became popular to have outside board members own some shares in companies they represented. The idea was that by owning a piece of the company—even if the company gave them the shares—they would be more motivated to serve the company's best interest. People recognize today that very capable people are willing to serve without equity enhancements, which is a plus for owners of closely held corporations who often have little desire for additional shareholders.

Partners should agree upon the number and composition of the board in the Partnership Charter. The optimal number of people on a board is five to nine. (Odd numbers prevent tie votes, though ideally actions are taken by consensus.) The partners should also determine how board members will be chosen or elected. Without an agreement to the contrary, board members are elected by either a partner with a majority interest or a majority vote of the shareholders. Partners can, however, select board members using any process they like.

SETTING A COURSE FOR THE BOARD

Co-owners need to give their board sufficient direction from its inception to ensure that it begins on the right course. At the broadest level, partners should communicate their vision for the company and any shared values they want to guide the company. Owners should decide and then communicate clearly to the directors the time commitment expected of directors, required activities between meetings, and remuneration.

The partners may want to offer guidelines for actions that will seriously affect them, such as making acquisitions and divestitures, changing dividends or distributions, or altering debt structure or liquidity. They must ensure that the board clearly understands its range of responsibility and authority. It is better for the owners of a closely held corporation to give too much direction to their board at the outset than to give too little and then micromanage. Just as boards do not manage the executives, partners should not try to manage the board. Competent, strong board members would not take kindly to being micromanaged by shareholders.

After partners agree on their expectations of board members, they need to agree on how they will judge their performance, which is not easy. Unlike the CEO, who can be held responsible "for the numbers," the board does not run the company, so it cannot reasonably be held responsible for how the company performs. Owners can evaluate the performance of board members based on stated expectations, such as attending meetings, serving on committees, responsiveness, holding the CEO accountable, and networking. At the same time, owners need to make sure they are giving directors the resources, information, and authority they need to do their job. If the board includes outsiders, that may require a degree of openness about financial data that owners of closely held businesses are not used to.

If the owners constitute the entire board, then of course evaluating the board is the same as evaluating themselves. Since I am an advocate of partners evaluating themselves as a team, this is just another angle on the same process. In addition to looking at how they perform as a group of *co-owners*, they look at how they are performing in their board capacity. The value of this exercise might be that they conclude that they never accomplish what a real board would and therefore need to rethink the idea that they can be the board.

The five founders of a transportation company in Illinois with $100 million in revenues and $11 million in annual profits had served as their own board since they opened the company's doors. After twenty-one years in business, two of the five partners had stopped working full time and a third had retired completely. All five were still on the board, but the meetings had been going downhill for about four years. It seemed that the better the company performed, the more contentious and alienated they became. As the partners' day-to-day contributions to the company had changed greatly since they started, they fought about what they each deserved. They would argue, yell, and sometimes storm out of meetings. There was little communication between meetings and little agreement during meetings. Threats of lawsuits and countersuits began to fly. When the partners grew fearful that they really could kill their golden goose of a company, they decided to use mediation to resolve their differences.

The two major outcomes from the four-day mediation retreat were a set of agreements related to employment, consulting contracts for the partners, and a restructured statutory board that would include three of the five shareholders and four outside members. They specified a procedure for working together to find the four outsiders and selecting them by consensus, with a backup plan if they could not agree on all of the new board members in nine months. In addition, they signed off on a set of guidelines for the responsibilities and authority of the board.

When the partners addressed their expectations for the outside board members, they considered something we routinely advise against. It's an idea we have heard other partners entertain, namely that the outside board members might intervene when the partners reach a stalemate. Some owners like the idea of outside members as referees for their wrestling matches, but few people of board stature want to serve as peacemakers or consider it their area of expertise; they wisely avoid taking sides between owners. No board member will be viewed by all the owners as perfectly neutral once the board is operating. Playing neutral is a losing proposition for anyone who serves at the owners' behest. One board candidate told a group of co-owners that he would demand "combat pay" if such interventions were going to be part of his job.

On the other hand, it was reasonable for these partners to anticipate that the addition of outsiders would greatly enhance and uplift the tone and quality of their board meetings, just as guests coming into a family's home for dinner can enhance the tone and quality of dinner conversation. One of the reasons this happens at the dinner table is that the guests' presence creates a clearer boundary between appropriate dinner conversation and that which is better dealt with elsewhere. Once the outside members joined the board, it operated with an efficiency and decorum that made all of them wish they had made the shift years before. Interestingly, the outsiders had a transforming effect even before they arrived. For years the partners had felt free to discuss any and all topics at their board meetings, including personal and operational issues. The final two board meetings before the outside members joined had none of the inappropriate conversation or the rancor that had characterized so many earlier meetings. Just anticipating the new members' arrival made it easier for the partners to stick to governance matters.

ADVISORY BOARDS

Advisory boards are established primarily to offer guidance, assistance, a fresh perspective, and good counsel to owners and managers of companies. They are more informal than boards of directors and do not have the responsibility of overseeing the management of the company. They do not have the authority to replace the CEO, for example, if he or she is performing poorly. Because the fiduciary and legal responsibilities of advisory boards are significantly less than those of statutory boards, some people will more readily agree to serve on them and will do so for less remuneration. Furthermore, companies are not obliged to purchase directors' and officers' insurance for advisory boards, which also makes them more affordable. Advisory boards can be extremely helpful to owners when they need expertise that none of the partners has. They can also assist with networking opportunities. Depending on the quality of the members, they can enhance the stature of companies, although they do not give them the same financial credibility that statutory boards do.

KNOW WHERE A BOARD FITS IN

While adding a governance structure can be advantageous to partners for all the reasons outlined above, it must be done with great care. (This is even true, though to a lesser extent, with advisory boards.) Boards need to understand where they fit into the bigger picture. Essentially, executives oversee employees, boards oversee executives, and the owners oversee—in a sense—the board. Boards have a significant amount of power, but partners have the option of replacing the board if they believe it is acting contrary to their interests or unsatisfactorily.

Paul Carlin, who served on the board of the United States Postal Service and later Mail2000, the company he co-founded, described his beliefs about where boards fit in like this: "It's important that managers running a company dominate the decision-making process—not the board. Companies need strong executive leadership and as long as they are doing well, they should not be second-guessed." They must be given free rein, otherwise, how can they be held accountable? "The tighter, more perilous the company's financial situation becomes, the less freedom the board is going to give the CEO." Carlin views boards as having a dilemma: "The board has a choice—do they want these people to run it, or don't they? If they don't, they should get somebody else to do that job." He believes that removal—not micromanagement—is the prerogative of the board, and if they cannot oust the problem managers, then board members can resign.

Just as boards of directors should not second-guess or micromanage their management, partners who have created boards with outside members should not second-guess their boards. If they consistently disapprove of how the outside members perform, they should replace them.

Like partnerships, boards must be designed and operated with care. Partners must be prepared to invest time and money in their boards to see worthwhile returns. If handled properly, a board can be a valuable asset for a group of partners.

PART THREE

THE INTIMATE SIDE
OF BEING PARTNERS

CHAPTER 8

Personal Styles and Working Together

The traits that make him appealing tend to make him appalling in the flash of an eye.

TODD PURDUM OF *THE NEW YORK TIMES,*
WRITING ABOUT FORMER PRESIDENT BILL CLINTON

"ONE OF THE CRITICAL skills for getting along is not getting hung up on other people's individual quirks." That was Arthur Sculley's answer to my question regarding the key to getting along well with partners. Sculley learned that lesson while climbing to the very top of the corporate ladder at J. P. Morgan. He says that lesson from corporate America is every bit as essential now that he has just two partners, his brothers John and David, who received their training in getting along at PepsiCo and Apple Computer (John) and H. J. Heinz (David). The three brothers became partners in a venture capital firm in New York.

ARE WE RIGHT FOR EACH OTHER?

Before people make a final decision to become partners, they should get to know each other better, no matter how long they've known each other or how well they believe they know each other. Research has demonstrated that people imagine that they know people better than they really do and that some people "are motivated to preserve misunderstanding." Before committing to one another, prospective partners need to clear the air, take a fresh look, and examine their styles.

It should come as no surprise that some personalities don't mix. "It was an odd marriage from the start," a *Washington Post* reporter wrote recently: "the old-time real estate developer and the new-school king of sports commercialism, Abe Pollin and Michael Jordan. Nearly 40 years apart in age and even more distant in approach, their partnership in the Washington Wizards often seemed like a Lincoln Town Car and an Aston Martin vying for the same parking spot." The end of their partnership in the spring of 2003 was like a controlled nuclear explosion. Pollin, the majority partner, told Jordan he was history, while Ted Leonsis, a Wizards minority owner and the person responsible for bringing Jordan into the partnership, looked on helplessly. People nearby reported that within seconds the rhetoric escalated to shouting and invective so bad that onlookers were half-surprised not to see fists flying.

It was quite different, of course, when the partnership was taking off. Pollin spoke effusively of Jordan, "He's a straight, honest, decent, wonderful human being, and in the short term, I've gotten to really know him." Perhaps he saw something of himself in Jordan.

As different as the two men were, it was their similarities that drove them apart. Both men were highly dominant and competitive—two qualities that can add strength and spice to partnerships. But if you merge dominance and competitiveness in any two people in the *same* partnership, sooner or later you'll see sparks fly. The polite explanations about differences in "work ethic" and "different directions for the team" after the final ouster were mere window dressing. It didn't matter in the end that Jordan had left his front-office job, donned a Wizard uniform, drew sellout crowds, and made an unprofitable franchise profitable. Nothing was enough to offset Pollin's difficulty with Jordan's *style*. And in the end, Pollin's $10 million offer to ease Jordan's departure did nothing to offset Jordan's antipathy to Pollin's style.

Styles are ways of describing people or their personalities. Personal, social, or leadership styles show how people operate—how they think, make decisions, use time, communicate, handle emotions, manage stress, judge others, influence others, and deal with conflict. They also suggest the kind of environment and support that people need to be effective. Although no two people are exactly alike, for practical purposes people fall into fewer than twenty categories, or styles. These systems for describing leadership styles are used extensively in the business world for personnel and executive selection and also for team development.

LEADERSHIP STYLES

Two of the most common leadership style inventories are the Myers-Briggs Type Indicator (MBTI) and the Personal Profile System, or DiSC test. BMC Associates has used both extensively with partners but prefers the DiSC because it provides a great deal of information partners can use to develop their agreements for working together more effectively.

The Personal Profile System or DiSC inventory is short and simple. It contains only twenty-eight items, each a set of four adjectives. For example, the four words might be *stimulating, patient, perceptive,* and *independent.* A person must pick one word from the four that most describes himself or herself in the workplace and one word that least describes himself or herself. The inventory is so well constructed that it is able to supply a wide variety of feedback from the information garnered from those few items. First, it reports the person's overall style. Every person will score highest on one or two of four dimensions; no one will be equal on all four, which is why it is possible to understand people. The four dimensions are Dominance, Influencing, Steadiness, and Conscientiousness (the source of the acronym DiSC, which is written with a lowercase "i" for historical reasons). It is easy to think of any potential or existing partner and guess which one or two dimensions predominate in his or her style. Very briefly, the four dimensions are as follows.

Dominance.   People high on this dimension are competitive, decisive, and quick to take action. They love challenges and are usually the first to reach for responsibility and authority. They are not afraid to struggle with opposition to achieve results. As hard as they push for what they want and believe in, if thwarted, they usually do not hold grudges. They prefer environments that offer prestige for accomplishments, freedom, and varied activities.

On the downside, partners with dominance as their highest dimension may get bored or frustrated quickly when things become too predictable. They may be blunt, sarcastic, and quick to find fault with another's performance. Being part of a team can present a challenge for them.

Influencing.   This dimension describes people who are enthusiastic, outgoing, and optimistic, and prefer working with people rather than things. They have a natural ease and charm about them, which makes them trusted and popular with others. They tend to be articulate and know how to entertain and motivate others. They organize people at work and then go home and organize after-hours activities with friends. They prefer environments that allow them freedom of expression and provide public recognition for abilities and accomplishments.

Although socially skilled, partners who score high on influencing have a tough time when personnel situations fail to run smoothly. They may avoid situations requiring confrontation or a direct approach. Their positive, affable approach means that they may trust people indiscriminately.

Steadiness.   People high on steadiness are known for being supportive, good listeners, generally amiable, and easygoing. They are skilled at cooperating with others and maintaining stability in order to get the job done. Their even tempers make them dependable and patient, particularly if they are able to approach tasks in a systematic manner. They are loyal and value the security that comes from identification with a group. They prefer work environments that allow them to work steadily and without being rushed or forced to alter their standard operating procedures.

These partners typically do not like change, preferring to maintain the status quo unless given very good reasons. They do not like conflict and when pushed, may give the appearance of conceding while subtly resisting.

Conscientiousness.   This dimension describes disciplined people who have the patience to sift through details that would make other people's minds numb. They are pros at quality control. These people make few mistakes because they've done their research and have weighed all the facts. They may be slow to take action, but once they've figured something out, they move ahead confidently. They prefer environments that include a businesslike atmosphere, defined performance expectations, and recognition for specific skills and accomplishments.

Partners with a conscientious style may get bogged down in processes and established ways of doing things. They hate being wrong and are sensitive to criticism. They may yield their position before it's warranted just to avoid controversy or conflict.

After reporting people's styles at this broad level, the DiSC then combines information from all four dimensions and comes up with one of fifteen profiles for each person. Whereas the four dimensions are broad, sweeping descriptions, the fifteen profiles are very specific and detailed. People contemplating partnership can easily get access to this information. Given the seriousness of the commitment, it makes good business sense for people to take the test and discuss it with the help of a psychologist.

I have used the DiSC frequently with medical practices contemplating taking on associates or partners. I help the practice owners analyze the fit between their own styles (and values) and those of the candidates. It is possible to see styles that complement one another as well as styles that are likely to clash.

Which personal or leadership styles fit together, and which are likely to clash? Unfortunately, psychological researchers warn us that there are often close links between the qualities that initially attract people to others and those that later generate annoyance or hostility.

TABLE 8.1   "Before" and "After" Partnership Perspectives

DiSC Dimension	Before, We See Our Partner's Strengths as:		After, We See Our Partner's Limitations as:
D	Courageous	⟶	Reckless
	Efficient	⟶	Workaholic
	Competitive	⟶	Overly aggressive
	Determined	⟶	Stubborn
i	Enthusiastic	⟶	Excitable
	Optimistic	⟶	Unrealistic
	Persuasive	⟶	Manipulative
	Spontaneous	⟶	Disorganized
S	Steadfast	⟶	Resistant to change
	Systematic	⟶	Slow paced
	Agreeable	⟶	Indecisive
	Good listener	⟶	Noncommunicative
C	Analytical	⟶	Critical
	Serious	⟶	Unsociable
	Orderly	⟶	Perfectionist
	Industrious	⟶	Workaholic

According to Dr. Diane Felmlee, "Like a moth to a flame, individuals are drawn to the very aspects of another individual that they eventually will dislike." Couple that unfortunate tendency with the fact that people actively try to get their potential partners to like them, and you have the makings of a high-risk situation.

People entering partnerships tend to see a potential partner in a warm glow reflecting only the best of the other person's leadership style, but over time the perception may shift to a harsh glare. What people initially perceive to be a partner's strength, they later perceive as a liability. Table 8.1 illustrates what happens. "Courageous" morphs into "reckless"—both characteristic of the dominance dimension. "Agreeable" becomes "indecisive"—both characteristic of steadiness. Many admirable qualities become ugly caricatures of their former selves, but in highly predictable ways. Why does this happen? Here is some of what we know.

Likes attract.   Similarity is one of the main factors that draw people to one another. Similarities may be related to attitudes; personality traits; ways of thinking, communicating, and working; or even places of origin. People tend to be comfortable with those like themselves.

Opposites attract.   Opposites do attract, though probably less often than likes. There is, however, a greater need to be cautious when attraction to another person is based on dissimilarity. While dissimilarity can challenge one's view of the world and make one more open, it can also raise fears that the other person will be *too* different, that is, will make decisions that are too different. Dissimilarity also leads to conflict more easily than similarity. Unless other people can see clear reasons for partners' dissimilarity, they are likely to be uncomfortable with those who are very different. Felmlee noted that in couples, the qualities of a partner that are viewed as dissimilar are more susceptible to disillusionment. "A difference that is initially appealing is likely to wear thin over time. In fact, dissimilarities that are attractive at the start of a relationship can be particularly fatal. . . . Considerable differences result in considerable disagreements, thereby facilitating . . . disenchantment."

Extreme traits.   Besides similarities and differences, people are also attracted to extreme traits in others. It is wise to proceed with caution around partners-to-be with extreme traits, even when they are virtues. Alexandre Dumas expressed it most pointedly in *The Count of Monte Cristo*: "Any virtue carried to the extreme can become a crime." Among partners, for example, a person who is extremely confident is more susceptible to being viewed as arrogant than a person who is only moderately confident. The qualities in a partner that are intense or extreme are more likely to cast a shadow that may doom the partnership.

In short, there is information about leadership styles that will help determine whether prospective partners will be a good match. For one thing, partners with similar styles may relate more fluidly because they are more likely to understand each other's thinking and feel empathy more readily. But because similar styles do not complement one another as well as diverse styles, similar partners may experience less creative tension. On balance, I've found that partnership teams with unlike styles have an advantage because they have people with different strengths that play to a broader range of activities. Dissimilar styles can reduce competitiveness by allowing each partner to shine in his or her own way. Teams with a mix of styles can get along well; however, the greater the differences, the greater the challenge.

When talking about similarities versus differences, the particular styles become important. For example, two steadiness types will have a much easier time getting along well than two people who both score high on dominance. Two steadiness types may have more trouble making decisions, but they will get along. Two highly dominant people can get along—despite what happened to Jordan and Pollin and countless other high-achieving entrepreneurs—but they will have to work harder than others at cooperating and making joint decisions. Dominant types will have special trouble in partnerships that aspire to be teams of relative equals. There's a joke about asking a dominant person if he is able to be a team player. He answers without hesitation, "Yes. Team captain." Competitiveness is a strength of dominant personalities and generally an asset in business, but between partners it can be toxic.

There are no simple dos and don'ts for partners taking a look at their respective leadership styles, except perhaps to slow down and take a look. A woman named Gretchen owned and managed a large auto dealership, which she had inherited from her father. She struggled for five years to reestablish its profitability, finally doing so after receiving significant help from a talented, entrepreneurial man named Skip. Skip wanted a piece of the ownership pie to help Gretchen expand her dealership, and she was willing to negotiate with him. She sought our help with their partnership discussions. When we recommended that they look at their respective styles, Skip balked at the idea, even after I went over the purpose and process with him. Gretchen quickly and wisely understood that his refusal to work with her at this level was a bad omen for their nascent partnership.

Good potential partners are not afraid to examine their styles and discuss them openly with another potential partner. Healthy partners have qualities similar to what psychoanalyst and consultant Manfred Kets de Vries has described as healthy qualities of leaders. They have a capacity for self-observation and reflection. They take personal responsibility, and importantly, they avoid blaming others for what goes wrong, a behavior that is particularly toxic in partnerships. They don't easily lose control or act impulsively. They know how to roll with disappointments, and if they become depressed, they can acknowledge it and work through it. Most important, they have the capacity to establish and maintain relationships—what partnerships are all about. Whether this last quality is present or not readily becomes apparent during the process of examining styles.

Each person contemplating partnership should ask the following question: Do I believe we can work in the highly collaborative manner that is usually required of partners, given what I have learned about our respective styles? The responses can spark a very useful discussion among potential partners. Since naiveté, or lack of information, may be the best predictor of the regrettable shift from pre-partnership glow to post-partnership disillusionment, spending time and energy on this subject is well worth the investment. This is equally or more true for friends and long-time associates.

UNDERSTANDING YOURSELF AND EACH OTHER BETTER

There are three main reasons for investigating leadership styles in the context of the Partnership Charter: to understand yourself better, to understand your partners better, and to learn how to work together more effectively.

While understanding oneself is always a worthwhile goal, it is particularly advantageous for people who will work closely with partners to have a clear picture of their own style. It is their personal due diligence. Style inventories help people understand their strengths better in order to capitalize on them. They help people see their shortcomings in non-judgmental terminology. They help people appreciate what it's like for others to work with them. They also help remove the "blind spots" that make people difficult to work with. The economist John Kenneth Galbraith once complained to President John F. Kennedy that he didn't see why the *New York Times* had called him arrogant. Kennedy replied, "I don't know why not, Ken. Everybody else does." Partners who know themselves well are better positioned to appreciate what they bring, as well as what other people bring, to their interactions.

We once provided feedback on leadership styles to eight members of a senior executive team. Seven were impressed by how accurate and specific the feedback was. The eighth told his partners, "This is way off; it's not me." The others asked him what it said. He read the description of his style to them, and they shot back in one voice, "That is you!" The description didn't say anything disparaging, but it was not how he saw himself. Gradually, it sank in and he was able to use the information to his own benefit and to the relief of the others.

As described earlier, the DiSC inventory combines the information from all four dimensions and comes up with one of fifteen profiles for each person. We suggest that prospective partners review their profiles and then, one at a time, share the information with the others. The appendix contains a synopsis of each of the three Star Systems partners' leadership styles.

From this wealth of information, prospective partners are then asked to address three specific topics that will form the basis of discussion. The topics, with sample responses from a different Star Systems partner for each, follow:

What I want in order to feel successful—*Jeff*
- I need people who can support me to follow through on the ideas that I have.
- Freedom to think outside of the box.
- Autonomy.
- Highly competent people around me.
- To be recognized when I have a great idea.

My fears related to the workplace—*Sarah*
- Being seen as the Wicked Witch of the West.
- Being boxed in and controlled by too much bureaucracy makes me crazy.
- Being too "soft," controlled.
- Being criticized unjustly.
- Staying the outsider in this group.

My limitations at work—*Beth*
- Not being "nice" enough, or diplomatic when it would help.
- I don't always see the big picture because I'm so focused on the bottom line.
- I can get set in my ways, be stubborn and inflexible.
- I don't always pick up when people feel hurt by something I did.
- I can burn out because I keep going too long on one project without a break.

DEVELOPING AGREEMENTS TO ACT DIFFERENTLY WITH EACH OTHER

With a better understanding of their own and each other's styles, prospective partners can now discuss and document what they are willing to do differently with each other in the hope of being a more effective team. Each dyad completes this exercise so that each pair has a set of agreements. Because what people request of one another is partly based on their styles, they are somewhat predictable. For example, any person with a style of perfectionist, like Beth, is likely to ask people not to surprise her at the last minute. Perfectionists have a fear of being caught off guard and being forced to scramble to get back on top of the situation. Along these lines, Jeff agreed to do the following with Beth: "I will let you in on more of my preplanning thinking, and I agree to be clearer about project expectations." People with a creative style, like Jeff, need a high degree of autonomy to feel successful. So Sarah agreed, "I will take care of the details of my area so you don't need to

TABLE 8.2   To Work Better, Smarter, and More Effectively with My Partner

Jeff with Beth	1. I agree to treat you like a real partner (not simply a key employee).
	2. I will let you in on more of my preplanning thinking and be clearer about project expectations.
	3. I'll tell you when I feel you're taking too much time to do something.
Jeff with Sarah	1. I agree not to be critical of you and to listen if you think I am.
	2. I will not talk to people about you like you're the new kid on the block.
	3. I will appreciate that you sometimes get more dominant and demanding when you're stressed out, and I will tell you when I see you getting that way.
	4. I agree to work out clear understandings about what you will have control of in the company.
Beth with Jeff	1. I will keep you apprized in *summary* fashion of everything important.
	2. I will back off when you say you've had enough of the details.
	3. I'll be straightforward—even blunt—with you when I think you're in left field.
	4. When people complain to me about your style (i.e., nasty and condescending), I'll encourage them to go straight to you with it.
Beth with Sarah	1. I'll let you know if I think you're being unreasonably demanding or manipulative.
	2. I'll do everything I can to make you part of the "Jeff–Beth thing."
	3. If you're not getting me the information I need fast enough, I'll let you know.
	4. I will tell you when I think you're being too optimistic about someone or something or being too pollyannaish about what you're trying to achieve.
	5. If I don't think you're working like a team player, I'll tell you right away.

(continues)

be bothered by them." Beth also agreed, "I will back off when you say you've had enough of the details." Focused behavioral agreements such as these can enhance communication among partners as no type of general communication training can hope to do.

TABLE 8.2   (*continued*)

Sarah with Jeff	1. I agree to not be put off by your "bite" and let you know when I feel unfairly criticized.
	2. I'll keep you informed of what I'm doing in my area and won't make decisions to change things without letting you know ahead of time.
	3. I will tell you "straight up" if I think you're excluding me from things that I should be involved in.
	4. I will take care of the details of my area so you don't need to be bothered by them.
	5. I agree to do whatever is necessary to keep from becoming manipulative and (unreasonably) demanding.
	6. If you call me on being manipulative, I will not get defensive, and I will talk about it with you.
Sarah with Beth	1. If I need your help on projects, I will be clear with you about what I'm asking for and provide what you need in a timely way so you can do your job.
	2. I will tell you when I think you're too much in the details and missing the bigger picture.
	3. I won't assume that just because you look cool, calm, and collected in a crisis, you actually feel that way.
	4. I'll tell you when you're missing people's feelings.

The majority of the agreements partners make with one another are highly individualized. The DiSC feedback gets partners started and makes it easier to recognize where they might have difficulties. It also makes it easier to articulate what they could do differently. Table 8.2 illustrates how unique and specific these agreements are.

That people can get to this high level of understanding and reach agreements with one another before conflicts arise is truly impressive. That two of the partners had only known one another for a few months makes it even more impressive. The feedback from the style inventory gives people a vocabulary to talk about themselves and information they can use to better understand their feelings and their interactions. Most people are not good at describing themselves, but armed with the style feedback, they become much more insightful and articulate. That's very important because, to paraphrase de Vries, great partners are capable, visionary, and inspiring, but that doesn't mean they're always rational.

Jeff, who had significant anxiety about his ability to get along with Sarah before they worked on the charter, later concluded, "If we hadn't done that piece of work on our leadership styles, our differences could have driven us apart." Recognizing how useful it had been to them, the three of them had their entire management team work on their styles at a daylong retreat.

Negotiating these agreements builds trust among prospective partners and gives them an enormous edge when they begin working together. They have learned things that other partners might take months or years to learn, and they have ironed out ways to deal with the most challenging aspects of their style similarities and differences. In the final analysis, what is most important about styles is not the similarities or differences themselves, but how people choose to capitalize on them.

CHAPTER 9

Partners' Personal Values

*A customer drops a $100 bill as he walks out of a neighborhood deli.
The co-owner of the store picks up the money, turns to his young son,
and asks, "What, my boy, is the ethical question that we need to ask
in this situation?" The son replies, "Do we chase the man down and
return the $100 bill?" The father shakes his head. "No, son. The
question is whether I tell my partner about it."*

THE CEO OF A $150 MILLION distribution company once
said to me of his partner: "At some point, you can't write off bad
behavior as just differences in personalities. It's about *values.*" He and
his partner had never had an easy time of it. It seemed they knocked
heads whenever they had to make decisions jointly, and given my understanding of the two of them, the CEO was quite right to identify it
as a values conflict. Personal values come into play in a myriad of ways
when partners are running a company together—from keeping the
books, paying taxes, and setting salaries, to making decisions about
people's futures. Personal values influence every level of the organization—from the partners' own relationships to the company's reputation in the community. Values are the underpinnings of most decision-
making processes. A "judgment call" is often a values call.

Values are underlying interests and intentions that matter most to
people. They are what motivate, interest, and drive people. Values are
guideposts that people rely on for charting their course through the

delicate situations they face every day. They color people's perceptions of the world and influence how they judge their own and others' actions. People may struggle to verbalize their values, but at the same time, it's easy for them to identify behavior that runs counter to them. Values can range from the commonplace, such as the belief in hard work, self-reliance, and punctuality, to concern for others, trust in others, and harmony of purpose.

People acquire most of their values early in life, though some develop values later as a result of significant experiences or contact with influential people. Some values remain constant throughout life, while others wax or wane with personal changes or changes in circumstances. Certain values may be repressed, or inactive, because the time is not right for them. For example, someone may have a burning desire to escape the legal profession and pursue a lifelong interest in a creative endeavor but decide to put it off "a few more years" until circumstances are more conducive to a lifestyle shift.

Some values become satisfied and diminish in importance, so that what motivates people today—for example, money—is not necessarily what will motivate them tomorrow. David Falk, the quintessential sports agent, is a perfect example. Falk is crystal clear about what got him out of bed for the first twenty years of his career: money. To keep the money rolling in, Falk says, he felt "a compulsion to go out and get the next big guy," which he certainly did. His client list includes the likes of Michael Jordan and Patrick Ewing. When the motivation to make money generates a sufficient amount of it, however, either the drive to play the game dies or the motivation shifts. "Now," Falk reports, "the money is irrelevant. What keeps me going now are the relationships with those people."

Comedian Jerry Seinfeld had been driven for years by fame and fortune until those drives withered through satisfaction. Then he moved on to a new game. He left his television series to pursue something more challenging and definitely more stressful—standup comedy. In a *New York Times* interview, he acknowledged that he didn't really have to put himself through the rigors of stand-up comedy. "I've kind of graduated from show business," he said. "I have no further need of this business. It's not about money any more, and it's not about fame. Now, it's just about maintaining a creative arc."

People committed to their values are usually happier and more active. Their values give them energy, direction, meaning, and goals. Achieving their goals feeds their happiness, which strengthens their values—a self-reinforcing loop. Leaders, in business as elsewhere, have strong personal values and know how to project them. People are attracted to strength, at least when it agrees with their own beliefs. Strong leaders demonstrate consistency with their values; they don't waffle. Weak leaders generally have weak values and act inconsistently; their behavior changes to suit the circumstances. Weak leaders may talk a straight line about values, but they walk a crooked one. Once others catch on to the inconsistency, they lose respect for such people.

Knowing other people's values is very important, especially if they might become your partners. That is not to say that partners must have exactly your values. Bill Hanna and Joe Barbera, the cofounders of the hugely successful cartoon studio that bears their names, probably had some very different values. Barbera reveled in the Hollywood social life, while Hanna was, literally, a Boy Scout scoutmaster as well as a devout churchgoer. But each partner happily went on his own way after working hours and let the other do the same.

Knowing one's partners' values and understanding how they relate to one's own is important. The discussions regarding values that I have been privy to have been some of the deepest, most thoughtful, and most heartfelt discussions I have witnessed. Values touch a deep chord in people, and learning about one's own and each other's values and using that information to create a stronger, healthier partnership is an integral part of the Partnership Charter process.

TAKING STOCK OF PERSONAL VALUES

Measuring personal values is not easy. For years potential partners would ask me to help them determine whether they would be a good fit in terms of getting along. In addition to assessing personal styles, I tried different tools to assess and compare personal values, but no tool worked particularly well with partners. Eventually I came across an instrument called simply "Personal Values," developed by Thomas C. Ritt Jr. The instrument asks people to respond to a few dozen statements and quickly produces a profile showing how a person prioritizes eight values. The usefulness of the survey is threefold. First, I've found that partners think these eight values, out of potentially dozens, are relevant to what they are primarily interested in, namely, working together and getting along as partners. Second, the partners' profiles (i.e., their rankings of the eight values) are easily compared. Finally, people generally agree with the objective results—the test seems accurate to them. The eight values, adapted from Ritt's book, *Understanding Yourself and Then Others*, are briefly described in Table 9.1.

My first occasion using the "Personal Values" tool was with the parents and four adult children in a family business who had been working together for varying lengths of time. The arrival of the last two children had precipitated two troubled years, climaxing with a fiery resignation from one of the kids. The next day I received a call from the distressed father, who reported that the one who resigned was furiously packing a car to leave for California. I talked with the son and persuaded him to stick around long enough for an associate and me to have at least two meetings with everyone.

Between the first daylong meeting and the second we asked them each to do some writing, including taking the "Personal Values" test. Though we weren't sure what the profiles would show, the results were surprising and revealing. Based on their value profiles, it wasn't difficult to identify which of the children had resigned and was itching to move across country. (See Table 9.2.)

As you may have noticed, everyone in the family, except for Roy, has "spiritual" as either the first- or second-highest value. People's top two values reveal the most about their interests and motivations. People's lowest values also reveal something, namely, what carries little or no weight for them. It's possible that "spiritual" was once high for Roy and equally possible that it will eventually rebound, but at that time it was his lowest value.

TABLE 9.1   The Eight Personal Values

Aesthetic	A desire to value beauty, make things attractive, and feel free to be artistic; a desire for harmony with people, places, and events; sensitivity to and perception of the nuances that contribute to creativity. May lack sense of urgency for getting things done.
Humanitarian	A need to find opportunities to give time, talent, and money, sometimes placing others' needs above one's own. A wish to be helpful and without the guarantee of personal gain. May be taken advantage of because of trouble saying "no."
Individualistic	A need for personal freedom and self-determination; self-reliance, self-confidence, and a willingness to take risks. May ruffle feathers and alienate even friends.
Materialistic	A desire to work hard, keep score by acquiring money and possessions, and have a return on one's investment. May become workaholic in pursuit of wealth.
Power-Seeking	A wish for control, recognition, and ego satisfaction more than financial gain; hard working and willing to be accountable. May have a fragile ego or seem impatient to get ahead.
Ritualistic	A need for structure, rules, and a "niche" in which to feel secure; usually exemplified by high ethical standards and working in an organized way. May become rigid and unapproachable.
Spiritual	A belief in a higher power and using faith to transcend reason; striving for unity with people, desiring to be of service to others and see the good in everyone. May only see the good in others.
Theoretical	An insatiable desire for knowledge and understanding of how things work; a desire for intellectual challenges and a propensity for incisive decision making. May move slowly and be a bit unrealistic.

TABLE 9.2   Value Profiles of Partners in a Family Business

Jack (father)		Marilyn (mother)	
Spiritual	72	Spiritual	67
Aesthetic	63	Theoretical	65
Humanitarian	58	Humanitarian	64
Individualistic	45	Aesthetic	58
Ritualistic	43	Ritualistic	52
Theoretical	41	Materialistic	43
Materialistic	33	Power-Seeking	35
Power-Seeking	26	Individualistic	33

Stan		Barbara	
Ritualistic	58	Theoretical	53
Spiritual	55	Spiritual	48
Aesthetic	47	Ritualistic	47
Humanitarian	47	Humanitarian	45
Theoretical	46	Aesthetic	39
Materialistic	41	Individualistic	37
Individualistic	35	Materialistic	36
Power-Seeking	27	Power-Seeking	13

Kara		Roy	
Spiritual	62	Aesthetic	57
Theoretical	60	Theoretical	53
Ritualistic	56	Humanitarian	52
Materialistic	53	Ritualistic	52
Humanitarian	53	Individualistic	46
Power-Seeking	53	Materialistic	43
Individualistic	52	Power-Seeking	39
Aesthetic	49	Spiritual	21

Before revealing the results in the second family meeting, we discussed values with them, pointing out that there are no better or worse personal values. People have different values, and they shift over time, but values are what motivate and energize them. It makes little sense to judge others' values; better to appreciate the differences and realize how some differences (and some similarities) can make it difficult to work together.

On seeing the differences in their profiles, the family members quickly understood what had been confusing and conflictual. It was as if the values profiles helped Roy say to his family, "I see the world differently than you do and I need to move on." With the mediators' assistance, the family continued to discuss what had happened, and by the end of the day they had given Roy their blessing. He left in peace with their good wishes—a far healthier exit than the one he almost made. The remaining three siblings then proceeded to work on their Partnership Charter.

COMPARING PARTNERS' VALUE PROFILES

While those family business partners' experience was unusually dramatic, my experience with hundreds of partners of all types since then has confirmed that the "Personal Values" tool is extremely useful for understanding the similarities and differences among people and helping to create agreements about working together more effectively. According to Ritt, the two highest-ranked values are the most salient; they are the ones that really motivate people. Values near the bottom of the list have little effect on behavior.

When partners see their own profiles, I encourage them to jot down a response to each of the following items:

1. Their immediate reaction, and then a second, more thoughtful reaction
2. Two ways that they can see their highest value play out in their workplace in a positive manner
3. One way that they can see their highest value play out in their workplace in a not-so-positive manner
4. Two ways that they can see their second-highest value play out in their workplace in a positive manner
5. One way that they can see their second-highest value play out in their workplace in a not-so-positive manner
6. Their best guess about their partners', or future partners', top two values

Partners should share their responses, going around the group, one item at a time. It gives them straightforward and important information about each other's strengths and weaknesses related to values—information that sometimes takes partners years to discover. When partners discover this information in the normal course of doing business together, it's not always pretty. That's what happened to Gary Frey, who describes how he lost nearly $250,000 in two different business partnerships before becoming president of Axiom Creative Group. "In my earlier partnerships," he says, "I was so eager to get the ball rolling that I made the mistake of hastily committing myself without paying enough attention to comparing our core values. Eventually I found out that certain values I held sacred were worlds apart from those of my partners and, in the end, it cost me dearly. I wound up losing $30,000 to one partner and nearly $220,000 to another because I didn't do a good job in evaluating the compatibility of our values prior to forging those partnerships."

Prospective partners' responses to items 3 and 5 can be quite revealing. I'm often surprised by how easy it is for people to articulate how their highest values can play out in not-so-positive ways. For example, one person noticed that his high spiritual value hinders his ability to terminate employees who need to be let go. Since one's highest values have a great deal of influence, being aware of their disadvantageous influences is very important. People who clarify their values with one another in this way are in a much better position to understand each other's behavior. Strange behavior becomes easier to understand, and discussing each other's actions becomes more straightforward.

Once they have discussed the six items, partners can begin looking at the profiles of the whole group. With everyone's eight values listed next to each other's on flip chart paper, it becomes easy to compare and notice the following:

1. Is there a value that everyone, or nearly everyone, has listed among his or her top values?
2. Are there values that no one, or nearly no one, has among his or her top four values?

3. Are there significant differences between people on certain values? (I consider a difference significant when it is five, six, or seven levels different, for example, "humanitarian" is first on one person's profile and sixth on another's.)

For a group of people who plan on working together closely, these questions invariably lead to important revelations about the group as a whole. For example, are there multiple partners who value power-seeking highly? (This could predict competition among the partners.) Is there no one with a materialistic motivation in the top half of his or her profile? (These people often provide an important push for accountability.) Is everyone high on the individualistic value? (It could be a very disconnected group.) What if one person's highest value is humanitarian, but it is another person's lowest? Remember that every value has something to contribute but can also create problems.

As Roy and his family illustrated, there is a higher potential for conflict when one person's highest values are another's lowest. On the other hand, with certain values, it can work out better if one person is high and another low. In the case of the Star Systems partners (see the appendix), Jeff and Sarah are both high in power-seeking, while this is Beth's lowest value. Beth gets along very well with both Jeff and Sarah. However, Jeff and Sarah had to discuss the implications of both of them having power-seeking among their top two values.

A partner with a high materialistic value can be a plus in a business because companies have to make money, and these individuals can keep a watchful eye on profitability. Roxanne Quimby, the co-founder of the highly successful company Burt's Bees, described this better than anyone: "What motivates me to keep building the company is not money. I live a simple lifestyle; rice and beans and the little Maine town I live in is fine. I'm in it for the challenge; it's about the game. The money is just kind of the score. I'm still very curious about how far I can push this." For other people, a high materialistic value is definitely not about beans and rice. People have to explore what the different values mean to them. This takes some candor and skill, but the survey's feedback is an excellent way to get the conversation going.

Once they've discussed these issues, partners are in a position to ask themselves two final questions and document the answers in their charter. First, given our unique mix of personal values, what agreements could we make (between each pair of partners and as a group) to help us work more effectively together? Second, are we willing to make a group commitment to one or two values that will guide us in our decision making as well as our day-to-day actions? Shared values can be a source of great strength for partners. The personal value systems of partners will eventually permeate their organization, intentionally or not. In time, their values will be apparent to all, so it's best for partners to make their implicit values explicit. Having the data, the discussions, and these understandings in hand, partners will be ready to operate more effectively together to maximize their potential.

IN PARTNERS WE MUST TRUST

Closely related to values is one of the most important factors in partnerships: trust. Ask people in a successful partnership what makes it work so well, and they are very likely to respond, "trust." Trust engenders cooperation, and cooperation builds trust—a positive feedback loop. Partners have an easier time trusting partners with similar values. People lose trust in their partners when they think they are not acting in accordance with the values underlying the partnership, whether these have ever been agreed on or not, as the following story illustrates.

In the middle of a mediation in which two 50–50 partners in a Florida marina were trying to determine whether they could remain partners, one partner, Nick, told the other, Frank, "I think a lot of this stuff is a result of the lawsuit." They filled us in about the lawsuit. A client of theirs had sued them for hundreds of thousands of dollars for damage to his ninety-foot yacht. The interrogatories and depositions had dragged on for two years, when finally Nick reported to Frank that he had discussed a settlement offer from the client's attorney. He got Frank's agreement, then called the attorney and told him it was over—gave his word that his partner and he both agreed to settle on those terms. At 7:00 A.M. the next morning Frank called Nick at home and reneged.

They were both recounting the story but suddenly Nick turned straight to Frank and cried out, "I gave my word to his attorney and you agreed. Never in my life have I gone back on my word! I should have said to you right then and there, we were through if you were going to renege on your agreement."

The lawsuit was settled about a year after this incident. It cost them many more thousands of dollars than it would have if they had gone through with the first settlement, but the real cost was to their relationship. What followed the "betrayal," as Nick called it, were five prickly years. Frank had apologized and admitted he'd made a mistake, but he would always add that their own attorney had told him "a verbal deal's never a deal 'til it's signed," and that they would have been giving away "millions."

Nick claimed there were many other times when Frank second-guessed him or stepped in his way, even though they had agreed that Nick was the one who would run the company. Interestingly, at the start of the mediation they had both taken the styles and values surveys. They found the results of the styles tests very useful in helping them to communicate better, even at this late stage. But because the mediation became a way to help them separate amicably, we never shared their values profiles with them. Not surprisingly, they were quite different. The most important difference was that power-seeking was Nick's second-lowest value and Frank's second highest. The way Frank's high power-seeking manifested itself was that even though he had agreed to have Nick run the marina, it was nearly impossible for him to follow through and not undermine Nick's decisions.

In Nick's mind, when Frank forced him to act dishonorably, it was the straw that broke the camel's back. Subsequently, he felt so little trust that there was nothing upon which to rebuild. Nick demanded an end to their twelve-year partnership. We helped them part amicably, which is a monumental challenge for partners who have sunk that low with one another. Nick bought Frank out, giving him the full value of his interest and plenty of time and assistance to reestablish himself.

Trust comes much more easily to people who share similar values. When values are different it is extremely important for partners to understand, discuss, and arrive at agreements about how they will work together so those differences never get in their way.

CHAPTER 10

Is It Fair?

Give me that which I want,
and you shall have that which you want.

ADAM SMITH

BARBARA LAZAROFF, WHO IS in partnership with her celebrity-chef husband, Wolfgang Puck, started feeling that something was not quite fair between them. It wasn't that she shouldered most of the responsibility for the business side of their food and restaurant operation. It wasn't the hours she worked. It wasn't even the money, she said. But something didn't feel fair.

When she talked to Puck about it, they focused on what was not working for her. She felt her efforts to make their partnership a success were overshadowed by Puck's notoriety. It became clear that she placed a high value on the fame and glamour bestowed upon him. Together they devised a plan to address the imbalance. They decided to hire a publicist, not to drum up more publicity for their restaurants, but to make sure that Lazaroff, the groundbreaking designer, was recognized for her contributions. This seemed to do the trick. They continued working side by side as business partners, and their restaurant empire grew, eventually surpassing the $300 million mark.

Now, years later, Puck and Lazaroff are divorcing, but they are trying to maintain their business partnership. Keeping the business partnership after ending the marital relationship is always an uphill climb, but perhaps they have created a formula for fairness in their company that works well for them.

Fairness is like breathing: We don't think about it until something goes wrong. But it is one of those issues that has to be dealt with *before* it erupts. In close to half the cases my colleagues and I have mediated (Puck and Lazaroff not being one of them), one of the partners says the partnership is not working because something doesn't feel *fair,* yet that person has trouble saying exactly what it is. Some partners have a visceral feeling of unfairness that they can't articulate. Others believe they know what is unfair but not what to do about it. Fairness is a subject that people need to address before becoming partners and review periodically after they are partners.

PARTNERS' INTERPERSONAL EQUITY

Just as partners examine their financial equity in the business, they need to examine what I call partners' interpersonal equity—fairness, conceived in both business and personal terms. The idea for partners' interpersonal equity occurred to me when I was reading a book by two University of Georgia professors of management called *Managing the Equity Factor.*

Partners understand fairness much better after they have been introduced to the concept of interpersonal equity. Interpersonal equity is about each partner's *perception* of the balance between what he or she thinks he or she is putting in and getting out and what he or she thinks his or her partners are putting in and getting out. Partners are perpetually—often unconsciously—weighing contributions and withdrawals and checking whether they are balanced. Among the contributions are how hard they work, the expertise they contribute, capital investments, business leads, business acumen, and the time they spend on the road. On the withdrawal side are money, of course, but also the ability to set their own hours, access to social activities, the percentage of ownership, a position that bestows special prominence in the community, and being in control. Both lists could be extensive. If the interpersonal balance sheet of one of the partners is in the red for long, trouble lies ahead, just as it would if his or her financial balance sheet lingered in the red.

As hard as it may be to come by, a positive sense of interpersonal equity is crucial to the long-term success of partner relationships. Partners who feel that their partners are *more* than fair have a great deal going for them. Such partners tend to have more trust and confidence in each other and in their collective ability to work through sensitive subjects. They have a strong belief in their ability to weather adversity because they believe that they will all look out for one another and treat each other fairly. Each partner is likely to feel satisfied and thus motivated to contribute more than he or she otherwise would.

Creating this sense of fairness in an entire group of partners is easier said than done. People don't always see what their partners are contributing, and everyone values things differently. Some people have a tendency to place a higher value on a contribution if they are the ones offering it. Maintaining a sense of fairness in a group of partners is also difficult because the balance of contributions shifts over time. Many partners have a "set it and forget it" approach to fairness that is unsuited to the rapidly changing business world. Other simple methods for achieving a sense of fairness, like trying to make everything equal, tend to fail because there are too many variables, and it's virtually impossible to make them all equal.

The concept of partners' interpersonal equity does not strive for an objective determination of what is fair. Instead, it acknowledges the importance of each partner's perception of what he or she is putting in and taking out, and it recognizes that his or her perception is dependent on what he or she sees his or her partners contributing and taking out.

Ben Cohen and Jerry Greenfield of Ben and Jerry's ice cream provided a perfect illustration of the importance of both of these pieces of the fairness puzzle during an interview about their partnership at their corporate headquarters in Vermont. They described how one night Jerry was in their ice cream factory mixing one of the very first batches of Oreo cookie ice cream—a flavor that Ben invented—and it was not going well. Jerry was exhausted and his arm was almost frozen from sticking it into the concoction to break up the cookies that were jamming the machine. He began feeling overburdened and unappreciated as he focused solely on the importance of his own contribution, which at that moment felt monumental.

Jerry then told me how a few minutes later, as dawn was beginning to break over the bucolic Vermont hillsides, he realized that Ben would soon be driving their company's "death-trap" delivery truck, with bad brakes they had no money to fix, up and down those steep hills to deliver their ice cream. His feeling that their relationship wasn't fair suddenly vanished. "We were both really in it together for better or worse and however hard I was working, he was working harder," he concluded. Ben chimed in to say that he felt the same way about how hard Jerry was working at that time.

Ben and Jerry's story illustrates that partners' contributions may be as different as night and day, or as different as their personalities. Ben had the brilliant idea of lacing their ice cream with Oreo cookies; Jerry had the ability to transform the idea into something other than gray mush. Jerry stayed up all night and risked frostbite; Ben got up before dawn and risked crashing into a tree. Neither of them could have done what came naturally to the other.

This is part of the magic of partnerships. I suspect that Ben and Jerry prefected it over many years of being together. When I interviewed them, before the company was sold to Unilever, Ben and Jerry each appeared to be concerned with making sure the other got everything he deserved. When that happens, the partnership is no longer about self-interest and protecting one's turf or rights; instead, it's about looking out for someone else and being supportive. Each person motivates the other, which creates the best of all possible worlds. Each person then accomplishes more—more than he or she thought he or she could, and more than he or she was capable of alone.

PARTNERSHIP DISTRESS

Partnerships infused with a generous, altruistic, and benevolent spirit are not that common. Partnership distress, a situation that develops when one or more partners begin feeling that the interpersonal equity is out of balance, is much more common. It is characterized by feelings of jealousy and resentment that someone is getting more than someone else. It may develop over a period of years; at other times, a single decision may immediately bring on partnership distress. All it takes is for one partner to feel that things are out of balance for partnership distress to occur. That all the others may feel pleased with the arrangement is immaterial. If one partner's distress is not addressed properly, either by that individual or the group, it will become everyone's problem.

Partnership distress may be a result of perceived inequities involving tangible inputs such as dollars invested and hours worked, or it may be a result of factors that are more difficult to quantify. For example, a co-owner in a Web design start-up company felt that her unique expertise (her programming skill) was worth far more than her two partners with marketing and administrative backgrounds had been willing to acknowledge by granting her only 33 percent of the equity. She believed she'd brought more to the table than either of them and yet she received the same amount of ownership and compensation. She was bothered by it and was underperforming as a result, which only reinforced her partners' feeling that they had been perfectly fair in dividing the company equally.

A key to understanding partnership distress is to remember that it is perception, not reality, that matters most. No one inside or outside the partnership may have agreed with the programmer's assessment of the value she brought to the venture, but her perception was central to the problem.

When partnership distress develops, the question is not *whether* it will be expressed but *when* and *how*, which depends on the partners' personalities and the intensity of their feelings. Paradoxically, partners are sometimes more reluctant to voice serious partnership distress than to raise less significant problems. There is more risk involved when discussing deeper concerns because of anxiety that the partnership will not survive, so the problem goes farther underground. But because these problems rarely resolve themselves, it behooves partners to pick up on each other's dissatisfaction early on.

There are six possible ways for partners to respond to partnership distress. Only two are positive, constructive responses. The four most common—though unfortunately less desirable—responses are to

1. give less to the partnership or business,
2. take more out of the partnership or business,
3. sabotage the partnership or business (intentionally or unintentionally), or
4. get out of the partnership or business.

Give less.   There are many ways that partners put less into the partnership in order to feel less taken advantage of. They can cut back on their hours, their effort, or their enthusiasm. The next time the business needs a capital infusion, they might say no. When there is a crisis, they may drag their feet in responding.

Take more out.   Similarly, there are many ways partners can take more out, often surreptitiously. They may take more vacation or sick days, swipe small amounts of petty cash, or embezzle thousands of dollars. They may begin to write off more of their personal expenses or borrow business equipment for personal use.

Sabotage.   Partners will sometimes sabotage their own business to get even, an action that often feels hateful and crazy to the other partners, who may not have a clue as to why it's happening. An angry partner may not return phone calls to clients, may complain about a partner to a third party or to an employee, or may be abusive to an employee or client. It does not matter whether the partner is harming himself or herself in the process; the point is simply to get even with the partners.

Get out.   Finally, partners may try to get out if they believe the situation is too unfair. They may have lost all hope that anything could correct the inequities. They may believe they have tried and nothing has worked. They may want to avoid conflict that might result if they voiced their dissatisfaction. It is always surprising when a company is profitable and partners appear to be getting along, yet a partner opts out.

Sometimes the partnership stops feeling worth it to all of partners and they all decide to get out. Many people in the legal community were taken aback when the partners at the prestigious and seemingly financially successful New York law firm of Shea and Gould voted to dissolve the firm after forty-three years of operation. Reports said the partners simply had had enough of trying to deal with one another. While they had succeeded at creating and maintaining a first-class reputation in the Wall Street legal marketplace, they failed to maintain interpersonal equity. Partners distanced themselves from one another. "We became a firm of solo practitioners," sharing only workspace, one ex-partner explained.

Milton Gould, who founded the firm with William Shea (of Shea Stadium), said that in its final, tumultuous years, the firm resembled "a harem" wracked with jealousies, and that partners were acting "high-handed and selfish"—all evidence of partnership distress. Gould described it as a "personal tragedy" that there were "so many personal antagonisms and tensions that the attorneys couldn't get along" and had to unwind. Before partners take such drastic action, it is best to get outside assistance to deal with the partnership distress and find a more positive method of restoring interpersonal equity. If these attempts fail, then the partners can always exercise the option to dissolve.

Happily, there are two ways for restoring interpersonal equity that are positive, constructive, and usually successful.

Recheck and reevaluate the data.   Contributions to and benefits from the business are often reflected in hard data. Partners who feel things are not fair can go back and check the data. For example, one person had long assumed that his partner was writing off her trips to her vacation home as business expenses. When he looked into it, he discovered that she had not written off any of them. Partners may also decide to change their interpretation of the data. They may conclude upon looking at the whole picture that their deal is not as bad as they thought. One woman was feeling increasingly resentful of her partner's taking off huge blocks of time to care for her sick mother. She felt forced to pick up the slack. Talking to a friend, though, helped her to see that she had similar freedom and might need to do the same thing someday.

Renegotiate the deal.   The second positive method for restoring interpersonal equity is to convince one's partners that they all need to sit down together and renegotiate some aspects of their deal. Hopefully, all of the partners appreciate the fact that if one partner is unhappy, the entire partnership is at risk. They will all be better off if they agree to discuss the problems, even if it's not an easy discussion.

To illustrate this point, two men in Florida, Roger and Terry, started an insurance agency as 50–50 partners, sharing profits evenly. After a few years, Terry no longer felt their deal was fair because he was bringing in over 80 percent of the business while Roger was primarily managing the office. Terry told Roger directly and clearly that he loved him dearly but that their arrangement did not feel fair. He asked Roger to take three weeks off to assess what his job was worth in the marketplace, and then they would talk about it. Terry told me, "I knew if I didn't address it, it was only going to get worse and in the end be unworkable." After Roger researched what he could make elsewhere, the partners talked. Terry suggested a 70–30 split and Roger agreed. Now, ten years later, they continue as partners at 70–30.

EXERCISES FOR ASSESSING INTERPERSONAL EQUITY

Over years of working with partners to restore a sense of interpersonal equity, my colleague and I have developed a set of exercises to help assess fairness problems. Partners use these to renegotiate things in a way that strengthens their belief in the fairness of their arrangement.

Contributions and benefits.   In preparation for the first exercise, each partner should create four lists, as follows:

1. All of the things you think you contribute to the partnership and business
2. All of the things you want out of being a partner in this business
3. All of the things you think your partner contributes
4. All of the things you think your partner wants out of being a partner

The lists must be as broad and also as specific as possible. The more comprehensive they are, the more beneficial they will be. Points 3 and 4 require that each partner make a separate list for every other partner. If a partner's lists are too general and similar for each of his or her partners, this may point to a source of a problem: that the partner doesn't appreciate individual colleagues' contributions.

When the partners come together as a group, one person begins by putting her first list on a flip chart. When that partner is finished writing what she thinks she contributes, she should use a different colored marker and continue adding to her list all the things her partners think she contributes. The partners take turns until everyone has a complete flip chart list of what he or she and everyone else thinks about that person's contributions to the partnership and the business. The same procedure is then used for the second list—what partners want out of being a partner. At the end this exercise, every partner has two long lists that include all the partners' ideas—one of what they contribute and one of what they want out of being in the business together as partners.

The lists of the three Star Systems partners are included in Tables 10.1 and 10.2 to illustrate the type of detail that this exercise commonly elicits. The number of items on the partners' lists is not critical when assessing interpersonal equity. What is critical is some combination of quantity and quality, and the relative importance that each person assigns to the items on everybody's lists. The exercise gives the partners the data they need to have thoughtful discussions about what is or isn't fair. With the lists compiled, they can debate each other's contributions and the relative value of them.

TABLE 10.1   What Each Partner Contributes to the Business and the Partnership
(Each partner's own ideas are listed above the line, and other partner's ideas are listed below the line.)

What Jeff Brings	What Beth Brings	What Sarah Brings
1. Ownership of a highly successful company	1. Twenty years' experience with SSI	1. $280,000 capital contribution over a period of time
2. Broad industry knowledge and experience	2. $280,000 over a period of time	2. Relationships and business with large, potential customers
3. High energy and huge capacity for hard work	3. Reputation in the industry for fairness and integrity	3. Willingness to share risk
4. Family values including trust and loyalty of employees	4. Head of finance department for many years	4. Marketing abilities
5. Vision for the company	5. Extensive contacts with clients and advisors	5. Relationships with vendors
6. Integrity	6. Stability, persistence, dependability, and consistency	6. Vision
7. Willingness to risk everything		7. Money
8. Zeal to improve client products and service	7. Ability to get things done right the first time	8. Technical abilities and education
9. Trustworthiness	8. Institutional history	9. Management experience
10. Positive, can-do attitude	9. Integrity and clarity	10. Honesty, trust, and ethics
	10. Good rapport with employees	11. Great work ethic
	11. High level of commitment	12. High energy
	12. Cooperative and positive attitude in the company	13. Potential for future
		14. Sound strategic ability
		15. Quick study
		16. Strong desire to be successful
		17. Generosity
		18. Fun
		19. Fresh viewpoint
		20. Credibility and stable record
		21. Can-do attitude
		22. Great verbal skills

TABLE 10.2 What Each Partner Wants from the Business

(Each partner's own ideas are listed above the line, and other partner's ideas are listed below the line.)

What Jeff Wants	What Beth Wants	What Sarah Wants
1. Salary of $425K	1. Opportunity to stay involved in acquisitions	1. Autonomy in my position
2. Mandate to focus on the big picture	2. $150,000 per year salary	2. Freedom to call my own hours
3. Ultimate control	3. Company car	3. Ability to increase ownership beyond 10 percent
4. Sufficient quality support so I don't have to get mixed up in routine work	4. Grow my staff with 2 new positions within the next 6–12 months	4. At least $200K annual salary
5. Be bought out at some time	5. Security and continuity —more than we've had in past years	5. Ability to spread purchase payments out over 5 years
6. More vacation time than I've taken in the past	6. Sufficient staff to run the finance department very efficiently	6. Car and other benefits as company can afford them
———	———	7. Plenty of vacation time
7. Feel secure that this partnership is going to work	7. Opportunity to own a larger share in the future	———
	———	8. Backup and support akin to what I've been accustomed to
	8. Final authority for staff decisions in her department	9. My life to be in balance
		10. Freedom to run her piece of the company
		11. Be viewed as an owner

Contributions that relate to the level of commitment or ambition that people intend to contribute deserve special note, because fairness is often assessed by how hard people work (their ambition, roughly) and their attitude (commitment). The default standard in many partnerships is the following: All partners will give their all, at all times and forever. Even if partners cannot demand equal performance of other partners, they believe it is reasonable to require similar levels of ambition and commitment.

The mandate, or expectation, that all partners give their all at all times is too rigid. It creates unhappiness for some partners because there's no flexibility. In many partnerships, perhaps especially law firms with their monomania about billable hours, it is almost impossible for partners to work out a different arrangement. For example, one partner in a Washington firm wanted to cut back his hours and compensation by 20 percent so he could have time for his personal life. His partners agreed but hated the deal they struck, I believe because many of them wanted a saner workload themselves but were unwilling to sacrifice the rewards in order to have it. After a relatively short period, the partner gave up and went back to full time until he found a firm more tolerant of individual differences. A senior partner in another firm confessed to me that he, too, wished to cut back on time and money but was afraid of being viewed with suspicion by his partners. He thought they would not take him seriously after cutting back and he'd lose his place "in the pecking order."

Cutting back hours could reflect dwindling ambition or commitment, but that should not be assumed. It is important to understand the motivation behind changes in hours. The lawyer who wants to work 80 percent may be every bit as dedicated as the lawyer who works full time. He may even get more accomplished than the person working full time. The experience of many lawyers, however, is that any deviation from full time and full pay is arduous to work out in theory and even more exhausting to execute day to day.

Partners can work out individual arrangements if they use the principle of fairness and look at the entire range of contributions and compare that with the entirety of what each partner will take out. We often see people breathe a sigh of relief when they realize they can work out unique arrangements for each person. The awkwardness, strain, and feelings of unfairness come most often when partners try squeezing themselves in rigid boxes that are all the same, usually with equal pay.

Developing thorough lists of contributions makes it easier to ascertain whether what partners want out of the business makes sense. Many partners find that this exercise helps them zero in on realistic ownership percentages because it provides a clearer picture of all the factors that come into play. By the time they did this exercise, Beth and Sarah had already negotiated 10 percent stakes in the company. Beth came to the conclusion during the exercise that she wanted the opportunity to own a larger share of the company, which led to a discussion and an agreement that each of the minority partners would have the option to purchase an additional 10 percent after three years.

People don't necessarily get what they want, and the Star System partners made that clear, too. Jeff wanted a salary of $425,000. His partners argued that the experience he was bringing to the table was not substantial enough to warrant that much compensation. He backed down to $375,000, and they all agreed that was acceptable.

The exercise is guaranteed to generate a great deal of discussion, as partners get a clear view of what each of them values, often for the first time. This puts them in a much better position to influence their partners' perceptions of interpersonal equity. Partners cannot give each other more of what they need and value without knowing what those things are. A partner in one consulting firm, for example, wanted more time to write articles for marketing purposes. Her partners were delighted that she was interested in doing that because they were not, though they knew it needed to be done. However, to be fair to them, they insisted and she agreed that they would sometimes coauthor the pieces so they would also share in the direct credit. Since she loved writing, the first partner's satisfaction went up much more than if she had received an increase in pay. Besides that, the other partners felt relieved that she was going to be responsible for the articles. Partners have the power to influence both the reality and the perception of their partners' equity factors, but only if they know what their partners really value.

When partners begin talking about the value they think each person brings, almost inevitably someone hears that he or she is recognized for contributing something he or she thought no one noticed. Partners sometimes begin to have individual and collective realizations about additional contributions people could make, and momentum grows about *adding* value.

In some businesses, the partners have become so completely focused on themselves that they think only in terms of what they are contributing and getting and have little appreciation for what their partners contribute and get. This exercise forces them to notice the value their partners are adding, maybe for the first time in years. It can be refreshing and rejuvenating for them to focus on each other for a change.

Fairness ratings.   In the second exercise, the partners rate their satisfaction with the various components of interpersonal equity and answer one overall fairness question. This exercise is especially relevant for partners who have been working with one another for some time.

1. How satisfied are you with what you are currently contributing?
2. How satisfied are you with what you are currently receiving?
3. How satisfied are you with what you put in compared to what your partners are putting in?
4. How satisfied are you with what you take out compared to what your partners are receiving?
5. How fair do you feel it is overall?

This exercise is also guaranteed to generate discussion. Its five short questions go directly to the heart of the fairness issue. If there is dissatisfaction, the answers will pinpoint what partners must change to improve the situation.

As partners strive to achieve a satisfying balance, they inevitably struggle with the fact that *equity* is not the same as *equality*. Partners will often start out paying themselves the same, but over time this begins to feel unfair. Someone begins to think that he or she is working harder or longer hours or shouldering more responsibility. If partners' contributions differ, then providing equal rewards is a disservice to some. Avoiding tough decisions about different rewards in an effort to prevent resentment can backfire and create resentment in those who feel that they deserve more and may eventually lead them to contribute less.

One such case involved four partners who had equal ownership and received the same pay, but one partner held a position with much less responsibility than the other three. He was also less motivated and worked far fewer hours. This created strong resentment among the other three partners. The fourth clung tightly to their original deal even though he admitted it wasn't fair because of their inequitable contributions. He would defend his stance by saying, "My partners set it up that way so they have to live with it." This attitude was shortsighted and eventually self-defeating. Working together was always unpleasant, and when the business was sold, the three partners managed to give the fourth partner the short end of the stick and then severed their relationships with him.

Equity has to do with assessing each partner individually: What is a fair reward, given each person's contribution? According to the standard of equity, the rewards each partner gets should be related to what he or she contributes. Of course, contributions fluctuate. Partners must realize when doing the exercises that they are taking a snapshot in time. Balancing contributions and rewards is never perfect and requires periodic attention. Ideally, over the lifetime of the partnership, each partner will feel that the partnership was fair by and large. At any given moment, things may not feel perfectly balanced, but that is not the point. Over time, things should feel reasonably balanced. If contributions grow temporarily unequal, partners should develop confidence that eventually the balance sheets will return to neutral—that, over the long haul, each partner will get out of the partnership as much or more than he or she put in. If not, adjustments need to be made. With the four partners just described, the inequities were serious and long-standing. In such situations, when one person refuses to renegotiate the deal, the end is probably not far off. I have seen this regrettable dynamic in many partnerships.

Fairness problems frequently arise when partners lose sight of the struggles, gifts, and contributions of their partners. We all see the world through our own eyes, but when we have partners we have to adjust our vision so it includes what our partners see. The exercises help open people's eyes to what they're missing. They help partners see why, to make a partnership work, it's sometimes necessary to compare apples to oranges. Different kinds of contributions, though equally necessary, cannot always be weighed on the same scale.

From Bonn comes a story of individuals in the Beethoven Orchestra who lost sight of their colleagues' contribution to the music they were making. The violinists sued to be paid more than their wind- and percussion-playing colleagues, because they claimed to be responsible for more music. Most orchestral works require much more production from string players than the other musicians. They do play more notes and thus, in this strict sense, there is a disproportionate workload. The violinists chose to focus on the number of notes.

I asked Luis Haza, a highly acclaimed high-producer of notes (that is, violinist) in the National Symphony Orchestra in Washington, for his thoughts about this apparent inequality. Haza explained that while it is true that violinists predictably play considerably more music and the job is physically strenuous, you have to look at it from many angles. An orchestra might have sixteen violinists playing together, yet at times the notes of one trumpet may be the only sound coming from the stage. "A trumpeter's head is on the line regularly in a way that mine is not." Also, while we don't usually think about classical music as a physical danger, Haza says that certain players are exposed to decibel levels that can put their hearing at risk.

The violinists in Bonn were missing the underlying purpose of the orchestra. The orchestra exists to produce music, which requires the participation and effort of all of the players. Viewing it as a collection of notes that you ascribe to various individuals, Haza feels, is almost laughable. "Counting notes from different sections would be like claiming that red is more important than blue in a Picasso. The hard thing to do, but the honest thing, is to fully appreciate all the elements and the nuance of every player's contribution."

CHAPTER 11

Getting What You Wish For:
The Power of Expectations

ALAN FUNT, THE PRODUCER of *Candid Camera*, once hid a camera inside an elevator for an episode called "The Rear of the Elevator." An unsuspecting victim enters the elevator followed by Funt's stooges. Once inside, rather than turn around toward the door, the stooges continue to face the person and the back wall. The awkwardness is palpable until the person slowly, sheepishly, turns back fully around so he's facing the same—backward—direction. As Funt was fond of doing, he repeated it over and over with new victims, each time with the same awkward, funny result.

People often communicate their expectations to others without uttering a word. As Funt demonstrated so comically, expectations literally have the power to turn people around. People do things they would never have imagined, all because of expectations.

Expectations, by definition, are what people look for and confidently anticipate. They often anticipate benefits. We all learn to form expectations early in life and take them with us wherever we go. Expectations help us to know—or at least *think* we know—what's going to happen next, and that makes us feel more secure.

How much we respect and admire people determines how much power their expectations have over us. Psychologist Robert Rosenthal and his colleagues have demonstrated this phenomenon, known as "interpersonal expectancy," in classrooms, hospitals, courtrooms, and the workplace. No matter how people come by their expectations of others, the expectations will be communicated and the recipients will live up to them. Students perform better, patients get healthier faster, workers accomplish more. This is also called the Pygmalion Effect, after the mythical king of Crete who fell in love with a statue of a maiden. He so wanted the statue to become warm flesh and blood that his wish was granted by Aphrodite, who brought the statue to life. In scientific terms, one person's expectations for another person's behavior come to serve as a self-fulfilling prophecy.

Expectations can also get us into trouble. A few years ago, a woman in Michigan called me in a panic. She told me that she and her husband had discovered that their thirty-something son thought that he was gong to inherit their company—soon. It *was* something she'd hoped would someday happen. He had grown to expect it, and that scared her now. This too, I thought, is the power of expectations: first hers for him and now his for her.

Expectations play an important role in partner relationships; they are like promises that certain things are going to happen. When they do happen, a positive loop is established. People who deliver on their promises can be counted on, and this builds trust among partners. However, if people are creating expectations in others, they'd better deliver, because people hate disappointment. Not fulfilling one's partners' expectations is tantamount to breaking a trust: It creates cynicism and sours people to the whole idea of partnerships. Not surprisingly, "unmet expectations" was one of the prime reasons why a majority of people think that having partners is a bad idea, according to an *Inc.* magazine poll taken a few years ago.

There are two primary causes of unmet expectations. One is promising more than one can deliver, and the other is failing to talk about expectations. The latter appears to be the more significant problem. Countless partners have forlornly admitted, "We never even had a discussion about what we expected of each other." Some partners like to think that they have discussed expectations but, when pressed for details, admit they've only exchanged a few words in passing.

Most people form their expectations of others without much thought or evidence. Though a person may never have said, "I agree to do X, Y, and Z," others pick up some sign or hint, and that is all they need to begin forming expectations. The whole process may be quite unconscious. If Stacey, for example, hears her partner-to-be Mike say that he has never known anyone more energetic than himself, Stacey may expect that Mike will put in sixty-hour weeks, an understandable but dangerous assumption. Many people form their expectations of others based on watching their actions, but that, too, can prove unreliable. For example, if Mary notices Greta's willingness to put an additional $50,000 into their operating fund, she may come to expect Greta will ante up again if necessary. Without talking about it, she has no way of knowing whether that is really true. Greta may have done it while promising herself that it was the last penny she was risking in the company. Interestingly, the more similar partners are, or think they are, the more likely they are to have unspoken expectations. When people think their partners are similar to them in background, disposition, and desire to be successful, they are more likely to think their partners will behave as they think they themselves would.

Partners are wise to talk in depth about their expectations and bring them into the light of day. Having thoughtful and thorough conversations helps to uncover expectations people may be unaware of. Having a structured conversation that addresses certain types of expectations is even more helpful. These conversations immunize partners against the destructive power of unmet expectations. In this section of the Partnership Charter, prospective partners engage in structured exercises to help them examine their expectations of themselves and each other and clarify their expectations for their partnership. By accomplishing these tasks, they create a sense of alignment that few partners can claim.

PARTNERS' EXPECTATIONS OF ONE ANOTHER

Partners can use these exercises to clarify their expectations of one another and also eradicate unrealistic and unstated assumptions. The exercises involve exposing hidden expectations, discussing which of these are realistic, and documenting the results. Both individual and group activities are involved. In the first step, each person individually lists the following sets of expectations:

A. Expectations I have for myself
B. Expectations I think my partners have of me
C. Expectations I have for each one of my partners

The participants are encouraged to be exhaustive—to think both broadly and specifically—when creating their lists. When the prospective partners then get together, one person begins by writing down on flip chart paper in front of the group the expectations he has for himself and the expectations he thinks his partners have of him. Then the rest of the partners tell him the expectations they actually do have of him. After each person has written all this on the flip chart, they all go back around the group and discuss which expectations each person is willing to commit to, or try to live up to, and which ones he or she does not accept.

To illustrate what this looks like, in the following table are the expectations of Jeff Davis of Star Systems. (Beth's and Sarah's lists can be found in the appendix.) Jeff's list of expectations for himself led the group to important discussions about his vision of his own future and specifically how he viewed his role as president, CEO, and the primary decision maker. Forcing Beth and Sarah to be explicit about each of their expectations for Jeff stimulated other discussions, including one about their fears of being second-class partners. As a result of these talks, Jeff agreed to specific actions he would take to help them become full-fledged partners in the eyes of the staff.

Prospective partners using this exercise have the opportunity to say that there are expectations of others that they do not agree with. Jeff, for example, said he did not want to agree that he would not take on too much. (This item has a question mark in the left column.) He believed that he had always taken on more than most people, including Beth, thought he should have. He didn't think that would change, es-

TABLE 11.1   Partner's Expectations

Jeff

Expectations I Have for Myself

* Keep focused on the overall growth of the company.
* Have a better than average job for the rest of my career.
* Be bought out in 10–15 years.
* Keep Star Systems on the cutting edge.
* Make decisions in best interest of everyone—not just myself.
* Lead others in the company by being the best example of a model employee.
* Make the ultimate decisions when necessary.

Expectations I Think Others May Have of Me

* Be more patient.

Beth's Expectations of Me

* Think of partners as co-owners and not simply employees.
* No hiding and more communicating.
* Be financially conscientious with personnel.
? Monitor personal workload and don't take on too much.
* Be more trusting of partners' intentions.
* Not be paranoid and think they're going to treat me like my siblings did.

Sarah's Expectations of Me

* Give me [Sarah] assistance getting on board and accepted by staff.
* Support me if challenged by people in established positions.
* Give Beth and me plenty of advance notice regarding any thoughts regarding any changes in the ownership of the company—before you talk with anybody else.
* Actively work to get employees thinking of Beth and me as owners too.
* Understand your shortcomings and take action to overcome them.

---

* Indicates an expectation the person agrees to live up to
? Indicates an expectation the person is not ready to agree to

pecially because he thinks he works best when he's got an overabundance on his plate.

For the exercise to pinpoint unrealistic expectations people have when entering a partnership, each partner must be very specific about what he or she expects from each partner and for himself or herself. If someone remains at a superficial or general level—saying, for instance, that he or she expects only hard work and honesty from a fellow partner—the exercise will not be useful. Similarly, if someone has identical expectations for every partner, the exercise will be pointless. People bring different strengths to their partnerships. If these differences are not recognized, partners will not perform up to their potential.

Some people find it difficult or threatening to be explicit about their expectations for their partners because of the power balance. It is far easier for them to generate a list of expectations for someone lower in the hierarchy, such as the office receptionist. "You must be at the reception desk five minutes before the office opens; answer the phone this way," and so on. Orders and expectations easily flow downward in organizations, but they rarely flow upward or among people on the same level. Sometimes it is awkward for partners who are technically on an equal footing to freely express their expectations of each other. If someone is stymied by a sense of a hierarchy within the partnership, that should be talked about and understood by everyone.

Disclosure can also be useful for long-time partners who have built up extensive expectations that may not be working to their mutual advantage. Two partners, Janet and Carol, who had not been getting along for years, were working on the charter process to help resolve their problems. While revealing the expectations she thought her partner had of her, Janet, who was most dissatisfied, said she thought Carol expected her to continue together indefinitely or would feel terribly abandoned if she left. Much to her surprise, Janet found out that Carol was fine with her leaving the business and had actually wondered why she was staying now that her interests had obviously changed.

As partners reveal their expectations, they frequently discover that what they had imagined were others' expectations of them were simply that—imaginings. When reality takes over, they get to relax. They also learn about others' expectations of them that they were oblivious of and thus were bound to disappoint. Sometimes people have wittingly or unwittingly nurtured other people's unrealistic expectations of them. It is advantageous to get these cleared up so they don't remain an inexplicable source of friction.

When BMC Associates has used this exercise with existing partners, we have had them complete one additional step. We ask them to rate on a five-point scale how well they think the expectations for each partner are being met. The exercise has the power to get partners talking *constructively* about each other's performance, what aspects have been disappointing, and how to resolve what hasn't been working but was not being discussed.

EXPECTATIONS OF THE PARTNERS AS A TEAM

After looking at their expectations for each other individually, partners can examine their expectations for themselves as a team. They begin this exercise by working individually on lists of their expectations for their group: what they expect of every partner by virtue of the fact that he or she is a partner, and what they expect of the group as a whole. People are encouraged to think of the expectations that existed in their previous partnerships too, and whether those expectations helped or hindered the group. Then they get together and, one by one, present these expectations to the entire group.

Some people will have many expectations, others only a few. Some will have notably high expectations for how the team will act and what they will achieve; others less so. Once they all have a chance to see the similarities and differences, they immediately begin discussing and negotiating, because they recognize that the results will have consequences. There is a difference between setting high expectations and setting low ones. High expectations can encourage engagement and hard work, but if they are too high they can result in disillusionment and cynicism. Likewise, expectations that are too low may cause partners to underachieve.

How these differences will play out is impossible to say in the abstract. Every partner group must struggle with this question. Essentially, partners are consciously managing their expectations and negotiating what they intend the team to be.

Partners essentially develop performance standards for the partnership itself when they have agreed upon a list of acceptable expectations. The rejected items should no longer be expected of anyone. An additional benefit of this clarity is that it helps prevent partners from engaging in opportunistic behaviors or actions that benefit them at the expense of other partners.

A woman partner in a retail store was questioned by her potential partners about her strikingly low expectations for the partnership. She ended up telling them about a previous partnership she had been in that ended in disaster. She opened her soon-to-be partners' eyes about certain financial traps regarding compensation and commissions that none of them had been aware of and that had not come up during their earlier discussions about compensation. The partners revisited their earlier discussion and decided to change the way they had planned to handle commissions. As partners talk about how to align their expectations, they often visualize steps they could take to help realize them. By taking this partner seriously and incorporating her concerns and past experience into their planning, the team convinced her that this set of partners could aim higher.

The partners at Star Systems developed the following shared expectations.

Our Expectations for Ourselves as Co-Owners

- We will work together as a team, meaning we will keep one another informed and involve each other in decision making whenever appropriate.
- We will do our best to foster trust among us and immediately address actions and circumstances that might erode it.
- We'll avoid two-against-one alliances ("triangulating") and instead deal directly with one another.
- We'll be extremely discreet about our partnership, not discussing matters among us with others in the company, with family, or with outsiders.
- Once per quarter the three of us will meet with the senior executive team for the primary purpose of critiquing and improving how we are communicating among departments.
- Once a year we will conduct an offsite weekend retreat that includes a review of our charter, focusing one entire day on how the three of us are working together and another day on how the company is working.

- We won't flaunt the fact that we own the company.
- We will value all the employees and will not show favoritism.
- Our relationships with one another will always be more important than anything else—including money.
- We will never allow a partner to learn about a crisis in our area from anyone other than a partner; we will always tell one another first if something major is wrong.
- We'll be patient with each other.
- None of us will do anything that might hurt the credibility of another partner, and if we're in doubt about it, we'll ask first.

There are many other issues that prospective partners can cover in setting out their expectations for their partnership, including how hard they expect partners to work, how much vacation time they will take, use of company property, access to perks, socializing with employees, and access to information. I have assisted many medical practices with selecting and integrating new partners, and I have seldom seen a practice that did not have specific expectations included for how much energy partners would put into cultivating and maintaining social contacts with both professional colleagues and the community at large.

Many company owners firmly believe in establishing performance expectations and goals for their top leaders but stop short of establishing the same for themselves. Obviously, what's good for the goose is good for the gander. Partners are more likely to succeed if they are in agreement about what is expected of everyone on the team. By extension, the *companies* of partners who have truly figured out how to work together are more successful than companies with partners who have not done this homework. In their book on employee teams, *The Wisdom of Teams,* Jon Katzenbach and Douglas Smith document that all teams achieve more with clearly articulated performance goals. It's no different for teams of co-owners.

Any group of partners that has worked through its expectations in this way ends up with a clear understanding of what their partnership means to them. They are in a better position to support one another in their individual and shared expectations and to succeed as a group.

HOW CLOSE DO PARTNERS REALLY WANT TO BE?

An important question for partners is how closely they want to work together. The range is enormous. At one end of the spectrum are partners who give each other such wide latitude that you wonder how they could be as successful as they are. I remember my father telling a story when I was young about how my mother's four brothers and he worked as a team in their Wisconsin construction company. He said that one winter, one of my uncles and his wife went on a month-long African trip and returned without any of his partners realizing he had been away. At the time it seemed that my father was telling me a story about how well they operated; unbeknownst to his partners, the president of the company left for a month and nothing untoward happened. If fact, they ran the business quite successfully. Now I suspect the story was slightly apocryphal, because at least one of my other uncles must have known he was away, even if it was their slow season. I came to see my father's story as a way of describing how independently they operated, which they could do because they were in charge of different divisions.

At the other end of this spectrum are partners who completely blend their business and personal lives. Some married couples and some non-family partners fall at this end of the spectrum. The expectations these partners have of their partner teams are usually quite high and involve trust, openness, and coordination. For example, in the early 1980s Dave Broach and Bob Sober bought out their four other partners in an architectural firm that had fallen apart over feelings of unfairness. As they began rebuilding the firm, they radically changed the ownership and compensation structures. However, they recognized that changes were needed beyond reorganization. They brought Bob Workman on board as an owner in 1989, formed the BSW Group, and together they took a close look at what else had to be changed.

"We realized that the quality of our business decisions was dependent on the decisions we were each making independently in our personal lives, and how we were conducting our personal and family affairs was affecting what we could and couldn't do as partners," Workman explained to me. There was an inescapable financial connection. "Why would we let an accident that's happening in one of our personal lives become an accident for all of us, our employees, and our clients?" They wanted to feel confident that if the business suddenly needed $1 million, "we could each walk in the next day with a personal check covering a third of it."

They decided as a group to revisit their expectations for their partnership. Through intensive soul searching, they came to the following conclusions:

1. They wanted transparency among themselves regarding their business lives and their personal and family finances.
2. In addition to sharing financial goals for the business, they would jointly develop a goal for personal financial independence—that each would aspire to.
3. They would not consider the goal satisfied until they all had achieved it.
4. They would all use the same financial planning and estate planning advisors for themselves and their families, to help ensure transparency. Those advisors would also meet with them as a partnership.
5. Their advisors would share information regarding each partner's financial, tax, and estate plans.
6. They would not make any decision that resulted in a burden on any partner or his family.
7. Their spouses would be part of the process and understand their agreements, effectively making them pseudopartners. If anything happened to the partner, his spouse would be less likely to need an attorney to protect her assets.

Regarding the final conclusion, Workman explained, "This was done to protect the company from after-the-fact spousal/attorney interference during the transition, as well as protect the spouse and the estate." Workman admitted that it wasn't easy for them to overcome their initial resistance to that level of mutual disclosure and the feeling that "some stuff is private." "The more we opened up, the more we realized we'd each made a lot of the same mistakes. But more important, we were pretty similar in terms of what we wanted for ourselves." They overcame the resistance and have felt thankful ever since. According to Workman, "Those commitments have since proven to be the bedrock of our partnership." It was in that process of defining their expectations for themselves as a team and committing to working so closely that "we became 'partners' for life," explained Workman. "The commitments we made go deep and last forever."

BE CAREFUL WITH YOUR EXPECTATIONS

A caveat is in order. As I have said, people will live down, as well as up, to their partners' expectations. If people believe their partners will cheat them, the partners are more likely to cheat. If people expect partners to do a poor job, they will. We have mediated numerous partner disputes in which one partner complained bitterly about the poor performance of the other. Undoubtedly there are many partners who are not up to the job, but many cases of underperformance are attributable to one partner's low expectations of the other. In one such mediation, the "underperforming" partner burst in at the start of the fourth session and informed her partner, who was running the company, "I am now clear about what I need to do. I'm buying you out, or you're buying me out." She wound up buying the company and has very successfully run it by herself for the past nine years. So much for underperformance.

We tend to think our expectations are a function of who the other person is, but *we* are the people having them. To a large extent, we are in control. If we appreciate the power of interpersonal expectancy, we may realize the wisdom of changing negative and neutral expectations to positive ones. If we can develop positive expectations for our partners, we will increase the likelihood of a positive outcome. It's as if we can get them halfway there. But these expectations have to be genuine, not faked. Expressing positive expectations simply to manipulate one's partners is sure to backfire. You have to do the heavy lifting yourself, meaning that you have to shift your thinking in order to create genuinely positive expectations for your partners. Accomplishing this can produce significant and lasting change for the better.

PART FOUR

THE FUTURE IS SOONER THAN YOU THINK

CHAPTER 12

Just Suppose:
Scenario Planning for Partners

All events should be crossed in imagination before reality.

SIGMUND WARBURG, FOUNDER OF UBS

For people to act, too often we must substitute catastrophe for imagination.

ALEXANDER BRIN, EDITOR AND PUBLISHER

"THINKING ABOUT THE unthinkable" is how Herbert Kahn at the Rand Corporation described what businesspeople need to do more often. Brian Miller, a co-owner in the marketing firm Miller White in Terre Haute, Indiana, discovered how important scenario planning can be a few years ago when he was diagnosed with leukemia. For seven months he had to battle for his health and life while counting on his partner, William White, to keep their firm viable. "After that experience, we realized there were many different situations we had not given the least bit of thought, much less planning, to."

In another example, two doctors who had formed a professional corporation were struggling both financially and emotionally after only one year of being partners. They agreed to call it quits but could not agree on how to separate. They had a shareholders' agreement, which,

194 THE PARTNERSHIP CHARTER

as one of them explained, "lists a lot of eventualities except the one we're facing—we're not making money." The shareholders' agreement, she said, "has exit strategies, but it never addressed the possibility that we'd be exiting without money."

If these two sets of partners had done some scenario planning while forming their businesses, they might have anticipated the situations they faced. That would have made their situations far easier to deal with. Every set of business partners should conduct scenario-planning exercises to reduce the risks inherent in co-ownership. While other sections of the charter aid prospective partners in preparing for dozens of situations that countless partners have had to deal with, scenario planning helps them prepare for the unpredictable. It helps partners catch potential problems they missed in the other sections.

ADVANTAGES OF SCENARIO PLANNING

Scenarios are stories to help people understand the uncertainties of the future. Anticipating possible events may cause them to alter their plans by taking preventive actions. By creating guidelines to deal with various scenarios, partners can "rehearse" how they would respond. If and when an out-of-the-ordinary event occurs, even when it is not exactly the scenario they had envisioned, partners usually make better decisions because they are not caught completely off guard. Having done scenario planning, partners can spot situations as they begin to unfold, before they become overwhelmingly complex or uncontrollable. The participation of partners in a systematic process of generating, discussing, and analyzing scenarios, and then creating guidelines for dealing with them, builds shared understanding.

The greatest advantage of scenario planning is that it is immensely easier for a group of people to agree on their actions in a challenging situation if the situation is purely hypothetical, meaning the situation has not yet begun to unfold in reality. When considered beforehand, no one knows who may be affected adversely. In contrast, when a real crisis strikes, emotions cloud the picture, personal agendas distort clearheaded thinking, and people have trouble acting like a team. Partners who fail to contemplate a situation ahead of time discover that negotiations become radically different and far more arduous than they expected.

For example, a few years ago a frustrated owner of a small clothing store chain called us when he wanted to hire his daughter, but his partner was adamantly opposed to the idea, calling it nepotism and claiming that it would precipitate an unmanageable situation. The father claimed that he understood his partner's trepidation but also resented it because he believed that if any of his partner's children had expressed an interest in joining their business, then his partner would have been in favor of the idea. It's impossible to know if he was right about his partner, but their situation illustrates how much better off they would have been if they had entertained the possibility ten years earlier, before they'd opened their first store. Having guidelines in place beforehand makes for a calmer, more rational, and more unified response to a challenge or crisis.

I suspect that most partners do almost no scenario planning. Many businesses, regardless of size, probably do almost no scenario planning whatsoever. In the summer of 1999, when a few dozen people got sick from drinking Coke in Europe, Coca-Cola blundered its way through one of the worst public relations nightmares in the history of corporate America. A company spokesperson was quoted in the newspapers as saying, "The crisis was bigger than any worst-case scenario we could have imagined." There is no better example of a corporate failure to anticipate the out-of-the-ordinary. All partners, boards, and executive teams can put themselves in a more advantageous position if they take the time and energy to anticipate the circumstances that could await them.

SCENARIOS

A scenario is a brief description of a possible but not probable future. The most useful scenarios speculate on a wide range of possibilities. Creating scenarios necessitates some tolerance for ambiguity. If people cannot break momentarily out of their present reality, they will have difficulty imagining possible future situations. Scenarios based only on what people currently know about their circumstances will offer little in the way of planning for the unpredictable.

There are many different approaches to scenario planning, most of which date back to the work of Herbert Kahn during the 1960s. These approaches differ in their emphasis because they serve various goals. The approach that we developed is designed to satisfy the needs of a team of partners who must plan their common future and share in the control and destiny of a larger entity. While the entire Partnership Charter is about planning in one way or another, scenario planning is geared toward those future events that are rarely planned for, less likely to occur, and not easy to control if they do happen—at least if no plans have been made for responding. It is also for catching situations that could have been planned for in one of the earlier sections of the charter but were not. Prospective partners have the option of adding these plans, or guidelines, to an earlier section or keeping them in this section.

SCENARIO PLANNING STEPS

Step 1.   Anticipating the out-of-the-ordinary is the first step in developing guidelines for coping with the unexpected. Each partnership is unique, and certain challenges that come the partners' way will also be unique. The first step calls for prospective partners to individually make lists of all the situations they can imagine that could challenge their company's security or the partners' ability to function optimally. They might include items like the following:

- One partner insists on hiring a key employee whom another partner dislikes.
- A partner is sued for sexual harassment.
- A partner demands that the company buy products from her husband's company.

- The company receives an unsolicited buyout offer from a competitor.
- The company runs out of money.
- Two major shareholders want to retire and cash out at the same time.
- An ongoing personal or family crisis interferes with the ability of one partner to perform.
- Two partners become close and ostracize a third partner.
- Three key employees exit and join a competitor.
- Partners disagree about letting employees buy into the business.
- One partner pushes relentlessly to take the company public.
- A partner rehires a niece to work for the company even though she did not perform satisfactorily the first time.
- The company suffers in a major economic downturn.
- One partner suddenly loses interest in the business.
- A partner is caught stealing from the company.

The forces that could threaten the health and security of the partnership or the business may have to do with the partners themselves; family; other people in the business; or economic, market, technological, or social forces. All of these should be considered when conjuring up scenarios.

Partners also need to consider positive scenarios. Success can strain partnerships, yet people rarely plan for what they would do if they were wildly successful. One BMC client explained, "Everything has changed now because there's money. It just wasn't a problem before, but when the money was finally there, the deal changed." Geoff Williams, an *Entrepreneur* columnist, pointed out that while success can sometimes come quickly and easily, reacting to that success isn't always simple. "If you don't react in the right way, success can overwhelm, control and humiliate you." Countless business owners have expanded rapidly following an initial rush for their products or services, only to become overwhelmed by massive debt and eventually dragged into bankruptcy. Anticipating such prospects and including them in a list of scenarios can help prevent such disasters.

Step 2.   The second step is for the group to pool their lists and expand them using brainstorming techniques. In other words, no one criticizes or attempts to eliminate the scenarios someone else puts forth. All the partners explain their own scenarios and work to understand the situations others propose. Then the group tries to come up with additional scenarios. Together, the partners will usually develop a wide array of hypotheticals. Steps 1 and 2 are very important to creating quality scenarios. If they aren't followed, the rest of the exercise will have little value.

Step 3.   In the third step, the group assigns people or teams the task of developing guidelines for handling the possible situations. A group of four partners-to-be, for example, may decide that the scenarios fall into four distinct categories and that they will each take one category and address the various scenarios within it. Some people decide to work in subgroups, and some may decide that they prefer to tackle all the scenarios as one group.

Step 4.   However the partners decide to organize themselves, the fourth step is developing and agreeing on the guidelines for action if any of the situations were to occur. Each partner team must determine how detailed to make their guidelines. A good rule of thumb is that the guideline for any particular scenario should leave all the partners feeling knowledgeable and confident about their own responses, and their partners', if the scenario began unfolding.

While one cannot know or control what, where, when, or how a challenge or crisis will strike, partners do have some control over their response. Guidelines should include agreements about how the partners should interact as well as what each person should do.

Creating guidelines is far from easy. Some items might sound simple to deal with—a light-fingered partner, for example—but in reality they are not. If an employee is caught stealing, a solution may present itself readily (firing the employee, turning him or her in to the authorities), but partner situations are always far more complex. The trick is to realize that guidelines should give direction by removing surprise and confusion. They need not dictate every step to be taken, but they should clearly illuminate the approach.

The scenario planning process does not dictate how the partners must handle a situation if it arises. Rather, it provides a baseline for how situations should be handled if they ever occur. Scenario planning is a staring point; it sets a direction. A month or a year after completing their charter, partners can agree to change their strategy. It is not cast in stone; in fact, all guidelines need to be reviewed whenever the charter is reviewed. Also, partners can certainly choose to respond differently if a scenario begins to play out. But if they cannot agree on a response in the moment of crisis, at least they will have clear guidelines to fall back on.

Many partners have noted that they learned who their partners really were when their first crisis occurred, because they could finally see the kind of decisions their partners made under difficult circumstances. But by then it may be too late. Because people often assume they know more about others than they actually do, an indirect benefit of scenario planning is that partners learn more about each other— sooner. Scenario planning gives partners a glimpse of each other's decision-making capabilities without the pressure of an actual crisis. Taking the time and energy to create guidelines for the unexpected during the Partnership Charter process allows people to reduce risk offensively rather than defensively, sooner rather than later, and with confidence rather than trepidation.

CHAPTER 13

Essentials of Resolving Conflict

SINCE ONE OF THE primary goals of the Partnership Charter process is preventing destructive conflicts from ever occurring, why have a chapter on conflict resolution? It sounds like I'm hedging my bets. Actually, as I discussed in chapter 12, it is important to plan even for highly unlikely events, partly because the act of planning often spurs people to take practical steps to reduce their likelihood. Partners need to think through the various methods for dealing with partner conflict and develop clear strategies in the event that conflicts emerge.

PATHS INTO CONFLICT, AND OUT OF IT

Co-owners can follow many paths into conflict, but only a few paths lead out of it. Two 50–50 partners may be deadlocked on a major decision, or a group of ten partners may be split over a performance issue related to one of them. Whatever the problem, the partners need an effective way to move beyond their impasse, because once relationships get off track, they have a tendency to stay off track. Disturbed relationships can spontaneously resolve themselves, but they are more likely to simply continue or deteriorate.

Whatever gets partners into conflict, the path out will determine not only what the outcome will look like but also who will participate, what the process of getting from conflict to resolution will involve, and how long it will take. Mediation—a process that focuses on collaboration—is often the best option for business and professional partners.

Methods of conflict resolution span a spectrum from negotiation to litigation. Those on the left side of the diagram provide the greatest degree of self-determination for the people involved. Outsiders have more influence when the methods on the right side are used, until, at the extreme, the participants surrender complete control over the outcome to a judge or arbitrator.

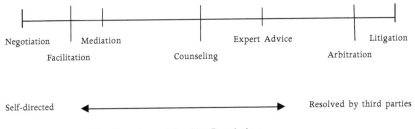

FIGURE 13.1   The Spectrum of Conflict Resolution

Negotiation.   Negotiation, when it works, is by far the easiest way to resolve disputes. This is simply talking it out, preferably with some measure of give and take. It's what partners do constantly and what they should do whenever they have a disagreement.

Facilitation.   When partners can't negotiate an end to a disagreement, they may seek assistance from a facilitator. The mere presence of a good facilitator can do wonders for some partners because the facilitator transforms a private, intimate exchange into a more public one, which causes some people to behave better. Any objective person can facilitate a more constructive dialogue. The higher the facilitator's stature in the eyes of the participants, the more effective his or her presence will be.

Facilitators carefully monitor the discussion and give feedback on the process that improves the parties' ability to communicate, thereby ensuring that partners are not only transmitting but receiving. But facilitators will typically stay out of the content of the discussion, in order not to lose sight of the process or be viewed as taking sides. Being neutral in everyone's eyes is at the very heart of both facilitation and mediation. Significantly, neutrality isn't a prerequisite of any of the other conflict resolution methods, including those of the counselor and the expert advisor.

Mediation.   Mediators, like facilitators, must be perceived as neutral by the parties. The main difference between the two approaches is that mediators must fully immerse themselves in the substance of the dispute, which is a significant difference in the case of conflicts among business partners. It is extremely advantageous for dispute resolution professionals to help the partners grapple with the nitty-gritty relationship, business, legal, and financial details of the dispute. Because mediation is widely accepted as the most appropriate method of resolving conflicts requiring the involvement of a third party, I describe how it works in more detail later in the chapter.

Counseling.   Therapists get called upon to help partners whose relationships are dysfunctional. Their role, though important for some partners, is more narrowly defined than one might imagine. Therapists who work with businesspeople are generally trained in individual and group dynamics. They are on the right side of the spectrum in the figure above because they are engaged to bring their knowledge and expertise to bear on the partners' interpersonal problems and are expected to offer their opinions and insights so that the partners can understand how to change; in doing so, they are rarely perceived by everyone as neutral or unbiased. While they do not have the power to impose resolutions, the expectation is that they will assess the situation and make clear suggestions regarding the most effective way to resolve the interpersonal issues.

Resolving partners' interpersonal problems may not be possible without dealing with business issues like ownership and management, because they may be causing the problems. Even when it is possible to resolve the interpersonal problems, that may not be sufficient to resolve difficulties in business relationships. It's difficult for experts who have entered the picture as therapists to shift gears and deal with complex and sometimes technical business matters. This would involve shifting from being one type of expert (therapist) to being another type (business consultant). It's far more complicated to shift from being an expert of any type to being a mediator because clients expect certain things from experts and different things from mediators. They expect expert advisors to recommend ways to resolve issues. If that means recommending what one partner wants and another does not, that's okay. They expect mediators to delve deeply into their disputes, to cajole and push them to reach detailed agreements, but they also expect mediators to maintain neutrality on the substance of their disputes.

Expert advice.   The role of business consultant is farther right on the spectrum because business owners surrender some control when they engage such professionals. Some business owners won't hire consultants because they aren't willing to surrender any control. Likewise, consultants occasionally "fire" business owners as clients because the clients won't follow their advice.

Business consultants can be immensely helpful to partners on a wide range of issues if the partners are open to receiving help. The process is relatively straightforward. Experts assess the situation by interviewing everyone involved, apply their knowledge and experience, and recommend a specific course of action. This process is very efficient when co-owners are getting along well and the advice is aimed at a business issue. Partners decide to follow or discard the consultant's advice based on their perception of the quality of the advice offered.

Expert advice is frequently *not* helpful when partners are at odds with one another. Partners experiencing differences often lose the ability to make simple business decisions together. Partners in a third-generation family in the resort business recently told an associate and me that they'd had "more top consultants than you'd ever imagine" to help them plan the future of their resort. Each time, they explained, one person or another opposed the recommended plan, so the resort continued its inexorable decline. Even the best business advice can be useless when the principals are not addressing their conflict directly.

Sometimes expert advisors are hired to assess partner conflicts and make recommendations to resolve them. This scenario reminds me of what the Swiss psychologist Carl Jung is reputed to have said: Good advice will never hurt anyone since nobody ever follows it. Expert advice rarely ends a festering conflict between partners because someone involved in the dispute inevitably resists the recommendation. This is how the dynamics of interpersonal conflicts work, unfortunately. Experts may be well qualified and their recommendations perfect, but the expert process is not optimal for resolving conflicts.

Partners sometimes pull in existing advisors such as accountants or lawyers to resolve their disputes. Before using professional mediators, Lon and Stan, whose battle over the direction of their business was described in chapter 3, had actually tried mediation with their accountant. This effort broke down when Lon examined the accountant's bills and noticed that he spent more time talking to Stan than to him. It didn't matter that the accountant had always talked to Stan more or that the accountant was being "neutral." It is nearly inevitable that a person with an existing relationship with the partners will be perceived by someone as biased when negotiations become difficult. Then the mediation will grind to a halt. The perception of neutrality is the sine qua non of mediation. (The partners' accountant or attorney will sometimes be part of a mediation, but his or her role will still be advising all of the partners.)

Arbitration and litigation.   At the far right of the spectrum are arbitration and litigation. Both are adversarial processes that take decision making out of the hands of business owners and put it in the hands of third parties, who base their decisions on laws and legal precedents, not subtle business realities.

The processes are very similar even though arbitration was initially billed as a major improvement over litigation. A *Harvard Business Review* article explained how alike they are. "The bad news," it reported, is that arbitration, "as currently practiced too often mutates into a private judicial system that looks and costs like the litigation it's supposed to prevent. [It] typically includes motions, briefs, discovery, depositions, judges, lawyers, court reporters, expert witnesses, publicity, and damage awards beyond reason." The two reasons to use arbitration, as opposed to litigation, are that arbitration usually results in a verdict in less time and is private.

Arbitration is often confused with mediation because both are called "alternative dispute resolution" techniques, but they are as different as night and day. The only similarities are that both employ neutral third parties and occur outside the courtroom. Unlike mediation, arbitration and litigation necessarily create winners and losers—and often leave partners' relationships in shreds. Rather than foster greater communication, they diminish and sometimes squash all direct communication. Partners are often instructed not to speak to one another, so the people who know most about the problem and are in the best position to resolve it have their hands tied, bringing the chances of resolving the conflict to near zero. Only the lawyers are left talking directly to anyone.

Rufus King III, a highly respected Superior Court judge in the District of Columbia, who has presided over the litigation of countless business partner disputes, agreed to discuss his views on resolving partner disputes. He believes that mediation is much more appropriate than litigation in most business partner conflicts, because "even a 'win' in court can be a loss for everybody involved." Even when one side prevails in an adversarial contest, the adversaries themselves often emerge severely damaged. Arbitration and litigation force participants to spend time, energy, and money trying to lay blame on the other side.

Judge King presided over a highly publicized dispute between father and son partners in the Dart Group (the Haft business empire) a few years ago. The family's ownership in the multiple businesses, worth more than $500 million, was rapidly unraveling, and the family was spiraling downward as well. The legal bills passed the $30 million mark, and it became difficult for family partners, board members, key employees, and others to find Washington lawyers who were not involved in the litigation. Judge King saw what was happening to the

Hafts and their businesses and tried to stop the bleeding by forcing the family out of his courtroom and into mediation. Unfortunately for the Haft family members, the solo mediator focused exclusively on the legal side of the resolution and did not, or could not, address the family side. The resolution they hammered out began falling apart within days. While the Hafts ultimately lost control of the business, and the Dart Group wound up in Chapter 11, the judge's dramatic maneuver probably helped them cut their losses. I believe the outcome might have been quite different if the family had had an agreement in place to use mediation at the first sign that they couldn't resolve an issue on their own, and if they had used co-mediators, one with legal or business expertise and one with family expertise.

HOW MEDIATION WORKS

Mediation's emphasis on collaboration is one element that distinguishes it from the other methods of resolving disputes. Getting partners to shift their mindset from antagonism, blame, and suspicion to recognizing that they're in their mess together is key to achieving resolution. Mediators plan at the outset of every engagement how they will create a spirit of collaboration among the parties involved. They do this in a number of ways.

1. *Mediators try to involve everyone who has a stake in the problem or might be instrumental in its resolution.* Spouses, key employees, and advisors may be asked to participate. In addition, anyone who has the power to block an agreement should be invited. (We learned this lesson the hard way when four key employees threatened to quit over Lon and Stan's first resolution, described in chapter 3.) Involving everyone who can contribute appreciably to a solution creates a spirit of collaboration that is essential to resolving disputes.

Sometimes a partner who owns more than a 50 percent share of a business is reluctant to use mediation for fear that sitting down with his or her minority partner, or partners, will dilute his or her power. Mediation does not alter the reality of the partners' situations or undermine someone with an advantaged position. It does give people an equal chance of speaking and being heard, which may not suit a controlling partner's wishes. Minority partners sometimes simply need and appreciate the opportunity to be heard and be part of the process; this can go a long way toward breaking an impasse among the partners.

2. Once the partners are together, mediators engage them in constructive dialogue. Partners are often skeptical that constructive dialogue is possible, either because they have been having plenty of dialogue but none of it constructive, or because they have been incapable of any conversation whatsoever. The secret to starting effective communication among warring partners is helping them shift from focusing on who is causing the problem to who can be part of the solution.

3. Mediators know how to spot underperforming partners and build them into the resolution. This, too, gets people energized and more willing to work together for the greater good. There is often a partner who has been marginalized and is not performing up to his or her potential. Mediators know how to get underperforming partners back onboard and up to speed.

4. Mediators create a safe environment by establishing ground rules and conducting caucus sessions that are useful for breaking impasses. Partners can drop their defenses (their anger, finger-pointing, denial, etc.) long enough to hear what the others are saying in this safe environment. They can then begin thinking more rationally and feel some compassion for one another.

The mediators meet in caucus sessions with an individual or a subset of the people involved to discuss something specific—usually something that cannot be said comfortably in the entire group—that can remain confidential if necessary. The mediators, or any of the participants, can initiate a caucus session. In these private sessions, mediators might coach a partner to say something he or she was afraid to say, or to apologize. These activities, which could mean the difference between success and failure, might never happen or would take much more time to achieve without the flexibility that caucus sessions provide.

Caucus sessions help partners to open up and reveal virtually everything, because if a partner withholds information that is important, it usually works to his or her disadvantage. The ability to engage partners in such caucus sessions is a distinct advantage that mediators have. Lawyers working with a set of partners do not have this freedom. Lawyers put themselves at risk for being sued for conflict of interest if they conduct individual meetings with partners who are at odds with one another. The individual sessions with mediators can unearth hidden agendas, shed light on secrets, resolve impasses, and reestablish collaboration. People open up to mediators in ways that surprise even themselves, revealing things that they may not have told anyone before. Then, for the first time, someone has all the information—all the pieces of the puzzle—and is in an ideal position to help the partners clear up misunderstandings and envision new options.

5. *Mediators define the solution as one that all of the partners will develop together.* Mediators control the process, but it's the partners who control the outcome. When partners understand they must work *together* to be successful, they begin thinking and acting differently and become more actively engaged. They take ownership of the resolution instead of surrendering it to advisors. Importantly, the chance for successful implementation is improved because everyone has a vested interest in seeing the plan succeed. Whereas decisions by others, even arbitrators and judges, can be undermined by warring partners, partners are more likely to accept and implement agreements they have developed themselves. An added benefit of being an integral part of the resolution is the therapeutic effect it has on the partners and others. When people reach their own agreements, reduce them to writing, and sign them at the mediation's conclusion, they feel a great sense of relief and become surprisingly willing to forgive the past. They often feel a renewed sense of hope about the future, and therein lies the healing power of mediation.

Successful business mediations usually require co-mediator teams that combine a mediator with a background in family dynamics and one with a business background (or sometimes law or finance, depending on the partners' dispute). Knowledge in these areas is critical because mediators must grasp the nuances of both business and personal issues quickly and be able to help partners brainstorm solutions that are practical. They must also assist in drafting detailed written agreements that capture the understandings reached by the partners and help prevent problems from developing in the future.

Mediation is considered the most effective method for resolving partner disputes in part because mediators have the freedom to dig in and grapple with the details of interpersonal and business issues. Mediators are not limited in terms of whom they can talk to or what they can discuss. They are free to raise issues that partners do not recognize and exert pressure on partners who are stonewalling or being unrealistic about their demands. Exerting pressure is the most delicate part of the process and what makes mediation very different from facilitation. Mediators must be very well versed in partnership issues and business to understand when, where, and how to get involved in the content of the dispute. Dealing directly with the substance of disputes allows issues to be resolved quickly. This is why business owners should look for co-mediators who have considerable experience with business–owner conflicts.

A typical mediation session lasts a half or full day. Extended periods are necessary because building collaboration and consensus cannot take place an hour or two at a time. (The extended meetings and the intensity of effort are additional reasons why co-mediators are necessary.) The total amount of time it takes to resolve partner disputes varies widely from case to case. The simplest cases can be resolved in a day or two. Other cases, which have been years in the making, may require many days to resolve. I tell people it depends on the complexity of the issues and the stubbornness of the partners. Even in complicated cases that take days to resolve, however, the cost—in time, money, energy, and personal anguish—is much less than the cost of the other procedures and far less than the conflict continuing unresolved. This is especially obvious when you consider the cost of the partners being distracted from productive work while the conflict drags on.

WHAT IS NEEDED IN THE CHARTER

We suggest that partners discuss and agree on the steps they will take to (1) establish a stepwise approach to resolving conflicts that might arise among the partners, on the board, or elsewhere in their organization; and (2) maintain effective communication. The section on effective communication should include any activities, tools, and techniques that the partners think will help minimize misunderstandings and make them more competent communicators. They might include things like carefully structuring meetings, helping partners who are having a problem talking directly to each other, or taking time to reinforce cooperation and collaboration during partners' meetings.

The section on resolving disputes usually documents a commitment to employing a three-step procedure for resolving all disputes: negotiation, mediation, and arbitration. Negotiation is always the method of choice, but if it fails or is stalled, then the partners engage co-mediators, preferably before positions have hardened. Arbitration is a last resort, but an important last resort. It is better to stipulate arbitration as a fallback strategy than to allow a partner conflict to go to litigation.

This section of the charter is the one that we have essentially prepared for partners. I suggest that you discuss it and decide whether you agree to follow it. If you do, you must also develop a list of mutually acceptable mediators and arbitrators, or a foolproof strategy for selecting them, so that you never have to choose third parties when you are in a state of conflict.

Setting up a sound process for resolving disputes is a mix of planning and insurance, like the entire Partnership Charter. Raising the issues that have tripped up so many partners, discussing them, negotiating agreements, and putting them in writing is the best insurance partners can buy. Besides good insurance, though, this process builds trust and confidence in one another and in the partnership.

APPENDIX: STAR SYSTEMS' PARTNERSHIP CHARTER

Note to the reader: This charter is meant to be an example only. Every set of principals will develop their own unique charter that coincides with their specific operations, personalities, and circumstances. No charter is perfect or can serve as a boilerplate for another partnership.

PREAMBLE

SECTION ONE:
BUSINESS ISSUES
  1. Vision and Strategic Direction
  2. Ownership
  3. Titles, Roles, and Managing the Company
  4. Employment and Compensation
  5. Governance

SECTION TWO:
THE RELATIONSHIPS AMONG THE PARTNERS
  6. Our Personal Styles and Working More Effectively Together
  7. Values—Personal and Corporate
  8. Fairness: Partners' Interpersonal Equity
  9. Expectations of the Partners

SECTION THREE:
THE FUTURE OF THE BUSINESS AND THE PARTNERS
  10. Creating Guidelines for the Unexpected
  11. Resolving Disputes and Communicating Effectively

PREAMBLE

Our broad goal in creating this charter is to facilitate a smooth transition from a company owned by one person to a company owned jointly by three partners. Our specific goals for our charter and our partner retreat include the following:

- Resolve any doubts that we should, in fact, become partners by learning more about each other—our styles and values—and undertaking this planning process.
- Build trust and confidence in one another and in our ability to jointly manage the company.
- Be clear with one another and ourselves about what we want from doing this together and what we are willing to contribute to make it a success.
- Explore the compatibility of our respective strategic visions for the company; the business tactics and practices we are each comfortable with; and our approach to dealing with employees, customers, and other stakeholders.
- Talk directly about our roles in the business, how we will make decisions together, our approach to compensation, and how the company will be governed.
- Discuss how to communicate effectively with each other and develop a system for resolving conflicts that might arise among us.
- Develop strategies for avoiding the pitfalls that are inherent in being business partners and create guidelines for how we will approach the myriad situations that could befall us as a team and as a company.
- Plan thoroughly for possible changes in, and the end of, our partner relationship.

We recognize that we have multiple roles with one another. Beth and Jeff have worked together for the past fifteen years, with Beth working directly for Jeff for many of those years. Since the time that Jeff became sole owner of the company, she has been his employee. Beth and Sarah have been close friends since high school. Now, all three of us are ready to become co-owners as well as members of the board of directors of the company. In the management of the company, Beth and Sarah will report to Jeff. Given this complicated mix of overlapping roles and relationships, we want to clarify the structure and meaning of these relationships to minimize confusion and possible conflict among ourselves, employees, and others.

We recognize that to be effective as co-owners and as the core of the board and the management team, and to be most valuable to the company and our clients, we must work together in a trusting and cooperative way. We recognize the need to be of one mind about our values, and we also recognize that we must have compatible goals for the company to maximize its chances of success—success that benefits all of us and many other people as well.

The ideas and agreements contained in this charter are meant to memorialize our discussions and serve as a guide for working together harmoniously. We also intend that it will help guide the drafting of the legal agreements we will have with one another regarding our joint ownership of Star Systems, Inc., and do not intend for this charter itself to be a legally binding document.

Finally, we intend that this charter will be a "living document," meaning that we will continue to work on it; expand it as needed; use it to refresh our memories; and review it periodically to add and change things as our circumstances, roles, and company change. We are dedicated to following through on this tremendous effort and capitalizing on our investment of time and energy.

This charter goes into effect this _____ day of _____, ____. It represents the work of the three of us: Sarah Kramer, Elizabeth Nelson, and Jeffrey Davies.

Sarah Kramer
Elizabeth Nelson
Jeffrey Davies

SECTION ONE: BUSINESS ISSUES

1. Vision and Strategic Direction

Star Systems has been in the medical instrument sales business for twenty-six years and has earned a reputation for quickly and efficiently providing high quality products. We are considered to have the most knowledgeable, experienced, and client-friendly sales force of any company in the northeastern United States. We have never tried to compete on price or convenience. Instead, we compete on service. Our sales force is extremely dedicated and strong on relationship selling.

Our strength as a company has always come from the sales staff. We have many long-term sales employees. Maintaining employee loyalty has always been a priority at Star Systems, and we will continue to provide and support programs that enhance employees' knowledge and skills. Even though the sales team has remained strong despite the recent turmoil, some rebuilding needs to take place. Sarah is currently working with the sales management team to assess the situation and develop a yearlong program to get the entire sales force back to their former high morale.

Something we always believed set us apart from many other sales organizations was the lack of tension between sales and administration. Since the beginning of the company, there has been an understanding that Star Systems was a sales company, but it took the combined effort of sales and administration, and harmony between them, to be the best. Jeff and Sarah and their respective management teams will work together over the coming year to repair the rifts that have developed.

We do not aim to change what we do or diversify in any ways that might confuse our existing client base. They view Star Systems as specialists even though we offer a very broad range of products. We have offered, and will continue to offer, new products and services, but only those that complement what we already sell and do for our clients.

While we have a reputation for being very responsive to the needs of our customers, we have not been viewed as being innovative. Our medical instrument management and protection products line was one attempt to change this view. We were one of the first to introduce and develop this, and it has done extremely well in the short time we have marketed it. It will be Jeff's responsibility to strengthen Star System's capability for innovation. To do this, he will be responsible for exploring relationships with new foreign manufacturers and expanding our training, service, and instrument repair work for clients.

While we have some national accounts, with Sarah's entry into the business and her extensive contacts in university hospital communities throughout the United States, we see an opportunity to expand our presence nationally, beyond our solid regional base. We anticipate this will be our main thrust for the next few years. We do not want to do this at the expense of our regional position, however. We are looking for controlled growth, at a pace the company can manage.

Although we want to remain open to acquiring a similar company in a strategically advantageous part of the country, we are not ready to actively pursue this strategy at this time, primarily because of financial reasons. We also want to see how the company develops over the next two to three years. Taking on new debt for any reason is not something we are willing to do in the near future unless there are compelling reasons and we are all in agreement.

None of us is particularly interested in being acquired. We dislike the prospect of working for a larger corporation. Since we are all relatively the same age, we agree that it makes sense to begin looking seriously at selling the company to a larger company in ten-plus years. Selling before that time would only make sense if the offer were extremely lucrative.

2. Ownership

We have discussed a full range of issues related to the ownership of Star Systems and have come to agreement on how to handle many of them. We have set forth our decisions on various ownership issues below.

A. Ownership—Buying In

At the suggestion of the company's accountant and because the company had bought Jeff's family out of the business, the corporation will issue additional stock to allow Beth and Sarah to each own 10 percent of the company. They each will pay the corporation for the shares they receive.

With the agreed upon value of the company being $4,000,000, a 10 percent share is worth $400,000. With a 30 percent discount for a minority interest and lack of marketability, the price is actually $280,000. Beth agrees to pay $80,000 now and the remaining $200,000 over five years. Sarah agrees to pay $100,000 now and the remaining $180,000 over two years. If she succeeds in bringing at least $1,000,000 of business to the company during her first year, then she can spread out the balance over five years. Beth and Sarah will pay the nominal interest required by the IRS on the debt.

Jeff agrees that at the end of three years, Beth and Sarah will both have the option of buying up to an additional 10 percent interest in the company. The purchase price for those shares would be determined according to the method described under section C (Valuation); however, the maximum price would be no more than 30 percent above the current price.

B. Ownership—Selling

If any one of us voluntarily elects to sell his or her shares, or is required to offer them for sale, then it would be done in the following manner: He or she must first offer the shares to the company at an agreed upon price, or according to the method described below. If the remaining two shareholders decide that the company will not buy the shares, then the shares must be offered to the remaining owners at the same price. If both remaining owners are interested in purchasing the shares, then the shares will be split on a pro rata basis among them (relative to the current ratio of their shareholdings) unless they agree otherwise. If only one owner is interested, he or she may buy the shares. Any buyout of equity will occur over a five-year period unless the purchasers agree to a different timeframe at the time of the sale.

The individual wishing to sell an interest in the company may sell shares to someone else at either the same or a higher price only if the company turns down the offer and neither other owner desires to buy the shares.

If an owner receives an offer from a third party for his or her shares, the company and the other owners have the right of first refusal, in that order.

Jeff has made it clear that he wishes to remain the majority owner of the company. Beth and Sarah accept his wish, with the proviso that they will have the right of first refusal if and when he wants to sell any of his shares. Beth and Sarah would increase their shares equally unless they agree to a disproportionate buy-in, or if one is unable or unwilling to purchase an equal number of shares.

Jeff agrees not to sell the company to any buyer within seven years without the consent of either Beth or Sarah. This is meant to serve as a protection for Beth and Sarah, who do not envision—at least at this time—wanting to sell the company in the short term and then needing to work for someone else. After seven years, if he still holds the majority of the shares, Jeff is free to sell the company without the consent of either of them. He will have a "drag-along" right, that is, he can require that Sarah and Beth sell their shares at the same price and on the same terms as his. Beth and Sarah will have a "tag-along" right so that they won't be left out of any deal that Jeff, as the majority shareholder, strikes with a buyer. They would receive the same terms as he receives. In other words, Jeff must arrange for the sale of their shares as well, if they want to be part of the transaction. If Jeff decides to sell even part of his shares, the tag along will give Beth and Sarah the choice to sell a proportionate number of their shares to the same buyer.

Beth and Sarah agree that Jeff will have the option to buy back either or both of their shares at any time over the next five years if he feels the partnership is not working satisfactorily. He would be required to pay the value of the stock—determined by the procedure described under Valuation—with the same discounts plus all interest that they had paid and one year's salary. After three years, he would have to pay an additional two years' salary.

If an opportunity for the company arises that is clearly in the best interests of the company and the shareholders, then we agree to entertain the possibility of a sale of the company.

C. Valuation

If we cannot reach unanimous agreement regarding the value of the company at the time we need to agree on the valuation, then we will use Robert Hanneman, a certified business appraiser who has experience in our industry. We agree to abide by his determination. The shareholders agree to use the dispute resolution methods described in this charter if any disputes arise in this process.

D. Key-Person Insurance

It is not our intention for any of us to become partners with anyone other than people we choose voluntarily. Therefore we will have the company maintain insurance policies on each shareholder to defray a portion of the cost for the company to buy back his or her shares in the event of death.

The value of the policy on Jeff will equal $2,500,000. The value of the policies on Sarah and Beth will equal $250,000 each. We will review the amounts of the policies annually and make appropriate adjustments as the company's value increases.

E. Dividends

The board of directors will determine whether or not dividends are to be paid; however, it is not our desire or intention for the company to pay dividends in the foreseeable future.

F. The Addition of New Partners

We want the owners of the corporation to always have the right to determine who their partners will be. We do not want shares in the company to be passed on to our children simply as an investment or for tax purposes, or by inheritance. In other words, we agree that none of us will sell, transfer, or give his or her shares in the company to any other party without the consent and agreement of the other partners.

The partners agree to the following prerequisite conditions for the consideration of any new shareholders. Minimally, any new partner will

1. have knowledge and expertise that can add value to the corporation;
2. be committed to the company;
3. share our values and a commitment to excellence; and
4. be desirable to, and have good "chemistry" with, the existing partners.

We would consider a financial, nonstrategic investor in the company, but any financial partner would also need to meet the above criteria (perhaps with the exception of number 1).

3. Titles, Roles, and Managing the Company

A. Titles

Jeff will continue with the titles of President and Chief Executive Officer. Beth will continue with the title of Chief Financial Officer; Sarah will have the title of Executive Vice President, Sales & Marketing. The three of us will comprise the Senior Executive Committee.

B. Roles

As president and CEO, Jeff is ultimately responsible for all aspects of the company. Specifically, he is charged with

- carrying out directives of the board and guiding the company toward its objectives;
- hiring and firing all officers, subject to the terms of employment contracts; and
- guiding the operations of the company.

As CFO, Beth is responsible for

- monitoring the accounting and financial operations of the company;
- managing the cash flow and lines of credit;
- establishing and managing budgets;
- managing contract negotiations and cost proposal preparation;
- working with the company's accounting firm;
- ensuring that accounts receivable and accounts payable are up to date; and
- supervising payroll services, wire transfers, and credit card processing.

As vice president of sales and marketing, Sarah is responsible for

- designing and implementing the marketing program,
- managing the sales force,
- training the sales force, and
- prospecting and business development.

C. Managing the Company

The Executive Committee

The executive committee will coordinate the leadership of the entire company and help ensure that all departments of the company are collaborating as much as possible. Executives will run and be responsible for their respective departments, but the executive committee will always be kept apprised of what is happening, especially problems, in all departments. One of the chief responsibilities of the executive committee will be to foster cooperation and teamwork throughout the company. They must ensure that there are no structural barriers to cooperation within or between departments, especially between sales and administration. It is expected that all employee-owners will constantly strive to improve the business by providing input to the appropriate individuals whenever possible.

We all agree to keep in mind that ownership status in and of itself does not give one the right to make changes or direct that changes be made. The people in charge of various areas have the responsibility to implement changes if they see fit to do so. If certain changes have a significant impact on other parts of the business, they will confer with the other executives affected before moving forward.

We are committed as a group to setting and maintaining the highest possible standards of performance. We agree that the executive committee will be responsible for performance evaluations of all the other company executives. They will be conducted on an annual basis, and the results will be shared with the board of directors.

D. Accountability

We agree that by six months from the signing of our charter, each of us will develop a list of five performance standards for ourselves. We will review them as a group and fine-tune them so that we can use them on an annual basis to hold one another accountable.

4. Employment and Compensation

A. Employment

It is our intention that we will all work full-time in the company and that full-time means at least forty hours per week on average. We are all entitled to six weeks of annual vacation.

For now, we have decided that all owners must work at least two-thirds time in the company to remain owners. Failing to do so for more than a year would necessitate the sale of that partner's stock unless, of course, the remaining shareholders decide otherwise at that time.

We will have disability insurance policies that will provide 75 percent of our salary over one year should any of us become disabled. It will be paid in the following manner: full salary for the first six months and 50 percent salary for the second six months.

As part of our employment agreements, we will include clauses that will protect the company from any of us going to work for a competing company or starting a similar company within a forty-mile radius of Star Systems for a period of two years.

In deference to Jeff, Sarah and Beth agree that the company shall not employ any owner's family members.

It is our intention that the shareholders of Star Systems will have employment contracts. The owners' contracts would terminate if and when ownership ceased unless the remaining shareholders are in unanimous agreement that the departing owner may remain an employee of the company. Employment would also terminate if an owner fails in his or her fiduciary responsibility as an officer, director, or shareholder, or is convicted of a felony or crime of moral turpitude. Jeff's contract will stipulate that he will hold the position of CEO for seven years unless he chooses to resign or is terminated. If Sarah or Beth's employment is terminated by the action of Jeff or the board, she will receive a year's salary if it occurs during the first three years and two years' salary if it occurs afterwards.

B. Compensation

We want to have a merit-based company. We will determine compensation—ours and other employees'—based on roles, and we determine bonuses based on performance in each role.

We have agreed that our salaries will be as follows: Jeff, $375,000; Sarah, $200,000; and Beth, $150,000. The owners will review compensation annually, but we all agree that short of some significant change in our respective roles or in the marketplace, these are reasonable salaries.

C. Bonuses and Perks

The board will review the bonuses along with compensation on an annual basis. We agree that each owner will be entitled to a company car.

5. Governance

The board of Star Systems is selected by the shareholders to oversee the management of the company. It is the company's governing body. It sets the strategic direction of the company and selects and oversees the officers. The board holds the CEO responsible for communicating its expectations for the company to the entire management team. It also holds the CEO responsible for the execution of its directives.

The three of us initially will constitute the board of directors of Star Systems. Each one of us has a right to continue on the board or to select a person to serve on the board in his or her place. Within one year we will add two outside board members, one of whom will be chosen by Jeff and the other by consensus of the three of us. They must be independent of management. Employees, regular advisors, or others who may have a conflict of interest or could not be relied upon for an unbiased view would not be eligible to serve as board members. One of the outside board members will serve as board chair.

We will strive to govern the company by consensus decision making, but recognizing that reaching consensus is not always possible or expedient, a majority of the board will rule. The following decisions will require board action:

- Significant increases in corporate debt (more than $20,000)
- Significant expansion (increasing revenue or personnel by more than 10 percent in any one-year period)
- Changes in by-laws or corporate governance rules

In conducting board meetings, we will be cognizant of our different roles as shareholders, employees, managers, and directors. We will strive to stay cognizant of the fact that as board members, each one of us has a fiduciary responsibility to the entire company and to all of the shareholders.

We recognize that divergent views on issues are not only appropriate but good for SSI. We will debate the issues in a manner that focuses on the facts, concepts, principles, economic and practical feasibility, and whether the proposal is in the best interest of SSI both short and long term. We will avoid personalizing our differences.

We recognize that full, open, and honest discussion can only be expected if the deliberations of the board are confidential. Decisions of the board will be made known to others (management, employees, etc.) on a need-to-know basis. Unless agreed to at board meetings and so noted in the minutes, the discussions leading up to decisions will not be shared with non-board members. Under no circumstances will any of us quote another board member. When the board acts, we agree to fully support the action of the board even if we were not in favor of the proposed action.

We have identified several responsibilities of the board, including to

- monitor and hold the CEO accountable;
- act as a sounding board and provide feedback to the CEO;
- approve the company's strategic plans;
- define and approve executive compensation packages;
- review and approve the company's budget and dividend distributions; and
- review and approve major company policies, actions, and initiatives.

As part of creating this charter, we have clarified some of our initial directives for how we want the company to be run. The company should

- position itself for growth;
- provide an enjoyable, pleasant, positive workplace; and
- maintain a solid depth of management by developing the next management team.

SECTION TWO:
THE RELATIONSHIPS AMONG THE PARTNERS

6. Our Personal Styles and Working More Effectively Together

We all appreciate that how well we work together as a team can make or break the company. It can also determine whether or not we enjoy working together. To increase the chances of having successful partner relationships, we wanted to understand our distinct personal styles better, and how we can all modify the ways that we interact so that we can be a better team. In the first section below we briefly describe our personal styles based on both the Myers-Briggs and the DiSC tests. We all felt the tests painted accurate pictures of the way we operate with people and wanted a brief summary of this information included in our charter so we'd have it available for reference.

We used all of the information from the two tests to help us develop concise summaries of (1) what we need to feel successful; (2) our fears related to the workplace; and most important, (3) the agreements we were willing to make with each other in order to work better, smarter, and more effectively with one another. This information is in the tables in section B.

A. Our Personal Styles

Jeff

I am your typical wired, high-energy, independent, spontaneous, creative idea person who loves being able to focus on projects and change things. I'm a big-picture type with a knack for predicting trends. I need challenges and authority to plan things and execute them. I like winning and do better under pressure. I like being a catalyst for other people who see what needs doing and go-for-it—people who are independent types.

I recognize that I can get so engrossed in the big picture and watching trends that I can lose sight of what's under my nose. It is not a strength of mine to slow down and make sure everybody around me is up to speed, and I'm not particularly diplomatic if they aren't. Some people see me as aggressive or aloof. I dislike routines and "SOPs." I'm not very hands-on, and I hate getting bogged down in details and follow-through. I want to study all the possibilities and then decide what way to go, but I can't stand making a wrong decision. Sometimes I take on too much and get overextended.

According to the MBTI, I'm an ENTP (Extroversion-Intuition-Thinking-Perceiving) and on the DiSC, I'm a "Creative" under normal and stressful conditions.

Beth

I like being organized and on schedule. I'm analytical and dispassionate about business things, and I always like knowing where I'm going, how I'm going to get there, and when I'll arrive. I am great with numbers and details. I thrive on analytical and technical challenges. The MBTI says that I am the "quintessential dependable, reasonable type," and that has always been true of me. I am independent and have no trouble being accountable for jobs assigned to me. I am very cost and bottom-line conscious, and that is part of what makes me particularly good at what I do. I am loyal and always follow through on my commitments.

Some people see me as a neat-freak and stubborn and inflexible, but I am flexible if someone can show me a better way to get something done. I prefer jobs that I can get done myself and do have trouble from time to time staying aware of the needs and feelings of those who work for me. Seeing the big picture and planning are not strengths of mine. I demand a great deal of the people who work for me, and sometimes I can drive them—and myself—to the brink to get things done. Even in times of crisis, however, I never lose my calm demeanor or look out of control, even when I may feel it on the inside.

According to the DiSC, my style changes from my normal "Investigator" profile to "Perfectionist," which seems perfectly accurate because I get even more focused on details under stress. I'm an ISTJ (Introversion-Sensing-Thinking-Judging) on the MBTI.

Sarah

I get along with people extremely well because I have a very outgoing and confident spirit, and I understand the way people and organizations work. Getting other people motivated and moving comes naturally to me. I am quick, energetic, direct, and like to take charge of situations. I can sell anything to anyone as long as I believe it is something of quality. Rarely does anything intimidate me, but I know that my style can be intimidating to others. I have a knack for cutting through confusion and complexity, getting rid of inefficiency, and reaching goals.

My goal-oriented nature can sometimes push people too hard, and then they see me as abrasive or arrogant. Also, if something needs to be said, I will say it and expect people to deal with it. I do get impatient when people can't handle an assignment and may have a tendency to overlook their needs and feelings. I'm a very positive, optimistic person, which is where I get my energy, and have trouble with negative people because they drag me down.

My DiSC profile changes from "Persuader" to "Inspirational" under stressful conditions because I can get more dominant and less patient when the pressure is on. My MBTI type is ENTJ (Extroversion-Intuition-Thinking-Judging).

B. Working More Effectively Together

TABLE A.1   What I Want to Feel Successful

Jeff	1.	I need people who can support me to follow through on the ideas that I have.
	2.	Freedom to think outside of the box.
	3.	Autonomy.
	4.	Highly competent people around me.
	5.	Be recognized when I have a great idea.
Beth	1.	I want things to run smoothly and be kept in an orderly fashion.
	2.	People to follow through on what they said they'd do, when they said they'd do it.
	3.	Clear directions when I'm expected to do something and then freedom to do it as I see fit.
	4.	Challenges.
Sarah	1.	The opportunity to experiment with the way things are done and alter the status quo.
	2.	Be in charge of my area.
	3.	Rewarded for my accomplishments and successes (and be held accountable for any mistakes or shortcomings).
	4.	Freedom to hire the best people.
	5.	Freedom to schedule my work as I see fit.

FIGURE A.2   My Fears Related to the Workplace

Jeff	1.	Being out of the loop—not knowing things I should know, and not being kept informed.
	2.	Being cramped. Too many people encroaching on my "space."
	3.	Getting bogged down in details.
	4.	People won't be straight with me.
Beth	1.	People being hostile.
	2.	I'll miss what people are feeling.
Sarah	1.	Being seen as the Wicked Witch of the West.
	2.	Being boxed in and controlled by too much bureaucracy makes me crazy.
	3.	Being too "soft," controlled.
	4.	Being criticized unjustly.
	5.	Staying the outsider in this group.

TABLE A.3   My Limitations at Work

Jeff	1.	I make decisions so quickly that I sometimes forget to consult with others first.
	2.	I can sometimes run too far with an idea that isn't worth it.
	3.	Being blunt and critical of people who aren't up to speed.
	4.	I can lose sight of everyday practicalities and necessities.
	5.	I don't always give people feedback—good or bad.
Beth	1.	Not being "nice" enough, or diplomatic when it would help.
	2.	I don't always see the big picture because I'm so focused on the bottom line.
	3.	I can get set in my ways, be stubborn and inflexible.
	4.	Don't always pick up when people feel hurt by something I did.
	5.	Can burn out because I keep going too long on one project without a break.
Sarah	1.	Can get demanding and manipulative when feeling stressed out.
	2.	Not always diplomatic or patient enough.

TABLE A.4   To Work Better, Smarter, and More Effectively with My Partner . . .

Jeff with Beth	1. I agree to treat you like a real partner (not simply a key employee). 2. I will let you in on more of my preplanning thinking and be clearer about project expectations. 3. I'll tell you when I feel you're taking too much time to do something.
Jeff with Sarah	1. I agree not to be critical of you and to listen if you think I am. 2. I will not talk to people about you like you're the new kid on the block. 3. I will appreciate that you sometimes get more dominant and demanding when you're stressed out, and I will tell you when I see you getting that way. 4. I agree to work out clear understandings about what you will have control of in the company.
Beth with Jeff	1. I will keep you apprized in *summary* fashion of everything important. 2. I will back off when you say you've had enough of the details. 3. I'll be straightforward—even blunt—with you when I think you're in left field. 4. When people complain to me about your style (i.e., nasty and condescending), I'll encourage them to go straight to you with it.
Beth with Sarah	1. I'll let you know if I think you're being unreasonably demanding or manipulative. 2. I'll do everything I can to make you part of the "Jeff–Beth thing." 3. If you're not getting me the information I need fast enough, I'll let you know. 4. I will tell you when I think you're being too optimistic about someone or something or being too pollyannaish about what you're trying to achieve. 5. If I don't think you're working like a team player, I'll tell you right away.

(continues)

TABLE A.4   (*continued*)

Sarah with Jeff	1. I agree to not be put off by your "bite" and let you know when I feel unfairly criticized.
	2. I'll keep you informed of what I'm doing in my area and won't make decisions to change things without letting you know ahead of time.
	3. I will tell you "straight up" if I think you're excluding me from things that I should be involved in.
	4. I will take care of the details of my area so you don't need to be bothered by them.
	5. I agree to do whatever is necessary to keep from becoming manipulative and (unreasonably) demanding.
	6. If you call me on being manipulative, I will not get defensive, and I will talk about it with you.
Sarah with Beth	1. If I need your help on projects, I will be clear with you about what I'm asking for and provide what you need in a timely way so you can do your job.
	2. I will tell you when I think you're too much in the details and missing the bigger picture.
	3. I won't assume that just because you look cool, calm, and collected in a crisis, you actually feel that way.
	4. I'll tell you when you're missing people's feelings.

7. Values—Personal and Corporate

We recognize that partners who co-own a business and work together can sometimes have serious troubles with one another because they have different personal values. Our personal values motivate us on a day-to-day basis and shape our decisions. We know we're not going to change our values to satisfy each other, but we can be clear about what values each of us holds near and dear; be aware of the differences; and make a conscious, concerted effort to respect each other's values. We do not want to fall into the trap of judging each other's values. To avoid that, we are trying to be open and honest about how we think our values will play out as we work and make decisions day to day—together. By understanding our values, we will understand better what each of us wants and how we each are likely to react to work situations, especially when we're under pressure.

In Part B below, we address our corporate values because we also see a need to come to a mutually agreed upon set of values and principles to guide how we operate the company. The company has had a statement of values for about ten years, so we started with those, debated, and finally agreed upon the values that are described below.

A. Our Personal Values

In the following table are the results of our "Personal Values" tests, which list our values from highest to lowest, meaning from most active, or motivating, to least relevant, or least motivating. The values that we consider significantly different are those that have five or more levels between them.

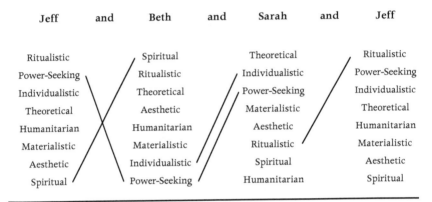

Jeff	and	Beth	and	Sarah	and	Jeff
Ritualistic		Spiritual		Theoretical		Ritualistic
Power-Seeking		Ritualistic		Individualistic		Power-Seeking
Individualistic		Theoretical		Power-Seeking		Individualistic
Theoretical		Aesthetic		Materialistic		Theoretical
Humanitarian		Humanitarian		Aesthetic		Humanitarian
Materialistic		Materialistic		Ritualistic		Materialistic
Aesthetic		Individualistic		Spiritual		Aesthetic
Spiritual		Power-Seeking		Humanitarian		Spiritual

Note: The lines denote differences of five or more levels.

FIGURE A.1   Comparisons of Partners' Personal Values

Each Partner's View of His or Her Own Values Based on the Results
Jeff (Ritualistic, Power-Seeking, and Individualistic)

I want freedom and the power to control what happens to the company. I need structure and like having rules and standard operating procedures, but I rely on Beth for all of that. It doesn't motivate me as much as it's just something I need to be effective. I want to be evaluated on the results that I create—my performance—and not on how neat my desk is.

Beth (Spiritual, Ritualistic, and Theoretical)

I am the ultimate team player, support person. To me, it's all about feeling useful, helpful, and like I can make a difference. I get immense satisfaction from organizing, systematizing, and making things work in the most neat, clean, effective way possible. My strong spiritual side is extremely important to me, but that's strictly personal.

Sarah (Theoretical, Individualistic, and Power-Seeking)

I get a big kick out of knowing everything I possibly can about our products and services and using that superior knowledge to create a strategic advantage—for the company and for myself. What I need is a place in the hierarchy of a top company that I can call my own. I'm a free spirit, but I like working with others. I want to direct and motivate others to accomplish everything they possibly can. I don't want to be second-guessed or held to rules that don't make sense to me.

Conclusions About How Our Personal Values Will Interact
Jeff and Beth

While Jeff *values* the order, the structure, and the standard operating procedures (ritualistic), it's really Beth who *provides* them. He's desperate for it because he knows he can't run the company effectively without it. For Beth, it's a really a personal value, something that is natural and emanates from within. For the two of them, it couldn't work better—she provides it and he values it. This helps explain why we seem so perfect for each other.

Jeff wouldn't have taken the company "private" if it hadn't been for his strong power-seeking, and it wouldn't have worked as well as it did between us if Beth had a strong need for control. We never have to struggle! The big difference in the individualistic value probably works the same way. The huge difference in the spiritual value is just not an issue, because it's private for Beth and Jeff respects it. Jeff's lack of concern for harmony in his physical environment (the low aesthetic score) is a problem for lots of people around him, including Beth. Jeff has stopped insisting on living with his piles of folders and mail and now lets someone help him with it.

Jeff and Sarah

Being so similar on the power-seeking and individualistic values could certainly be a problem for us. We both like freedom and being recognized for our brilliance! We're both hard working, but we're both competitive and like to win. Our strategy for avoiding clashes over this will be to clearly define our areas of responsibility and authority and to *talk about it* on an ongoing basis.

We're actually very similar on most of our values. The one value we are very different on is ritualistic. But Sarah is on the "un-neat" and disorganized side of the spectrum just as Jeff is in his behavior. She just doesn't value it in the same way he does. She knows it has hurt her in the past and agrees to work on it and have someone help her with this so it doesn't detract from her effectiveness.

Beth and Sarah

For being such good friends, we have a lot of different values! The spiritual has just never been a problem. Ritualistic may never have been a problem because as friends it didn't really matter. Maybe now it could be a problem, but Sarah agrees to try to get a handle on it. The individualistic and power-seeking values are the same differences as between Beth and Jeff, so we think it's not likely to be a problem here either.

B. Star Systems Company Values

With clients, we will

- keep their best interests at heart (including listening carefully to their needs);
- provide high-quality, professional service and first-class products; and
- honor our commitments and nurture a reputation for integrity.

With employees, we will

- promote and encourage mutual respect, open and honest communication, and a culture where mistakes are not hidden and people do not work in fear;
- encourage a spirit of teamwork with all employees in which people take responsibility for their own performance, are considerate of the problems and needs of others, and strive to help everyone succeed;
- nurture a culture of loyalty for, and from, our employees;
- encourage employee growth and development;
- maintain a positive working environment in which people approach every task with optimism, enthusiasm, and flexibility; and
- recognize and reward excellence.

8. Fairness: Partners' Interpersonal Equity

We recognize that each of us contributes a variety of things to the company that help to make it a success. We want to be aware of the range of things that each of us brings. These are listed in the first table below. We are committed to giving recognition to each other for these things because we know that receiving recognition from our partners for the value we bring will help all of us feel more satisfied and motivated.

We also recognize that our satisfaction in owning and running the company together is based on receiving many things from each other and the company in addition to purely monetary compensation. In the second table, we examine what we want out of working together for the company. We know that we all want job satisfaction and fair compensation, and we all want a balance between work and family life (though this is clearly most important to Sarah). We have each identified other important needs in that table.

TABLE A.5 What Each Partner Contributes to the Business and the Partnership
(Each partner's own ideas are listed above the line, and other partner's ideas are listed below the line.)

What Jeff Brings	What Beth Brings	What Sarah Brings
1. Ownership of a highly successful company	1. Twenty years' experience with SSI	1. $280,000 capital contribution over a period of time
2. Broad industry knowledge and experience	2. $280,000 over a period of time	2. Relationships and business with large, potential customers
3. High energy and huge capacity for hard work	3. Reputation in the industry for fairness and integrity	3. Willingness to share risk
4. Family values including trust and loyalty of employees	4. Head of finance department for many years	4. Marketing abilities
5. Vision for the company	5. Extensive contacts with clients and advisors	5. Relationships with vendors
6. Integrity	6. Stability, persistence, dependability, and consistency	6. Vision
7. Willingness to risk everything		7. Money
8. Zeal to improve client products and service	7. Ability to get things done right the first time	8. Technical abilities and education
9. Trustworthiness	8. Institutional history	9. Management experience
10. Positive, can-do attitude	9. Integrity and clarity	10. Honesty, trust, and ethics
	10. Good rapport with employees	11. Great work ethic
	11. High level of commitment	12. High energy
	12. Cooperative and positive attitude in the company	13. Potential for future
		14. Sound strategic ability
		15. Quick study
		16. Strong desire to be successful
		17. Generosity
		18. Fun
		19. Fresh viewpoint
		20. Credibility and stable record
		21. Can-do attitude
		22. Great verbal skills

TABLE A.6   What Each Partner Wants from the Business

(Each partner's own ideas are listed above the line, and other partner's ideas are listed below the line.)

What Jeff Wants	What Beth Wants	What Sarah Wants
1. Salary of $425K 2. Mandate to focus on the big picture 3. Ultimate control 4. Sufficient quality support so I don't have to get mixed up in routine work 5. Be bought out at some time 6. More vacation time than I've taken in the past ―――― 7. Feel secure that this partnership is going to work	1. Opportunity to stay involved in acquisitions 2. $150,000 per year salary 3. Company car 4. Grow my staff with 2 new positions within the next 6–12 months 5. Security and continuity —more than we've had in past years 6. Sufficient staff to run the finance department very efficiently ―――― 7. Opportunity to own a larger share in the future 8. Final authority for staff decisions in her department	1. Autonomy in my position 2. Freedom to call my own hours 3. Ability to increase ownership beyond 10 percent 4. At least $200K annual salary 5. Ability to spread purchase payments out over 5 years 6. Car and other benefits as company can afford them 7. Plenty of vacation time 8. Backup and support akin to what I've been accustomed to ―――― 9. My life to be in balance 10. Freedom to run her piece of the company 11. Be viewed as an owner

We know that if we structure our deal with one another in ways that help all of us to get more of the important things that we want from the business, then we'll be more motivated to contribute our best effort. To do this, we have to know what each person is contributing; then, we must try to structure our arrangement with one another to maximize what each of us gets to take out of the business; finally, we have to keep these things in mind as we work together.

We are also making a commitment to one another to speak up if things begin to feel unfair so that we can discuss the problem and make adjustments if necessary.

TABLE A.7   Jeff's Expectations

Jeff

Expectations I Have for Myself

* Keep focused on the overall growth of the company.
* Have a better than average job for the rest of my career.
* Be bought out in 10–15 years.
* Keep Star Systems on the cutting edge.
* Make decisions in best interest of everyone—not just myself.
* Lead others in the company by being the best example of a model employee.
* Make the ultimate decisions when necessary.

Expectations I Think Others May Have of Me

* Be more patient.

Beth's Expectations of Me

* Think of partners as co-owners and not simply employees.
* No hiding and more communicating.
* Be financially conscientious with personnel.
? Monitor personal workload and don't take on too much.
* Be more trusting of partners' intentions.
* Not be paranoid and think they're going to treat me like my siblings did.

Sarah's Expectations of Me

* Give me [Sarah] assistance getting on board and accepted by staff.
* Support me if challenged by people in established positions.
* Give Beth and me plenty of advance notice regarding any thoughts regarding any changes in the ownership of the company—before you talk with anybody else.
* Actively work to get employees thinking of Beth and me as owners too.
* Understand your shortcomings and take action to overcome them.

---

* Indicates an expectation the person agrees to live up to
? Indicates an expectation the person is not ready to agree to

9. Expectations of the Partners

A. Expectations of Each Other Personally

We are aware that each person's unmet expectations of others can be a source of friction. The problem often results from *not knowing* what each other's expectations were in the first place. To lessen the likelihood of this problem we are trying to be explicit about the expectations we have for ourselves and for one another. We have discussed the expectations in the tables below. Each of us is committed to living up to the expectations that are marked with an asterisk. The expectations with question marks are ones that we have not taken on for ourselves, are still under consideration, or require further clarification.

TABLE A.8   Beth's Expectations

Beth
Expectations I Have for Myself

* Will work diligently to secure a healthy future for the owners and employees.
* Continually improve at my job.
* Be discrete and confidential.
* Maintain a healthy balance between home and work (working 50–55hrs./wk.).
* Strive to optimize performance by getting adequate sleep and exercise.
* Focus on highest priority items—strategic planning and business development.
* Focus on regularly self-assessing my contribution level.

Expectations I Think Others May Have of Me

* Be a better listener and connector.

Jeff's Expectations of Me

* Network more.
* Provide sound leadership and direction and communicate it to all.
* Protect company from liability and manage risk.
* Schedule regular feedback time with direct reports.

Sarah's Expectations of Me

* Not let work get in the way of our friendship.
* Be a better listener.

TABLE A.9   Sarah's Expectations

Sarah
Expectations I Have for Myself
* To grow the company nationally.
* To improve my management skills.
* Develop the highest client satisfaction ratings in the industry.
* Clone myself so I'm not indispensable (share my skills with others).
* Create a cooperative but competitive sales team.
* Work with Jeff as needed to spot new areas of opportunity.

Expectations I Think Others May Have of Me
? Walk in with at least $3 million in business.
? Not act precipitously and "like a cowboy" like Stuart [author's note: Stuart is Jeff's brother].
* Manage work effectively.

Jeff's Expectations of Me
* Learn the corporate culture before you try to change it.
* Be patient with corporate change.
* Be responsible for no less than $750,000 of new business within 2 years.
* Don't assume I'm not listening to you; check it out.

Beth's Expectations of Me
* Take time to develop respect from others.
* Don't take things personally.

B. Expectations for the Partners as Co-Owners

As the owners of the company, we realize that it behooves us to fully understand the role of owner and how it differs from the role of employee. To that end, we have discussed and negotiated our common or shared expectations for ourselves related to our positions as co-owners of the corporation. We—as a group—understand and agree on the expectations in the following table for ourselves as shareholders of Star Systems.

TABLE A.10   Our Expectations For Ourselves as Co-Owners

We will have a proportional risk equal to ownership shares.

We will work together as a team.

We will do our best to foster trust and address actions and circumstances that erode it.

We'll avoid two-against-one alliances ("triangulating,") and instead will deal directly with one another.

We'll be extremely discreet about our partnership, not discussing matters among us with others in the company.

We won't flaunt the fact that we own the company.

We will value all the employees and not treat those we work with any better than any others.

We'll keep our relationships with one another more important than anything else, including money.

We'll be patient with each other.

We'll revisit our expectations for ourselves annually.

SECTION THREE:
THE FUTURE OF THE BUSINESS AND THE PARTNERS
10. Creating Guidelines for the Unexpected

While we understand that we cannot anticipate every eventuality, there are many circumstances that we can anticipate so we're not blindsided. Anticipating events, strategizing about them, and creating guidelines for dealing with them has helped us get to know each other better and given us more confidence that we can succeed together. Not to mention that our planning should eliminate unpleasant surprises in the future.

Wild and Crazy Success I

(The business is wildly successful, has a value that we never dreamed of, and one of us wants to cash out.)

> Since our deal isn't to be in this business just to get rich quick, if it happens and one of us wants out, we will try to accommodate that person, but we agree that no buyout will happen in a way that compromises the financial health of either the company or the remaining shareholders.

Wild and Crazy Success II

(The business is wildly successful, is making a lot of profit, and one of us wants to increase salaries to get the money out.)

> We're in agreement that our number 1 priority is to grow the company, not grow rich (too quickly), so we will raise our salaries modestly no matter how good the company's profit picture.

A Major Project Tanks

(We suffer a significant monetary loss on a major project and it puts us in the red in a major way, a recession hits causing several bad years, or there is some other reason why a major capital infusion is needed.)

> We agree to be as ready as we possibly can be to inject capital into the business or provide loan guarantees if necessary. If all of the partners are unable to meet the challenge, then we expect that whoever does will be rewarded for his or her effort.

Co-ownership Becomes Popular

(Other employees want to buy in.)

> We all agree that we will wait five years and then evaluate whether having other employee-owners is something we wish to do. We are not opposed to

the idea of having one or two other employee shareholders, or even giving a larger number of employees the opportunity to own a small piece of the company. We would entertain the idea, though, only if it meets the criteria we set for adding partners in the Ownership section.

Owner in a Pinch
(One of the owners is involved in a messy divorce or some type of financial disaster and feels a huge financial pinch.)

While none of us wants the company to act as a bank for the owners, we recognize that the owners make significant sacrifices for its success, and therefore it is reasonable to have the resources of the company be available to the owners if there is a short-term need and it doesn't put the company in jeopardy. All such loans would carry the lowest interest possible and be repaid in twelve to eighteen months unless circumstances are dire.

Owner Rift
(A rift among the owners causes multiple factions in the business.)

Because of the seriousness of any rift among the three of us, we're going to adhere to the philosophy that if any one of us believes there is a problem among us that necessitates mediation, then the others are obliged to participate and make a best effort to resolve the matter to everyone's satisfaction.

Employee Lawsuit
(One of the owners is sued by an employee for sexual harassment.)

If an owner acknowledges sexually harassing an employee or is found guilty of sexual harassment, then he or she agrees to resign, forfeit his or her severance package, and sell his or her stock either to the company or the other owners according to the agreed upon procedures. Legal fees and other expenses will be deducted from the sale price. These will be the default consequences unless the rest of the members of the board of directors unanimously agree that the allegations were fallacious and without merit (regardless of a court verdict).

Family Crisis
(An owner has some sort of personal or family crisis that interferes with the ability to work day to day.)

Any owner is automatically granted a paid six-month sabbatical in the event of a personal or family crisis. We all agree that the person in that position will try to put in reduced hours rather than not work at all. Sabbaticals beyond six months would necessitate a cut in pay to 50 percent. Beyond twelve months, the partner would not continue to be paid.

A Directional Dispute

(We have a disagreement over the direction of the business.)

We all agree that the business is on the right track currently and should continue basically as it is. If market and industry conditions change, then of course we would have to reevaluate what we're doing. If we come to disagree on the direction the business is going and cannot resolve our differences ourselves, then we would ask the board to review the business's strategic plan. If it's more of a personal clash among the partners, then we will use mediators to help us resolve the matter.

Jeff Wants to Bail Out

(Someone makes him an offer for the company that he doesn't want to turn down, and he doesn't need or want a contract with the new company.)

Jeff agrees never to conduct any discussions with any person or company without informing Beth and Sarah beforehand. He also agrees that regardless of whether he has, or wants, a stake or position in the acquiring company, he will help negotiate the best possible benefits and positions for Beth and Sarah.

11. Resolving Disputes and Communicating Effectively

A. Resolving Disputes Among the Partners and Within the Company

There are many ways to handle disputes when they arise. Some methods are better than others because they make it more likely that issues will be resolved quickly and effectively. We already have certain conflict management procedures in place and look to augment them with additional procedures as backups, for use in case the regular methods are not sufficient. The following are procedures that we plan on using among ourselves if conflicts arise and also plan on using within the company as a whole to promote healthier conflict resolution and fewer formal grievances and lawsuits.

The best procedure for resolving disputes in organizations is a stepwise approach with three distinct methods:

Negotiation   ⟶   Mediation   ⟶   Arbitration

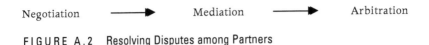

FIGURE A.2   Resolving Disputes among Partners

1. **Negotiation.** If we find ourselves in a destructive type of conflict with another owner, we all agree to do everything we can to work out our differences
   side-by-side. Also, when one of us sees a conflict persisting between the
   other two, we will encourage them to negotiate their differences directly and
   avoid "triangles." We recognize that it is important to keep our emotions from
   taking over and to balance emotions with rational dialogue. Accordingly, we
   will endeavor to abide by the following guidelines in resolving disputes:

   A. Clarify the issues in dispute.
   B. Provide each person an opportunity to express his or her opinion on
      the issue and encourage active *listening*.
   C. Collect data if needed.
   D. List the pros and cons of each person's position.
   E. Identify alternatives that maximize advantages and have minimal draw-
      backs.
   F. Reach consensus on the best resolution.

2. **Mediation.** If negotiation between the parties themselves does not seem
   to resolve the matter or results in lingering resentments, we agree to hire
   business mediators to help resolve the problem. We agree to take this step
   before matters have a chance to get so bad that positions harden, other
   people get dragged in, or the unresolved conflict compromises the company's productivity or morale. We will hire co-mediators who will be neutral third-parties with no stake in the conflict, whose role is simply *assist-
   ing* the parties in their own negotiations. Control over the outcome is still
   in the hands of the parties themselves; the mediators are in control of the
   process. All agreements reached by the parties will be confidential, written, signed, and binding on the parties.

   To make this dispute resolution program as effective as possible, we are
   selecting the co-mediators *before* a dispute arises. The third choice is a
   backup in case either of the first two cannot serve. The list may be reviewed and changed by the partners at any time.

   (1) _____
   (2) _____
   (3) _____

3. **Arbitration.** If neither negotiation nor mediation is successful, arbitration is the final method for coming to a resolution. Like mediation, arbitration utilizes a third party. Different from mediation, the third-party arbitrator *is* in charge of the outcome. The arbitrator will listen to both sides and make a ruling, and it will be final and binding. The arbitrator will be selected by the mediators. He or she will have experience in business arbitration and will have no knowledge of the parties involved or the substance of the mediation that occurred.

B. Effective Communication

We recognize that we are a group of dominant personalities and need to be vigilant in following certain guidelines to ensure that we communicate effectively, thereby reducing the likelihood that misunderstandings will arise. Also, certain tools and techniques can help us communicate better with one another. These include the following:

1. use effective and considerate verbal and nonverbal feedback during meetings when one of us is too loud, not listening, talking too much, or otherwise not communicating effectively;
2. rotate leadership at meetings among the owners;
3. have a facilitator or mediator at an owners' or board meeting if the issues are contentious;
4. present only one idea at a time so that everyone has an opportunity for input;
5. set and circulate an agenda in advance of each meeting, with approximate times allotted for each agenda item so that we can adequately prepare for the meeting and stay focused at the meeting;
6. review individual goals at the start of each meeting so that we can help each other improve our communication styles;
7. reinforce cooperation and collaboration during meetings; and
8. use "thumbs-up" or "thumbs-down" to get a quick read on how partners are thinking on a particular issue.

NOTES

PREFACE

x **Family businesses form the bulk of the world's economy:** Joseph H. Astrachan, ed. "Editor's Note," *Family Business Review* 2004, 16, no. 4 (2004): v.

CHAPTER 1

4 **dominate *Entrepreneur's* annual list of the "hottest" companies:** Conversation with Steve Cooper, research editor at *Entrepreneur* magazine, February 4, 2004.

4 **founded only 6 percent of the "hypergrowth" companies:** Leslie Brokaw, "The Truth about Start-ups," in *Inc. Magazine's Guide to Small Business Success* (Boston: Gruner and Jahr, 2000), 29–33.

6 **the single owner in most cases:** A. C. Amason, "Distinguishing the Effects of Functional and Dysfunctional Conflict on Strategic Decision Making: Resolving a Paradox for Top Management Teams," *Academy of Management Journal* 39 (1996): 123–48.

6 **or what some researchers call "affective conflict":** Ann Mooney and Patricia Holahan, "Managing Conflict in Teams: Gaining the Benefits and Avoiding the Costs." Working paper, Stevens Institute of Technology, Howe School of Technology Management, 2004.

9 **partnerships were a bad idea:** "Are Partners Bad for Business?" *Inc.* (February 1992): 24.

9 **A poll by researchers:** Paul Rosenblatt, Leni de Mik, Roxanne Marie Anderson, and Patricia Johnson, *The Family in Business* (San Francisco: Jossey-Bass, 1985).

13 **the nightmare that it was meant to replace:** Todd B. Carver and Albert A. Vondra, "Alternative Dispute Resolution: Why It Doesn't Work and Why It Does," *Harvard Business Review* (May 1994): 120.

14 **their family's culinary legend, Manganaro Foods**: Tara Bahrampour, "Family Feud: Manganaro's against Manganaro's," *New York Times,* May 14, 2000, p. B1.

CHAPTER 3

56 **That ended in failure**: Jayne Osborne, ed., "Stepping into the Fray: Mediating Client Disputes," in *CPA Administrator's & Manager's Report* (New York: Aspen Publishers, 2000), 5–6.

59 **Make Your Values Mean Something**: Patrick M. Lencioni, "Make Your Values Mean Something," *Harvard Business Review* (July 2002): 5–9.

59 **"Your Personal Best Makes Enron Best"**: Jon R. Katzenbach and Douglas K. Smith, *The Wisdom of Teams: Creating the High-Performance Organization* (New York: HarperBusiness, 1993), 113.

60 **which shapes their strategic plans**: John L. Ward and Craig E. Aronoff, "How Family Affects Strategy," *Small Business Forum* (Fall 1994): 85–88.

60 **a reported $100 million**: Martin Kady II, "UPS's $100M Delivery," *Washington Business Journal,* May 25–31, 2001, 76.

63 **people range from profligate spenders to hoarders**: Olivia Mellan, *Money Harmony: Resolving Money Conflicts in Your Life and Relationships* (New York: Walker, 1994).

65 **angel investor funding or venture capital**: John May and Cal Simmons, *Every Business Needs an Angel: Getting the Money You Need to Make Your Business Grow* (New York: Crown Business, 2001).

65 **using credit cards**: Bobbie Gossage, "Charging Ahead," *Inc. Magazine* (January 2004): 42.

65 **family-friends-fools' money**: Conversation with John May, New Vantage Group, Vienna, Virginia, February 28, 2004.

CHAPTER 4

71 **I'm interested in learning from them**: Timothy Egan, "The $6.5 Billion Man," *New York Times,* October 29, 1995, sec. 3, p. 1.

75 **according to attorney Henry Krasnow**: Henry C. Krasnow, "What to Do When Talking Fails: Strategies for Minority Owners to Turn Stock Certificates into Money," *Family Business Review* 15, no. 4 (2002): 259–68.

78 **Dean Martin the entertainer**: *Dean Martin: That's Amore* (videotape) (Hollywood, Calif.: Capital Records, Inc., June 5, 2001).

83 **Philip Leslie and Raymond Cesmat**: John R. Emshwiller, "Desire for Revenge Fuels an Entrepreneur's Ambition," *Wall Street Journal,* April 19, 1991, p. B2.

85 **even though the book value was substantially higher:** Harold Reuschlein and William A. Gregory, *The Law of Agency and Partnership*, 2nd ed. (St. Paul, Minn.: West Publishing, 1990).

86 **One caveat with a noncompete covenant:** Conversation with Henry C. Krasnow on July 7, 2003.

88 **Not long ago all six partners in the Washington law firm:** David Segal, "From Allies to Adversaries: The Fall of Nussbaum & Wald," *Washington Post*, August 25, 1997.

CHAPTER 5

92 **based their partnership on that division of roles:** Collin Street Bakery Web site, http://collinstreetbakery.com, 2003.

94 **Philip Purcell of Dean Witter:** Charles Gasparino, "Morgan Stanley's Mack Steps Down after Rift," *Wall Street Journal*, January 25, 2001, C1.

95 **The Split Brain at the Top:** Warren Bennis, "The Split Brain at the Top," *Across the Board* (September 1989): 10.

97 **His company's stock had appreciated nineteen-hundred-fold:** George Anders, "Groomed to Lead, Fund Clan's Scion Veered into Trouble," *Wall Street Journal*, November 18, 2003.

103 **A *Fortune* article featured their partnership:** Patricia Sellers, "Divorce Corporate Style," *Fortune* (May 1999): 106.

105 **Follett President Richard Litzinsinger commented on the dismissals in *Forbes:*** Marcia Berss, "A Family Affair," *Forbes* (March 27, 1997): 136.

105 **Social psychologist David Dunning:** Tori DeAngelis, "Why We Overestimate Our Competence," *Monitor on Psychology* (February 2003): 60–63.

106 **a real opportunity to support one another:** Rick Maurer, *Why Don't You Want What I Want? How to Win Support for Your Ideas without Hard Sell, Manipulation or Power Plays* (Baltimore, Md.: Bard Press, 2002).

106 **Rick Maurer, who consults on building cooperation in organizations:** Rick Maurer, "The Leader's New Role," *Executive Excellence* (April 1993): 8.

107 **Prestigious job titles:** "Extreme Measures: Short on Cash? 'Up-title'." Edward Lowe Perspectives Web site, at http://peerspectives.org (accessed October 13, 2002).

CHAPTER 6

119 **the bifurcation of Anderson Worldwide:** David Leonhardt, "Arbitrator Splits Arthur Andersen into 2 Companies," *New York Times*, August 8, 2000, p. A1.

119 **the essential components of individual reward systems:** David H. Maister, *Managing the Professional Service Firm* (New York: The Free Press, 1993).

119 **creates more problems among partners than it solves:** Alfie Kohn, "For Best Results, Forget the Bonus," *New York Times,* October 17, 1993, p. F11.

120 **Law firms using this system:** Barbara Buchholz, "Firms Look for Lawyers Who Arrive with Clients," *New York Times,* August 25, 1996, p. 11.

CHAPTER 7

122 **A *Harvard Business Review* article:** Jay W. Lorsch and Rakesh Khurana, "Changing Leaders: The Board's Role in CEO Succession," *Harvard Business* Review (May-June 1999): 97–105.

126 **in military jargon "incestuous amplification":** Paul Krugman, "Delusions of Power," *New York Times,* March 28, 2003, p. A17.

126 **companies with strong directors:** Ron Anderson, "The Balance of Power: Who Monitors the Family?" Working paper, The Kogod School of Business at American University, 2004.

126 **and run the companies at the expense of minority shareholders:** Barbara Marsh, "Minority Shareholders Stand Up, Demand to Be Heard," *Wall Street Journal,* February 23, 1993.

CHAPTER 8

135 **The traits that make him appealing tend to make him appalling in the flash of an eye:** Todd Purdum, "Present and Paradox," *New York Times Sunday Magazine,* May 1996, p. 36.

136 **people imagine that they know people better than they really do:** Alan Sillars, "(Mis)Understanding," in *The Dark Side of Relationships,* ed. Brian H. Spitzberg and William R. Capach (Mahwah, N.J.: Lawrence Erlbaum Associates, 1998).

136 **It was an odd marriage from the start:** Rachel Nichols, "Competitive Personalities, Difficult Divorce," *Washington Post,* May 8, 2003, p. A1.

137 **the Myers-Briggs Type Indicator (MBTI):** Otto Kroeger and Janet M. Thuesen, *Type Talk at Work* (New York: Dell Publishing, 1992). (The MBTI can be purchased from CPP, Inc., 3803 East Bayshore Rd., P.O. Box 10096, Palo Alto, CA 94303, (800) 624-1765.)

137 **the Personal Profile System, or DiSC test:** Tom Ritchey, *I'm Stuck, You're Stuck* (San Francisco: Berrett-Koehler Publishers, 2002). (The Personal Profile System may be ordered from Inscape Publishing,

6465 Wayzata Blvd., Ste. 800, Minneapolis, MN 55426, www.inscapepublishing.com, (763) 765-2222.)

140 **According to Dr. Diane Felmlee:** Diane H. Felmlee, "Fatal Attraction," in *The Dark Side of Relationships,* ed. Brian H. Spitzberg and William R. Capach (Mahwah, N.J.: Lawrence Erlbaum Associates, 1998), 14, 26.

143 **described as healthy qualities of leaders:** Dian L. Coutu, "Putting Leaders on the Couch: A Conversation with Manfred F. R. Kets de Vries," *Harvard Business Review* (January 2004): 65.

147 **to better understand their feelings and their interactions:** Mike Stadter, "Persecutory Aspects of Family Business," in *Self Hatred in Psychoanalysis,* ed. Jill Savage Scharff and Stanley A. Tsigounis (New York: Brunner-Routledge, 2003), 205–24.

CHAPTER 9

150 **"Now," Falk reports, "the money is irrelevant:** Cynthia Hobgood, "Floating on Air," *Washington Business Journal,* March 8, 2002, p. 32.

151 **Now, it's just about maintaining a creative arc:** Rick Lyman, "Going Hunting in Seinfeld Country, Just for Laughs," *New York Times,* September 15, 2002, Arts and Leisure, p. 1.

151 **Barbera reveled in the Hollywood social life:** Joe Barbera, *My Life in 'Toons: From Flatbush to Bedrock in Under a Century* (Atlanta, Ga.: Turner, 1994).

152 **I came across an instrument called simply "Personal Values":** Thomas C. Ritt Jr., "Personal Values" (Tequesta, Fla.: People Concepts, 1980). (This test can be ordered through People Concepts, P.O. 3902, Tequesta, FL 33469. (561) 746-4817.)

157 **I'm still very curious about how far I can push this:** Roxanne Quimby, as told to Susan Donovan, "How I Did It," *Inc.* (January 2004): 76.

CHAPTER 10

161 **and you shall have that which you want:** Adam Smith, *The Wealth of Nations* (London: J.M. Dent, 1954), 13 (first published 1776).

162 **The idea for partners' interpersonal equity:** Richard C. Huseman and John D. Hatfield, *Managing the Equity Factor: Or, "After All I've Done for You . . . "* (Boston: Houghton Mifflin, 1989).

167 **"We became a firm of solo practitioners":** Martha H. Peak, "Ersatz Fable," *Management Review* 83, no. 5 (1994): 1.

167 **Gould described it as a "personal tragedy":** Jerome Cramer, "'Bad Management' Topples a Firm," *American Bar Association Journal* (May 1994): 30.

175 **From Bonn comes a story:** James R. Oestreich, "Beethoven: Unfair to Labor!" *New York Times,* March 28, 2004, Business, p. 7.

CHAPTER 11

178 **interpersonal expectancy:** Robert Rosenthal, "Covert Communication in Classrooms, Clinics, Courtrooms, and Cubicles," *American Psychologist* 57 (2002):839–49.

178 **according to an *Inc.* magazine poll:** Editor, "Are Partners Bad for Business?" *Inc.* (February 1992): 24.

185 *The Wisdom of Teams:* Jon R. Katzenbach and Douglas K. Smith, *The Wisdom of Teams: Creating the High-Performance Organization* (New York: HarperBusiness, 1993).

CHAPTER 12

193 **All events should be crossed in imagination before reality:** Sigmund Warburg, quoted by Ron Chernow in a keynote speech at the Family Firm Institute's Annual Conference in Chicago, October 1999.

193 **For people to act, too often we must substitute catastrophe for imagination:** Joshua Hyatt, "Fathers and Sons," *Inc.* (May 1992): 62.

193 **Thinking about the unthinkable:** Herman Kahn, *Thinking About the Unthinkable* (New York: Horizon Press, 1962).

194 **alter their plans by taking preventive actions:** David Stauffer, "Five Reasons Why You Still Need Scenario Planning," *Harvard Management Update* (June 2002): 3–5.

195 **any worst-case scenario we could have imagined:** Constance Hays, "A Sputter in the Coke Machine," *New York Times*, August 6, 1999, p. C1.

195 **speculate on a wide range of possibilities:** Garry D. Peterson, Graeme Cumming, and Stephen R. Carpenter, "Scenario Planning: A Tool for Conservation in an Uncertain World," *Conservation Biology* 17, no. 2 (2003): 358–66.

197 **Geoff Williams, an *Entrepreneur* columnist:** Geoff Williams, "Crash Course," *Entrepreneur* (January 2000): 89.

199 **it provides a baseline for how situations should be handled if they ever occur:** Conversation with David Mesco, an MBA student in a class on managing family-owned businesses at American University, March 2003.

CHAPTER 13

202 **Methods of conflict resolution span a spectrum:** David Gage and Scott Meza, "Achieving Collaboration Through Mediation," in *The Family Business Conflict Resolution Handbook,* ed. Barbara Spector (Philadelphia: Family Business Publishing, 2003), 190–93.

203 **But facilitators will typically stay out of the content:** Roger M. Schwartz, *The Skilled Facilitator: Practical Wisdom for Developing Effective Groups* (San Francisco: Jossey-Bass, 1994).

205 **Expert advice rarely ends a festering conflict:** David Gage and John A. Gromala, "Not All Business! Mediating the Personality Differences Behind Internal Business Disputes," *American Bar Association GP Solo* 19, no. 2 (2002): 10.

205 **Partners sometimes pull in existing advisors:** Jayne Osborne, ed., "Stepping into the Fray: Mediating Client Disputes," in *CPA Administrator's & Manager's Report* (New York: Aspen Publishers, 2000), 5–6.

205 **A *Harvard Business Review* article explained how alike they are:** Todd B. Carver and Albert A. Vondra, "Alternative Dispute Resolution: Why It Doesn't Work and Why It Does," *Harvard Business Review* (May 1994): 120.

206 **Rufus King III, a highly respected Superior Court judge:** David Gage, "The Hafts and Mediation: Lessons for Businesses," *Washington Business Journal* 13, no. 5 (1994): 23.

209 **do not have this freedom:** Laura Bachle, "Estate Planning and Family Business Mediation," *Bureau of National Affairs ADR Report* 5, no. 6 (2001): 11–14.

ACKNOWLEDGMENTS

For more than ten years I've had the privilege of working with hundreds of partners—co-owners of every type of business imaginable—who not only gave me the idea for this book but then taught me what to put in it. Many of them also gave me encouragement to tell their stories, if in disguised form, so that others would not have to trudge through the same missteps they had endured. The clients who in recent years created Partnership Charters deserve special thanks. While undergoing their "road test" to see if their partnerships could really fly, they persuaded me that the way I was conceiving and constructing the charter was on the right track. They helped with the book's road test.

I also wish to give special thanks to the many partners who gave generously of their time to be interviewed for the book. Their names and wisdom—lessons from their partnerships—can be found throughout the book. Thank you.

Writing this book has been a solo task, but the team of associates I have at BMC was as supportive a group as any writer could hope to have. Among those who took scant free time to review chapters and offer their wise counsel are Harry Linowes, John Gromala, Scott Meza, Lois Stovall, Michael Stadter, Richard Yocum, Melinda Ostermeyer, and Dawn Martin. Other people who helped out with research and editing include Ken Rubio, Ari Tuckman, and Charles Campbell.

During the last weeks of editing the book, an associate of seven years, Ed Kopf, decided that he wanted to become my partner. We knew that meant a Partnership Charter was in our future, but neither one of us fully appreciated how challenging and enriching an experience it would be. I think we both believed that after having helped so many clients with their charters, writing our own would be like taking the test when you've already seen the answers. Not even close. We debated, negotiated, struggled, regrouped. We examined our styles and values and saw how they were manifested in our intense interaction. We dealt with money and percentages like the best of them and imagined everything that could possibly go awry. Like our clients, we had our doubts and fears, but like them, we could see the tremendous advantage of combining our different backgrounds, styles, and talents, and knew that the result would be worth far more than the sum of its parts. We have our shared vision of the future of BMC Associates. Though I can't say exactly where it will lead, I do know that my world has already been enriched by our association.

A number of my colleagues in the Family Firm Institute have been helpful and encouraging, especially Birch Douglas, Marty Fetch, Haven Pell, David Morris, Marshall Orr, and Kathy Wiseman. Henry Krasnow and Sam Davis read chapters and offered cogent comments that have improved the finished product. Despite the feedback from everyone who has contributed over the past years of writing, the responsibility for any remaining deficiencies belongs to me alone.

My sister Jacquie Rubio was unstinting in lending her considerable editorial skills, and another sister, Katie Franco, provided a keen eye for grammar. It seemed to me that the head of my editorial team at Basic Books, Bill Frucht, was true to his promise of being "the most meddlesome editor in New York," and for that I am grateful. My agent, Gail Ross, was extremely helpful in finding the right publisher. Mike Barrier was instrumental with numerous partner interviews. Barbara Bird at American University, Amy Fox, Charlie Ritchie, Helen Bensimon, Rick Maurer, Peter Wylie, James E. Hughes Jr., Sharon Nelton, and Thomas Ritt Jr. were all encouraging and supportive.

As in business partnerships, there is an emotional as well as a technical side to completing a task as consuming as writing a book. I want to acknowledge the interest and encouragement I've received over the course of many years from the clients in my therapy practice, who will of course go unnamed, but not unappreciated. My friends Alison Baker and Jim Colwell contributed both their interest and technical expertise. My dear friend Jody Whitehouse proved to be ruthless at slashing unnecessary adverbs while also being kind and generous with her approval and praise. Finally, I wish to thank my wife, Cathy Bock, for her love, support, and endless reading on a project that neither of us suspected would take so much time and energy. As the late Bart Howard, who wrote "Fly Me to the Moon," once said, "It took me 20 years to find out how to write a song in 20 minutes."

INDEX